Introduction to Computer Organization and Data Structures

MCGRAW-HILL COMPUTER SCIENCE SERIES

RICHARD W. HAMMING *Bell Telephone Laboratories*

EDWARD A. FEIGENBAUM *Stanford University*

BELL AND NEWELL *Computer Structures*
COLE *Introduction to Computing*
GEAR *Computer Organization and Programming*
GIVONE *Introduction to Switching Circuit Theory*
HAMMING *Computers and Society*
HAMMING *Introduction to Applied Numerical Analysis*
HELLERMAN *Digital Computer System Principles*
KAIN *Automata Theory: Machines and Languages*
KOHAVI *Switching and Finite Automata Theory*
LIU *Introduction to Combinatorial Mathematics*
NILSSON *Artificial Intelligence*
RALSTON *Introduction to Programming and Computer Science*
ROSEN *Programming Systems and Languages*
SALTON *Automatic Information Organization and Retrieval*
STONE *Introduction to Computer Organization and Data Structures*
WATSON *Timesharing System Design Concepts*
WEGNER *Programming Languages, Information Structures, and Machine Organization*

Introduction to Computer Organization and Data Structures

Harold S. Stone

Associate Professor of Computer Science
and Electrical Engineering

Stanford University

McGraw-Hill Book Company

New York   San Francisco   St. Louis   Düsseldorf   Johannesburg
Kuala Lumpur   London   Mexico   Montreal   New Delhi   Panama
Rio de Janeiro   Singapore   Sydney   Toronto

This book was set in Monotype Modern 8A, printed and bound by The Maple Press Company. The designer was Michael A. Rogondino; the drawings were done by Judith L. McCarty. The editors were Richard F. Dojny and Marge Woodhurst. Charles A. Goehring supervised production.

Introduction
to Computer
Organization and
Data Structures

Copyright © 1972 by McGraw-Hill, Inc. All rights reserved. No part of this publication may be reproduced, stored in a retrieval system, or transmitted, in any form or by any means, electronic, mechanical, photocopying, recording, or otherwise, without the prior written permission of the publisher.

Printed in the United States of America.

Library of Congress catalog card number: 75-167560

234567890 MAMM 798765432

07-061726-0

Contents

For Jan and Jeremy

"And still they gazed, and still the wonder grew
That one small head could carry all he knew."

Goldsmith

PREFACE

The development of computers and computer programming over two decades has brought with it large programming systems, particularly compilers and executive programs, of enormous complexity. The construction of such systems would have been an impossibility without the concurrent development of the discipline of computer science. In the infancy of computers computer science was hardly more than "a bag of tricks," a collection of clever but unrelated techniques devised by good programmers. The problems that faced the computer pioneers were usually "existence" problems. That is, is there an algorithm that computes X?

With time, the problems changed from existence problems to those of good design and practical application. Now we seek the best algorithms for computing X, where we measure the quality of an algorithm in terms of its storage requirements and execution time. The body of knowledge that constitutes computer science today is no longer an unorganized bag of tricks; rather it is a highly structured discipline that includes tools for analysis and synthesis of programs.

The purpose of this text is to introduce the student to the most primitive actions of a computer and then show how the primitive actions can be put together to construct most of the complex actions that computers regularly perform. This text takes the student through an introductory treatment of Turing machines, into machine and assembly languages, number representation, and elementary programming. Data structures and input/output programs are the major concerns of the central portion of the text, and the concluding chapter develops techniques for analysis of programs through examples of algorithms for searching and sorting.

One of the primary objectives of the latter chapters is to show

how the representation of data strongly influences both time and space requirements for processing the data. A variety of data structures are presented, together with an analysis of their good and bad characteristics and typical applications for which they are well suited.

The scope of the text is sufficiently broad to cover most of Course B2, Computers and Programming, in ACM's Curriculum 68 as well as roughly half the material in Course I1, Data Structures. The material is intended primarily for college juniors and seniors with some computer experience. Very little mathematical background is needed, although a knowledge of elementary calculus and combinatorial analysis is helpful for understanding Chapter 11. Because college freshmen have also used this text successfully, it is likely that in time it can be used at the freshman level as more and more students receive their first exposure to computers before entering college.

This book reflects the contributions of many people. The author expresses his appreciation to these people in general, and in particular to Donald Chamberlain, Robert Fabry, John Wakerly, Gio Wiederhold, William McKeeman, Edward McCluskey, Frederick W. Terman, Donald Knuth, and David Van Voorhis for their comments, suggestions, and encouragement.

Thanks are also due Phyllis Winkler and Judy Demetre for their meticulous care in typing the manuscript. The author also acknowledges the contributions of Hewlett-Packard, whose equipment donations made this work possible.

Harold S. Stone

Instructor's Preface

The material in the text is suitable for a semester course in machine language programming and data structures. Prerequisites ideally should include at least one course in computer programming with a compiler language such as FORTRAN, ALGOL or PL/I. An ALGOL-like language is used throughout the text for descriptive purposes, but specific knowledge of ALGOL is not necessary. The descriptive language is developed in stages, so that the student learns the language along with the central course material. A short description of this language is given in the appendix. Calculus and statistics are desirable prerequisites, but not necessary. Only the material in the last chapter depends on these subjects. The mathematically oriented aspects of the last chapter can be skipped if necessary without marring the presentation of the search and sort algorithms.

The Hewlett-Packard 2116 and IBM System/360-370 computers are used as running examples throughout the text. It is clearly advantageous for students to have access to either of these computers for programming assignments. However, other computers may also be used for this purpose. For example, the Digital Equipment Corporation PDP-8 is quite similar to the HP 2116 and is a suitable vehicle for student programs. Subject matter is developed in a general framework and is then made specific through examples for the HP 2116 and System/360-370. The simplicity of the HP 2116 permits students to master the examples for this machine without having to program it, so that they can learn to apply their knowledge to more complex computers such as the System/360-370 or to computers not described in this text.

At Stanford University all programming assignments are done on a HP 2116, and each student operates the computer from the console. In this environment the student gains insight and learns to appreciate many aspects of the computer that are hidden from him in a batch or time-sharing environment. This is essentially the only environment in which it is possible to construct interrupt-driven input/output programs. Hands-on computer facilities are somewhat of a luxury, however, and so it is likely that the usual programming environment will be time-sharing or batch processing. For either environment the early assignments should be based on the most primitive facilities. For example, in a time-sharing environment, a console linked to the computer can be made to appear to be the operator's console of a stand-alone computer. The student ought to be able to simulate the actions of pressing buttons and reading and writing the contents of memory cells in octal or hexadecimal representation. The objective here is to give him his first, and possibly his last, opportunity to program the computer directly, without the intervening levels imposed by compilers, link editors, loaders, and executive programs.

For any particular programming environment, this text must be supplemented with one or more reference manuals. For HP 2116 installations we recommend "A Pocket Guide to Hewlett-Packard Computers," published by Hewlett-Packard, Palo Alto, California. For System/360-370 computers the student should obtain "Principles of Operation," Form A22-6821, and "Assembler Language," Form C28-6514, both available as part of the IBM System Reference Library. The instructor may have to supplement this reference material with a description of the input/output subroutines in use at his installation.

The programming assignments should be designed to introduce one new concept at a time during the course. A particularly effective first assignment, suggested by William McKeeman, is to have the student enter a short program at the console using the bit switches. The program is to flash the console lights in an interesting pattern. This assignment can be done after only a week of instruction in basic principles. An assignment in assembly language requires one to two weeks more preparation and is considerably more difficult as a first assignment than as a second assignment.

A typical set of program assignments for a one-semester course are:

1   Write a short program that flashes the lights in an interesting pattern. Enter this program by means of the console bit switches.

2   Write a nonrelocatable program in assembly language. Load and execute the program. The program should take input

from the console switches and produce an output in the registers or through an automatic dump. Multiplication and division algorithms, simple numeric processing, and number conversion are suitable types of programs.

3   Write two or more relocatable programs that have to be linked to each other. Load the programs with a linking loader and execute them. This assignment can make use of library subroutines for input/output. It should cover one or more of the data structures in Chapter 6.

4   Write an input/output program that uses wait loops. This program can do simple operations on input data before transmitting it to the output device. This assignment can also cover one or more of the data structures in Chapter 6.

5   Write an interrupt driven input/output program. This assignment covers material in Chapters 7 and 8.

6   Write a program that demonstrates some nontrivial process on linked data structures.

7   Write a program that performs Floyd's tree sort algorithm.

8   Write a program for searching with hash addressing.

To use this book for a one-quarter course, instead of a one-semester course, Chapter 1 may be omitted and the material in Chapters 9 to 11 may be treated selectively. The core material for one quarter is in Chapters 2 to 8.

A hands-on minicomputer to support this text should be configured as indicated below:

1   Processor with a minimum of 4K words, preferably 8K words of storage

2   Teletype or console typewriter

3   Card reader

4   Auxiliary memory for system program storage (cassette tape or disk)

5   Input/output devices for storing and reloading student programs (paper-tape reader and paper-tape punch or cassette tape)

6   A line printer or similar device for program listing

The line printer is not a necessity in many university environments, since programs can be assembled and listed on a central facility even when they are to be executed on a stand alone minicomputer. The Hewlett-Packard user's library contains an assembler for the HP 2116 that executes on System/360-370. Similar assemblers that also execute on System/360-370 are available for other computers.

Harold S. Stone

Introduction to Computer Organization and Data Structures

1

Algorithms, Turing Machines, and Programs

One of the major purposes of this book is to investigate the typical primitive instructions that are found in computers and to explore techniques for using sequences of such instructions to do computations. In this chapter we introduce the mathematical foundations of computation through abstract models of computing devices. In later chapters we shall turn our attention to real computers.

1·1 Algorithms

Let us adopt the point of view that a computer is a robot that will perform any task that can be described as a sequence of instructions. In this section we shall focus attention on the properties of sequences of instructions that can be obeyed by a computing robot.

Within the acceptable set of instructions are those which tell the robot to do simple arithmetic operations such as addition, subtraction, multiplication, and division. Moreover, the instructions must permit conditional actions to be taken by the robot, as in the instruction "Divide by A if A is not equal to 0."

In order to give the widest possible flexibility in forming acceptable instruction sequences, we allow the robot to obey instructions that cause it to obey other instructions. For example, instead of obeying the sequence of instructions

1. Output the number 0.
2. Output the number 0.
3. Output the number 0.
4. Halt.

the robot could obey the equivalent instructions

1. Repeat instruction A three times.
2. Halt.
A. Output the number 0.

A sequence of instructions of this type, or in fact any sequence of instructions that can be obeyed by a robot, is called an *algorithm*. Our discussion thus far suggests the following slightly more formal, but tentative, definition.

Definition An *algorithm* is a set of rules that precisely define a sequence of operations.

Although this definition of algorithm is rather vague, it is useful for introducing the concept of algorithms. Later we shall proceed to a more rigorous mathematical definition.

It is often the case that algorithms are directed to people rather than robots. For people to follow the rules of an algorithm, the rules must be formulated so that they can be followed in a robot-like manner, that is, without the need for thought. For example, the following set of rules is an algorithm for finding the roots of the equation $ax^2 + bx + c = 0$:

1. The roots of the equation

$$ax^2 + bx + c = 0$$

are found by evaluating the expressions

$$\frac{-b + \sqrt{b^2 - 4ac}}{2a}$$

and

$$\frac{-b - \sqrt{b^2 - 4ac}}{2a}$$

where $a \neq 0$.

2. If $a = 0$, then the equation has at most one root, which may be found by evaluating the expression

$$\frac{-c}{b}$$

where $b \neq 0$.

3. If both $a = 0$ and $b = 0$, then the equation has no roots.

Notice that all the operations that we have to perform to find the roots of a quadratic equation seem to be well defined, since they involve only the usual simple arithmetic operations, the ability to determine if a number is 0, and the operation of taking a square root. However, if the instructions are to be obeyed by someone who knows how to perform arithmetic operations but does not know how to extract a square root, then we must also provide a set of rules for extracting a square root in order to satisfy the definition of algorithm.

Cooking recipes, travel directions, and college registration instructions are also algorithms. Sometimes, however, these examples do not satisfy our definition of algorithm, for they may include questionable instructions such as "use a handful of flour" or "turn a mile after the last bridge"; you should have no difficulty in finding examples of college registration instructions that fail to satisfy our definition.

Algorithms, as pointed out earlier, may specify iterative behavior in that a particular instruction may be carried out several times. Moreover, the number of times that an operation is to be performed need not be stated explicitly. It may depend on the particular context in which the algorithm is applied. Consider the word description of a sorting algorithm in Example 1·1.

EXAMPLE 1·1

To sort a list of numbers into ascending numerical order, proceed by scanning the list from beginning to end. Each step of the scan consists of inspecting a pair of adjacent numbers in the list. If the first number of a pair is greater than the second number, then the two are interchanged. After inspecting a pair of numbers, and interchanging if necessary, the scan of the list continues by examining the pair of adjacent numbers beginning with the second number of the pair that has just been examined.

Scans of the list are repeated until a scan is performed during which no interchanges occur.

The sorting algorithm of Example 1·1 does not specify how many times to scan the list. If the list contains n numbers, then what is the most number of times that the list will be scanned? What is the fewest?

Clearly, not all instructions are acceptable, because they may require the robot to have abilities beyond those that we consider reasonable. For example, we may instruct a computing robot to "Output the number 0 if Henry VIII was a King of England, otherwise output the number 1." Intuitively we should not expect a robot to obey that instruction unless it has somehow previously been instructed to store the fact that Henry VIII was a King of England. It is even less reasonable to expect the robot to respond to the instruction to "Output the number 0 if Aristotle was a King of England, otherwise output the number 1." In this case either the robot must specifically have the information that Aristotle was not a King of England, or it must have the names of all English kings so that it can search the list of names for the name Aristotle. Suppose the robot has the names of only five English kings. If it cannot find Aristotle's name on that list, what should it do? Obviously in this case the robot cannot determine whether Aristotle was an English king, and so it cannot obey the instruction.

The problem exemplified above is that the instruction requires the robot to have particular information, so that if the information is not given to the robot, it cannot obey the instruction. It may guess what to do, of course, but guessing cannot be permitted if we are to be sure that the robot performs computations correctly. An intuitive definition of an acceptable sequence of instructions is one in which each instruction is precisely defined so that the robot is guaranteed to be able to obey it. With this definition the King of England instruction could be included in an instruction sequence only if the robot were given sufficient information about English kings to determine how to obey the instruction. We say that an instruction is *effective* if there is a procedure that the robot can follow in order to determine precisely how to obey the instruction. In our example the Aristotle instruction is effective when the robot has a list of all Kings of England, but if the list of Kings of England is incomplete, the instruction is not effective.

The effectiveness of an instruction is sometimes dependent on a finiteness property. For example, consider the instruction "If every map can be colored with no more than four colors so that no two adjacent countries have the same color, then output the number 1, otherwise output the number 0." This instruction embodies the famous *four-color conjecture*, which has challenged mathematicians for over a century. Either every map can be colored with four or fewer colors and satisfy the adjacent-country constraint, or there is some map that requires at least five colors to satisfy the constraint. No one has been able to find a map that needs five colors, nor has anyone proved that four colors are sufficient for all maps. Our computing robot could consider every possible map with one country, then two countries, then three countries, etc., and consider every possible way of coloring each of these maps with four or fewer colors. Since there is only a finite number of different ways that n countries can share boundaries, and since for each map with n countries there is only a finite number of different ways it can be colored with four or fewer colors, if there is a map that requires five colors, our robot will surely find it. So our robot can definitely output the number 0 if the four-color conjecture is false. Conversely, if the conjecture is true, then our robot will never discover this. Since the procedure we have given is not guaranteed to terminate in a finite number of steps, the four-color instruction is not an effective instruction.

With a slight modification we can form a similar instruction that is effective because it is finite. Consider the instruction "If every map with fewer than 26 countries can be colored with no more than four colors so that no two adjacent countries have the same color, output the number 1, otherwise output the number 0." Since we have limited the number of countries to 26 or fewer, our computing robot can examine every possible way that 26 or fewer countries can share boundaries and can decide if the four-color conjecture is true for 26 or fewer countries. Clearly the new instruction is effective, and it is effective if we replace the number 26 by any integer we care to name.

The preceding discussion illustrates that every algorithm must have the property of *finiteness;* that is, it must terminate in a finite number of steps. The first of the four-color procedures above is guaranteed to settle the four-color conjecture, because each map will eventually be examined unless the robot finds a counterexample to the conjecture. It could be shown by a tedious exercise that each instruction in the procedure is both finite and effective; yet the procedure as a whole is not an algorithm because it will not terminate in a finite time if the conjecture is true.

There is one more property that we require of algorithms. Each instruction of an algorithm must be precisely defined so as to avoid any ambiguity or misinterpretation. Algorithms that satisfy this property are said to be *definite.* An example of a definite instruction is "If x is greater than 1, then output 1, otherwise output 0." Suppose, however, that the instruction is "If the number x is very much greater than 1, then output 1, otherwise output 0." Now, we know that the robot must output 0 if $x = -2$, and we feel rather sure that it will output 1 if $x = 1,000,000$. However, what should it do if $x = 17$? And if it produces a 0 when $x = 17$, should it also produce a 0 when $x = 343$?

To summarize the discussion in this section, we define an algorithm to be a set of rules that precisely defines a sequence of operations such that each rule is effective and definite and such that the sequence terminates in a finite time.

1·2 Turing Machines

In order to make the definition of algorithm more rigorous let us consider the *Turing machine.* This "machine" is an abstract mathematical model that takes its name from A. M. Turing, who first introduced the concept in 1936 in a paper dealing with the theory of computation.

A Turing machine algorithm will be composed of rules drawn from a very restricted set. We shall suppose that the rules are obeyed by a computing device called a Turing machine. Since the actions of the Turing machine are motivated by the actions of a human being in carrying out an algorithm, the Turing machine is given "scratch paper" in the form of an infinite tape such that each square on the tape can contain only one symbol from a finite alphabet of symbols.

The Turing machine can read and write on its tape by means of a *head.* At any instant of time the head can read or write a symbol only in the square of the tape that is directly under it, but the Turing machine can be instructed to move the head left or right along the tape, one square at a time, to place any square under the head. Besides the tape memory, the Turing machine contains one other cell. This cell holds a symbol called the *state* of the machine, and this symbol is drawn from a finite alphabet that is different from the tape alphabet. An algorithm for the Turing machine consists of a set of rules that involve head motion, tape operations, and change of state. The state of the machine at a particular instant of time identifies the instruction that the Turing machine is carrying out at that time. Figure 1·1 shows a conceptual diagram of a Turing machine, with the head represented by an arrow pointing to a square on the tape and the state of the machine shown as a number attached to the head.

The actions of the Turing machine are determined completely by rules that specify the actions to be taken for each possible state and each possible observed symbol.

To be more precise, each rule for a Turing machine is a five-tuple of the form

$$(q_i, s_j, q_{ij}, s_{ij}, d_{ij})$$

where q_i is one of the states of the machine and s_j is one of the symbols that may appear on the tape of the machine. For each state-symbol pair the rule gives the next state of the machine, q_{ij}; the symbol to write in the currently observed cell, s_{ij}; and the next cell to observe on the tape, d_{ij}. By convention, $d_{ij} = 1$ if the next cell is the cell to the right of the current cell, -1 if it is the cell to the left, and 0 if the current cell will be observed again as the next cell. Also by convention, one of the states is distinguished as the stopping state and is given the name HALT.

An algorithm for the Turing machine consists of a set of five-tuples such that there is exactly one five-tuple for each state-symbol pair, excluding the HALT state. Such an algorithm is known as a *Turing machine program*.

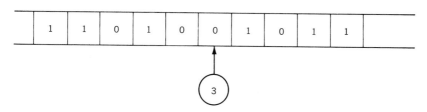

Figure 1·1 A conceptual view of a Turing machine

The computation of a Turing machine is described by stating:

1. The tape alphabet
2. The form in which parameters are represented on the tape
3. The initial position of the head of the Turing machine
4. The initial state of the Turing machine
5. The form in which answers will be represented on the tape when the Turing machine halts
6. The machine program

EXAMPLE 1·2

The following machine adds 1 to a positive integer and then halts.

Tape alphabet: 0,1.

Input representation: The integer i is represented by a string of i adjacent 1's bounded by 0's.

Head position: On the leftmost 1 of the input parameter if the parameter is nonzero, otherwise on a 0.

Initial state: State 1.

Output representation: The integer is represented by a string of adjacent 1's bounded by 0's.

Machine program:

q_i	s_j	q_{ij}	s_{ij}	d_{ij}
1	0	HALT	1	0
1	1	1	1	1

Example 1·2 illustrates a very simple Turing machine algorithm that has one state other than the HALT state. This algorithm adds 1 to an integer by the following strategy. The representation of an integer is a *unary* representation; that is, the integer i is represented by i consecutive 1's bounded on each side by 0's. To add 1 to an integer the head is moved right until a 0 is found. The machine replaces the 0 by a 1 and then halts. The algorithm works equally well if the head is moved left instead of right.

EXAMPLE 1·3

The following machine compares two positive integers for equality.

Tape alphabet: 0,1.

Input representation: Unary (same as Example 1·2), two numbers placed on tape separated by a single zero.

Head position: On the 0 between the two numbers.

Output representation: The head is reading a 0 if equal and a 1 if unequal.

Initial state: State 1.

Machine program:

q_i	s_j	q_{ij}	s_{ij}	d_{ij}	ACTION
1	0	2	0	1	Move to right of center mark.
1	1	—	—	—	Impossible state-symbol pair.
2	0	3	0	−1	No 1's to right of center, look to left of center.
2	1	4	1	1	Found a 1 on right, move to end of string of 1's.
3	0	HALT	0	−1	Move left and point to answer.
3	1	—	—	—	
4	0	5	0	−1	At end, back up one square
4	1	4	1	1	Scan over 1's.
5	0	—	—	—	
5	1	6	0	−1	Erase the rightmost 1.
6	0	7	0	−1	At center, move to check left parameter.
6	1	6	1	−1	Scan left to center marker.
7	0	HALT	1	0	Mark unequal and stop.
7	1	8	1	−1	Scan to leftmost 1.
8	0	9	0	1	Back up one square.
8	1	8	1	−1	Scan to leftmost 1.
9	0	—	—	—	
9	1	10	0	1	Erase leftmost 1.
10	0	1	0	0	Go back to start.
10	1	10	1	1	Scan right to center marker.

Example $1 \cdot 3$ is a Turing machine program for comparing two numbers for equality. The two numbers are placed on the tape initially so that they are separated by a single 0, and the algorithm begins with the head reading that 0. The strategy of this algorithm is to subtract 1 from each of the numbers until one of them becomes 0. The two numbers are equal if they both become 0 after the same number of 1's are subtracted from each. Notice in particular that the 1's are subtracted from the far right and far left on the tape. This guarantees that the two numbers are always separated by a single 0 until one of them becomes 0. If 1's were subtracted from the middle, then there would be a string of several 0's separating the numbers, and this string would grow in length as more 1's were subtracted. Consider what would happen in this program when the last 1 of a number were subtracted. The next time that the machine tried to subtract 1 from that number, it would start the head moving over the string of 0's looking for a 1, and the 1 would never appear, causing the machine to repeat the same instruction forever. Of course, there are ways of preventing this behavior if 1's are subtracted from the middle, but the point here is that there are a number of subtle aspects of Turing machine programs which are related to the problem of positioning the head on the tape. The strategy of subtracting the outermost 1's was selected for Example $1 \cdot 3$ primarily because it neatly disposes of the head-positioning problem.

It is rather interesting to investigate other computations that can be done by a Turing machine. Turing machines can be programmed to do addition, subtraction, multiplication, and division of numbers by using strategies similar to those of Examples $1 \cdot 2$ and $1 \cdot 3$. It is not surprising that they can perform more complex operations such as the extraction of the square root of a number, since such operations are based totally on the arithmetic operations and the ability to make conditional changes in an instruction sequence.

Turing machine algorithms that are guaranteed to halt in a finite time satisfy the definition of algorithm presented earlier. Since our definition did not specify the form of the rules of an algorithm, there is sufficient latitude in our definition to allow other abstract models of algorithms. As we examine the form of rules we may use for algorithms, we find it is very difficult to identify a set of rules that is truly different from the rules that define the behavior of Turing machines. For example, we may seek a set of rules that permit arithmetic operations such as addition and subtraction. Although Turing machines cannot perform arithmetic operations as single steps, they certainly can perform all of the arithmetic operations. Hence arithmetic operations alone cannot increase the power of computation of a set of rules beyond the power of the rules that govern the behavior of Turing machines.

Several mathematicians have proposed models of algorithms that use rules substantially different from the Turing machine rules. Nevertheless, all the abstract mathematical models have proved to be equivalent in that the sets of computations that can be described by algorithms within each model are exactly the same. The evidence seems to indicate that every algorithm for any computing device has an equivalent Turing machine algorithm. In fact, Alonzo Church has formulated a famous conjecture which says in essence that everything that is computable is computable by a Turing machine. So far Church's thesis has not been shown to be either true or false. If the conjecture is true, then it is certainly remarkable that Turing machines, with their extremely primitive operations, are capable of performing any computation that any other device can perform, regardless of how complex a device we choose.

REFERENCES

Readers interested in pursuing the study of the theory of computation will especially enjoy Minsky (1967), from which some of the material in this chapter is drawn. Minsky's book contains very good discussions of Church's thesis and noncomputable functions, among other topics. Davis (1958) is a much deeper text on this subject and may be of interest to the advanced student. Rogers (1967) contains a thorough discussion of Church's thesis and its importance in the study of recursive functions. The original definition of a Turing machine appeared in an article by Turing (1936).

EXERCISES

1·1   Several state-symbol pairs are not used at all in Example 1·3. Find a way to reduce the number of states by modifying the five-tuples. Simulate your program on a tape that contains the number 5 to the left of the marker and the number 3 to the right. Show the contents of the tape, the state of the machine, and the position of the head at just those instants when the head is about to change direction.

1·2   Write a Turing machine program that doubles an integer. Use a binary tape alphabet. Simulate your machine as described in Exercise 1, given the number 4 on its tape.

1·3 Write a Turing machine program that computes the product of a pair of operands. Use a four-symbol tape alphabet $\{0,1,X,Y\}$ and a unary representation of input and output data. Simulate your machine given the numbers 2 and 3.

1·4 Write a Turing machine program that compacts disjoint sequences of 1's into one contiguous sequence. Assume that the sequences to be compacted lie to the right of the initial tape head position, that they are separated by a single 0, and that at least two 0's lie to the right of the rightmost sequence. Simulate your program on the tape $\cdots 001101011100 \cdots$ and show that it produces the tape $\cdots 001111110000 \cdots$.

1·5 Prove that the following Turing machine program will never reach the HALT state when started on the all-0's tape (Lin and Rado, 1965).

q_i	s_j	q_{ij}	s_{ij}	d_{ij}
1	0	2	1	1
1	1	HALT	1	1
2	0	3	0	−1
2	1	2	1	−1
3	0	1	0	1
3	1	2	1	−1

2

Basic Aspects
of Computer
Organization

The previous chapter describes the Turing machine as an abstract model of a computer. In this chapter we shall see that the Turing machine, in spite of its abstract qualities, has many characteristics in common with modern digital computers. Figure 2·1 shows a block diagram of a typical computer. The memory component is the counterpart of the Turing machine tape. The module labeled processing unit corresponds roughly to the portion of a Turing machine that executes instructions. The representation in Figure 2·1 is greatly oversimplified, primarily to emphasize the similarity of computers to the Turing machine. When we investigate the detailed behavior of computers we shall see that they are in fact somewhat different from the Turing machine.

The material that follows describes the characteristics of a typical digital computer, particularly its instruction repertoire, the in-

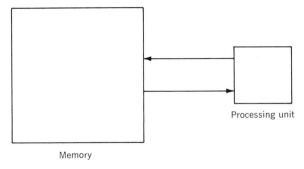

Processing unit

Memory

Figure 2·1 The structure of a digital computer

struction-execution mechanism, and the representation of numbers. The Hewlett-Packard 2116 computer serves as a running example throughout this chapter, but the treatment is sufficiently general to encompass a wide variety of computers.

2·1 Computer Memories

One of the difficulties encountered in programming Turing machines is the problem of storing intermediate results on the tape and retrieving the information later. When information must be copied from a storage area on the tape to an active computation area of the tape, the Turing machine must follow a complex sequence of instructions to move the head back and forth between the two portions of the tape. The head might make several trips between the two tape areas, one trip for each symbol of information. Fortunately advanced technology has provided storage media for computers that are far less cumbersome than Turing machine tapes. Digital-computer memories provide access to any specified storage position in a single operation. Moreover, the time required for a memory operation is independent of the location of the last item accessed. This mode of access is known as *random access*.

Figure 2·2 shows a block diagram of a computer memory which is typical of most computer memories. There are computer memories which are not organized precisely as indicated in Figure 2·1 or which do not behave exactly as the following description indicates. Nevertheless, the presentation here is sufficiently accurate for our purposes.

18

The memory contains a storage area, two registers designated T and M, and two control inputs designated GO/IDLE and READ/WRITE, respectively. The storage area is divided into cells called *words*, which are very much like the cells on the Turing machine tape. Each word is uniquely identified by a number called the word *address*. If the memory has N words, then the addresses are 0, 1, 2, . . . , $N-1$. Each word has the ability to store one datum, which corresponds to the symbol stored in a cell on the Turing machine tape.

An important aspect of computer memories is the manner in which they can be controlled by the processing unit. Figure $2 \cdot 2$ depicts some of the details of the control circuitry. The T and M registers are two special memory cells whose function is described below. We use the

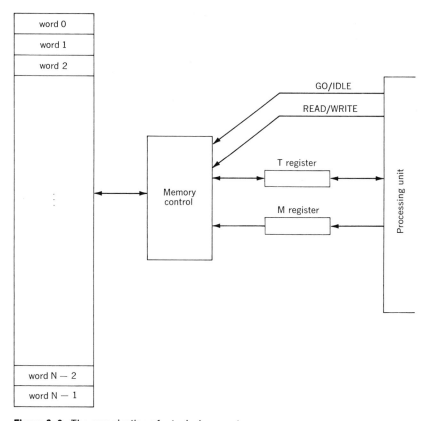

Figure 2·2 The organization of a typical computer memory

word *register* to identify a memory cell that is used for specialized functions, in contrast to a memory cell in the main computer memory, which is used for general-purpose information storage. In most computers, registers are constructed for higher-speed operation than the main computer memory, usually at a higher cost per component when the extra cost is justifiable. As we shall see, the speed of the entire computer depends critically on the speed at which we can modify the contents of the T and M registers.

The memory shown in Figure 2·2 looks somewhat like a Turing machine tape because it is one-dimensional, but there are essential differences. Naturally, real computers cannot have infinite memories, and so there is an upper limit on the amount of information that can be stored in a computer memory. No such limit exists for Turing machines. The use of addresses for computer memories is another distinguishing feature. We can speak about the contents of "the word with address 106" in a computer memory, and the address distinguishes this word from all the others. Since the Turing machine tape does not have addresses associated with each cell, we can only identify a specific piece of information on the tape in terms of its surrounding environment. For example, we might refer to the "datum immediately to the right of the first pair of adjacent 0's that lies to the right of the present head position."

The GO/IDLE control line shown in Figure 2·2 controls the activity of the memory. It can be in one of two states that are designated GO and IDLE. When the control line changes state from IDLE to GO, the memory begins a cycle of operation. At the completion of an operation the memory sets the control line to IDLE and awaits a new request.

To store a datum at a particular word in memory, the address of the word is placed in the M register and the datum is placed in the T register. The READ/WRITE control line is placed in the WRITE state, and the GO/IDLE control is set to GO (these operations are all performed by the processing unit of the computer). When the memory senses the GO signal, it begins its operation cycle. The WRITE signal on the second control line causes the memory to erase the datum found at the address indicated by the M register and replace it by the datum in the T register.

Retrieval is performed by placing an address in M and setting the second control line to READ. When the GO signal is issued, the memory copies the datum at the location given by M into the T register. The contents of the memory are not changed by this operation.

A more compact way of expressing the behavior of the memory is given by the following symbolism:

WRITE: MEMORY[M] ← T;
READ: T ← MEMORY[M];

The notational conventions used here follow those of the programming language ALGOL. Here we represent the N words in memory as MEMORY[0], MEMORY[1], . . . , MEMORY[N−1]. The bracketed items are analogous to subscripts. Then MEMORY[M] refers to the word in memory at the address that is stored in the M register. The left arrow signifies data movement. When an item appears to the left of a ←, as does MEMORY[M] in the WRITE action, we treat it as the name of the destination of data. Hence MEMORY[M] in the WRITE action signifies that MEMORY[M] receives the data. When an item appears to the right of ←, it is treated as a value. Hence the MEMORY[M] that appears in the READ action refers to the contents of MEMORY[M].

Thus far we have not discussed the physical mechanisms involved in storage of data or the technical details of the design of a computer memory. A complete discussion is beyond the scope of this text, but some technological characteristics deserve comment because they influence the organization and the programming of computers.

Nearly all computers use a magnetic medium for storing data in memory. The most common memory device in use today is the *magnetic core*, a small doughnut-shaped piece of ferrite with a diameter about one- or two-hundredths of an inch. When a core is magnetized, the magnetic domains can be aligned either clockwise or counterclockwise around the central hole. Thus a core can assume one of two magnetic states. By convention, one state is said to represent the symbol 0 and the other the symbol 1. A typical computer memory may contain from 10^5 to 10^7 magnetic cores.

As mentioned previously, computer memory is organized into words, each of which can hold a single datum. For several reasons it is not practical to associate a single magnetic core with a word. It is much more convenient to associate a fixed number of cores with each word, so that a datum stored at a word in memory consists of a vector of 0's and 1's, where the length of the vector is the number of cores per word. The individual components of a datum are called *binary digits* or *bits*. The number of bits per word in memory varies from computer to computer and may be as small as 8 or as high as 64, with multiples of 6 and 8 the most common. The Hewlett-Packard 2116, for example, has 16 bits per word.

In a later section we shall discuss how numbers are represented and manipulated in a binary number system. For the present we shall continue to assume that each word in memory can hold a single number.

2·2   Structure of the Processing Unit

The *processing unit* is the portion of a computer that executes program instructions, and thus it corresponds to the part of a Turing machine that performs the actions specified by five-tuples. The processing unit contains a few special registers which are used for holding data in active computation. Each processor register serves a particular function, in the same manner that the T and M registers serve special functions. One such register, called the *P register*, identifies the instruction currently being executed. The P register is thus the computer counterpart of the current state of a Turing machine.

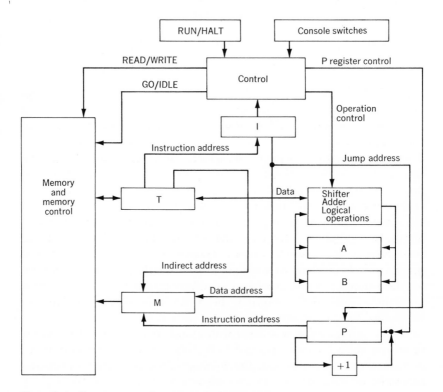

Figure 2·3   The structure of a typical processing unit

The processing unit also contains one or more data registers that serve as temporary storage and are used for arithmetic processing of data. In particular, the Hewlett-Packard 2116 computer has two data registers, designated as the A and B *registers*. Figure 2·3 shows the gross structure of the processing unit and its interconnection with memory.

To illustrate the behavior of the processor we shall consider a few instructions in the instruction repertoire of the Hewlett-Packard computer. Instructions for other computers are similar, but not necessarily identical, to those given here.

Each instruction described below specifies an operation and an address in memory. Associated with each instruction is a short mnemonic code called an *operation code*, or simply *code*, which is an abbreviation for the operation. Thus LDA is the code used for the load A register instruction. Addresses are designated by such symbols as X, MAX, and HEAD. Each such address is actually a number that is used to form a memory address.

INSTRUCTION	CODE	EXAMPLE	ACTION
Load A register	LDA	LDA X	A ← MEMORY[X]
Load B register	LDB	LDB MAX	B ← MEMORY[MAX]
Add to A register	ADA	ADA Y	A ← A+MEMORY[Y]
Add to B register	ADB	ADB Y	B ← B+MEMORY[Y]
Store A register	STA	STA Z	MEMORY[Z] ← A
Store B register	STB	STB HEAD	MEMORY[HEAD] ← B

The two load instructions copy a designated word of memory into a register in the processing unit. The contents of memory are unchanged by these instructions. The add instructions differ from the load instructions in that a datum is not merely copied into a register, but is added to the current contents of a register. The two store instructions copy a register into a designated word of memory. The contents of the register referenced by the store instruction are left unchanged by the execution of the instruction.

The column labeled ACTION is intended to show the effect of the execution of the instruction. However, the execution is actually more intricate than indicated there. Recall that every load and store operation must set an address in the M register and must transfer data to or from the T register. A more detailed description of the LDA X instruction is the following:

```
M ← X;
READ;
GO;
T ← MEMORY[M];
A ← T;
```

The instructions above are unlike those for Turing machines, but all aspects of Turing machine instructions are present. Notice that the memory address portion corresponds to that part of the Turing machine instructions that specify head movement. Instead of using a sequence of head-movement instructions to find a datum, as we might do with a Turing machine, we can access the datum in one operation by specifying its address in an instruction.

The portion of a Turing machine instruction that specifies the symbol to be written on the tape corresponds roughly to the operation code of the instruction. The load instructions, for example, copy data from memory to the A or B register. The data in memory may be viewed as symbols in remote areas of a tape that are rewritten as they are read. The A register may be viewed as a portion of a tape whose previous contents are erased as a copy of the remote data is written into it.

There is one other aspect of Turing machine instructions that bears discussion. Recall that each Turing machine instruction specifies the next state of the Turing machine. As mentioned earlier, the P register contains a number that corresponds to the state of the Turing machine. As we might expect, the digital-computer instructions specify how to modify the contents of the P register to change the state of the processing unit. For a full understanding of how this is done we must consider the notion of the stored program.

2·3 The Stored Program

Up to this point we have discussed instructions for computers without considering how they are stored in the computer. The computer memory provides an ideal place to store instructions, since, when a program has run to completion, the memory can be erased and replaced with a new set of instructions. Moreover, random-access addressing of memory guarantees that the successor of each instruction can be retrieved in one memory cycle, regardless of its location in memory.

The P register in the processing unit contains the address of the instruction that is undergoing execution. All the instructions described thus far cause the P register to be incremented by 1, so that the next instruction to be executed is the instruction at the next higher address. The following instructions cause different behavior of the P register:

INSTRUCTION	CODE	EXAMPLE	ACTION
Jump	JMP	JMP X	$P \leftarrow X$
Compare A, skip if unequal	CPA	CPA MAX	**if** $A = \text{MEMORY[MAX]}$ **then** $\quad P \leftarrow P+1$ **else** $\quad P \leftarrow P+2;$
Compare B, skip if unequal	CPB	CPB MAX	**if** $B = \text{MEMORY[MAX]}$ **then** $\quad P \leftarrow P+1$ **else** $\quad P \leftarrow P+2;$
Increment, skip if zero	ISZ	ISZ COUNT	$\text{MEMORY[COUNT]} \leftarrow \text{MEMORY[COUNT]}+1;$ **if** $\text{MEMORY[COUNT]} \neq 0$ **then** $\quad P \leftarrow P+1$ **else** $\quad P \leftarrow P+2;$
Jump to sub-routine	JSB	JSB SINE	$\text{MEMORY[SINE]} \leftarrow P+1;$ $P \leftarrow \text{SINE}+1;$
Skip on sign of A	SSA	SSA	**if** $A \geq 0$ **then** $\quad P \leftarrow P+2$ **else** $\quad P \leftarrow P+1;$
Skip on sign of A, reverse sense of skip	SSA,RSS	SSA,RSS	**if** $A < 0$ **then** $\quad P \leftarrow P+2$ **else** $\quad P \leftarrow P+1;$
Skip on sign of B	SSB	SSB	**if** $B \geq 0$ **then** $\quad P \leftarrow P+2$ **else** $\quad P \leftarrow P+1;$
Skip on sign of B, reverse sense of skip	SSB,RSS	SSB,RSS	**if** $B < 0$ **then** $\quad P \leftarrow P+2$ **else** $\quad P \leftarrow P+1;$

At the completion of any of the above instructions—or, for that matter, of any instruction—the computer executes the next instruction at the address contained in the P register.

The following program illustrates how the JMP and CPA instructions operate. The instruction labeled LOOP is executed 11 times:

ADDRESS	CODE	OPERAND	COMMENTS
	LDA	ZERO	Initialize A register to 0.
LOOP	CPA	TEN	Does A register contain 10?
	JMP	NEXT	Yes, continue with other processing.
	ADA	ONE	No, increase A register by 1.
	JMP	LOOP	Repeat, starting at CPA.
NEXT	. . .		

The memory cells identified as ZERO, TEN, and ONE contain the decimal numbers 0, 10, and 1, respectively.

We may also use the ISZ instruction to control repetitive portions of a program. The instruction labeled LOOP in the example below is repeated 11 times. The memory cell identified as MINUS11 contains the decimal number -11.

ADDRESS	CODE	OPERAND	COMMENTS
	LDA	MINUS11	
	STA	COUNT	Initialize COUNT to −11.
LOOP	ISZ	COUNT	Increase COUNT, skip next instruction if result is 0.
	JMP	LOOP	
NEXT	. . .		

The JSB instruction not only causes the instruction sequence to be changed, but it also leaves behind the address of the instruction following JSB. The saved address provides a mechanism for returning to the instruction after the JSB instruction. The JSB instruction and its uses are described in detail in Chapter 7.

The SSA and SSB instructions provide a means for testing the sign of an operand. Note that no memory address is specified for these instructions. In some contexts it is more efficient to reverse the skip behavior of SSA and SSB, and for such contexts we can make use of the instructions SSA,RSS and SSB,RSS.

In order to store instructions in memory we must be able to encode them into combinations of bits. Similarly, we must also encode numbers as combinations of bits. Moreover, since the contents of a memory cell are simply a collection of bits, there must be a mechanism that decides whether the bits are to be interpreted as a number or as an instruction, because a memory cell may contain either entity. Both these facets of computers are treated in the sections that follow.

2·4 Number Representations Based on a Binary Radix

The decimal notation 1234 is interpreted as a number that is the sum of one 1000, two 100's, three 10's, and four 1's, or more succinctly,

$$1234 = 1 \cdot 10^3 + 2 \cdot 10^2 + 3 \cdot 10^1 + 4 \cdot 10^0$$

The abstract notion of *number* is quite independent of decimal representation. It is a matter of convention that we represent the numbers by a sequence of decimal symbols. Because of the inherent binary characteristic of computer components, numbers in computer systems are represented internally by sequences of binary symbols rather than decimal symbols. Binary representation and decimal representation of numbers are both examples of *radix representations*.

Given any positive integer b, where $b \geq 2$, the radix-b representation of a positive integer N is the sequence of digits $n_{m-1}, \ldots, n_1, n_0$, where $0 \leq n_i \leq b-1$, $N < b^m$, and $N = \Sigma n_i b^i$. It is a relatively straightforward exercise in algebra to show that the radix-b representation of a positive integer N is unique, except possibly for leading 0's. Hence 1234 is the unique decimal representation of our example number, except that an arbitrary number of 0's may be prefixed to the representation. We shall indicate the radix of a representation by subscript, as in 1234_{10}, when it is not clear from context.

Decimal arithmetic generalizes to other radices. For example, radix-b addition is similar to decimal addition, except that carries are generated whenever a sum digit is b or larger instead of 10 or larger. For example, the usual arithmetic operations would be as follows in the radices indicated.

$$
\begin{array}{r}
34112_5 \\
+24441_5 \\
\hline
114103_5
\end{array}
\qquad
\begin{array}{r}
75314_9 \\
-66525_9 \\
\hline
7678_9
\end{array}
\qquad
\begin{array}{r}
21332_4 \\
\times \quad 133_4 \\
\hline
131322 \\
131322 \\
21332 \\
\hline
10311002_4
\end{array}
\qquad
\begin{array}{r}
12_3 \\
212_3 \overline{)11021_3} \\
212 \\
\hline
1201 \\
1201 \\
\hline
\end{array}
$$

Although binary representation is basic to computers, for practical convenience radix-8 and radix-16 representations are used as shorthand notation in the computer world. They are easily derived from binary representation by partitioning binary symbols into groups of three or four and finding their base-8 or base-16 equivalents. For example,

$$101001110100_2 = 101\ 001\ 110\ 100_2$$
$$= 5\quad 1\quad 6\quad 4_8$$

The letters A to F are used to represent integers 10 to 15 in radix-16 representation. Hence

$$1010\ 0111\ 0100_2 = A74_{16}$$

Representation of fractions in nondecimal radices is a natural generalization of decimal-fraction representation. To the right of a binary point, for example, the symbols in a binary fraction representation are the coefficients of 2^{-1}, 2^{-2}, etc. Thus 101.1101 is the binary representation of 5.8125_{10}, computed as

$$1 \cdot 2^2 = 4$$
$$0 \cdot 2^1 = 0$$
$$1 \cdot 2^0 = 1$$
$$1 \cdot 2^{-1} = .5000$$
$$1 \cdot 2^{-2} = .2500$$
$$0 \cdot 2^{-3} = 0$$
$$1 \cdot 2^{-4} = \underline{.0625}$$
$$5.8125_{10}$$

2·5 Representation of Negative Numbers

Representation of negative numbers has not been standardized in the computer industry. Four alternative schemes are discussed in this chapter. Their relative advantages and disadvantages are related mainly to the cost and speed of operation of the arithmetic processor. Since this aspect is beyond our present scope, no attempt is made to evaluate the various schemes. The computer specialist is likely to come in contact with all four representations in the course of his career.

2·5·1 Two's-complement Representation

We use the notation $\bar{X}$ to mean the *complement* of X, where X is a vector of 0's and 1's. To obtain $\bar{X}$ from X we change the 0's in X to 1's and the 1's to 0's. The complement operation is of central importance in the representation of negative numbers.

Let X be the binary representation of a number N. Then the number $-N$ in two's-complement representation is defined to be $\bar{X}+1$. By assumption in our discussion of the various methods for representing negative numbers, the representation of a number has exactly m binary bits, where m is an integer constant and is equal to the number of bits per memory word. We have to be careful to consider what happens if adding the integer 1 to $\bar{X}$ causes the representation to exceed m bits. The two's complement of X is defined so that carries that leave the most significant bit position are lost. For example, the two's complement of $00 \cdots 0_2$ is $11 \cdots 1_2 + 00 \cdots 01_2$. When we do the addition, we obtain a carry out of the leftmost bit position; this is disregarded, yielding the result $00 \cdots 0$. Since the number whose representation is $00 \cdots 0_2$ is the number 0_{10}, we see that the negative of 0_{10} is 0_{10}, as it should be. To distinguish between positive and negative numbers, it is usual practice to use the leading bit of the binary representation for a sign bit. If the sign bit is 0, the number is positive; if the sign bit is 1, the number is negative.

What is the range of integers that can be represented in two's-complement form when m is the number of bits per word? To answer this, note that positive integers can be represented by setting the first bit to 0 and using the remaining $m - 1$ bits to represent the integer magnitude. All integers in the range $0 \leq x < 2^{m-1}-1$ can be represented as positive integers. For negative integers the sign bit is 1, and the remaining $m - 1$ bits are available to represent the magnitude of the integer. The representation of -1 is $111 \cdots 1$, and the representation of the most negative integer is $1000 \cdots 0$, which is the representation of -2^{m-1}. Hence all numbers in the range $-2^{m-1} \leq x \leq 2^{m-1}-1$ are representable.

Addition of two numbers in this representation system follows two rules:

1. First add the two numbers and observe if a carry occurs into the sign bit and if a carry occurs out of the sign bit.

2. If no carries occur or both carries occur, the sum is in range. If one, and only one, of the two carries occurs, there has been an overflow.

EXAMPLE 2·1

The following arithmetic operations use a word length $m = 4$:

0101	5	Carry into sign bit, overflow.
0110	6	
1011	11	

0101	5	
0010	2	
0111	7	

0101	5	
1010	−6	
1111	−1	

0110	6	Carry into sign and out of sign bit, no overflow.
1011	−5	
0001	1	

1011	−5	Two carries, no overflow.
1111	−1	
1010	−6	

1011	−5	Overflow, true result is negative because of carry out of sign
1010	−6	position.
0101	−11	

Example 2·1 shows that arithmetic in two's-complement representation leads to consistent results. That is, when we add the representations of two numbers, we obtain the representation of their sum, provided that no overflow occurs. It is easy to see why this is so. Let the radix representation of the positive integer N be $n_{m-1}, \ldots , n_1, n_0$, so that $b = \Sigma n_i 2^i$. We say that the digit n_i has a *weight* of 2^i, since it is the coefficient of 2^i in the summation. Two's-complement representation is a representation in which the sign digit n_{m-1} has a *negative weight* of 2^{m-1} instead of a positive weight of 2^{m-1} (see Exercise 2·9). Since arithmetic with ordinary radix representations is consistent, two's-complement arithmetic is consistent, except possibly for arithmetic operations which generate carries into and out of the sign position. The overflow rules specify the conditions for correct results in these cases.

To clarify the overflow rules let us consider what happens when we add two positive integers. The sum of two positive integers must be positive, and to be representable, this sum cannot exceed $2^{m-1}-1$. If it should exceed $2^{m-1}-1$, a carry into the sign position occurs without an accompanying carry out of the sign position. Hence this particular carry condition is an overflow condition. It is easy to check that the sum of a positive and a negative number can never overflow, and such a sum always produces either 0 or both carries that involve the sign position. The last case to consider is the sum of two negative numbers. When does such a sum overflow, and how is the overflow condition distinguished by the carries?

Most computers have an instruction that permits the programmer to test for overflow. In the HP 2116 computer, if an overflow is sensed by the processor, according to rule 2 above, an overflow indicator is turned on. The state of the overflow indicator can be sensed by the instruction skip on overflow set (mnemonic code SOS), which causes the computer to skip the next instruction if the indicator is on. The instruction skip on overflow clear (mnemonic code SOC) causes the computer to skip the next instruction if the overflow indicator is off. Prior to an addition operation that could cause an overflow, the overflow indicator must be turned off with a clear overflow instruction (mnemonic code CLO).

EXAMPLE 2·2

The following program shows how to add two numbers and test for overflow:

CLO	Clear overflow indicator.
LDA X	Load A with X.
ADA Y	Add Y.
SOS	Skip if overflow occurred.
JMP EXIT	Normal exit.
. . .	First instruction of overflow processing sequence.

When it is known that overflow cannot occur, or that it is of no consequence if it does occur, then the only instructions necessary are the LDA and ADA instructions.

Most computers have instructions that subtract the contents of a specified memory location from a machine register. During execution of such instructions the computer adds the negative of the subtrahend to the contents of the machine register. The HP 2116 computer does not have such an instruction, so that the negative must be computed explicitly. For this purpose we make use of the instructions complement A (code CMA) and increment A by 1 (code INA). These two instructions can be combined into a single instruction as follows in a program for computing $X - Y$:

LDA Y	Load Y into A register.
CMA,INA	Complement A, then add 1.
ADA X	X—Y Is now in A register.

Two's-complement representation is preferable to other representations for the HP 2116 computer because the programming is slightly easier, as we shall see later. Computers that have subtraction, multiplication, and division built in are based on a particular representation of negative numbers and do not permit the programmer to select the representation.

2·5·2 One's-complement Representation

In the one's-complement system, if X is the binary representation of the integer N, then $-N$ is represented by $\bar{X}$. Since a 1 is not added to the complement of a number, as in two's-complement arithmetic, special action is necessary to ensure that computations will generate answers in the proper representation. With respect to addition, no action need be taken if two positive numbers are added, but if two negative numbers are added, the answer will be too small by 1. To see this compare the addition of two negative numbers in both one's-complement and two's-complement arithmetic. Let X and Y be the positive integers, and calculate $(-X) + (-Y)$. Note that the results below show a numerical difference of 2 in the representations when there should be a difference of only 1.

$$\begin{array}{r} \bar{X} + 1 \\ +\bar{Y} + 1 \\ \hline \bar{X} + \bar{Y} + 2 \end{array} \quad \text{Two's complement}$$

$$\begin{array}{r} \bar{X} \\ +\bar{Y} \\ \hline \bar{X} + \bar{Y} \end{array} \quad \text{One's complement}$$

The following rules for addition state precisely how to determine when

1 must be added to the sum and how to determine whether overflow occurred:

1. Add the two operands.

2. If a carry out of the sign occurs, then add 1 to the sum (this is called an *end-around carry*).

3. Inspect carries into the sign and out of the sign. If only one of the two carries occurs, then overflow has occurred.

EXAMPLE 2·3

The following examples show one's-complement addition for operands of length $m = 4$:

0101	5	Carry into sign bit. Overflow.
0110	6	
1011	11	

0101	5	
0010	2	
0111	7	

0101	5	
1001	−6	
1110	−1	

0110	6	Two carries occur, end-around carry added to intermediate
1010	−5	sum.
0000	1	
+1		
0001		

1101	−2	Two carries occur, end-around carry added to intermediate
1100	−3	sum.
1001	−5	
+1		
1010		

1101	−2	End-around carry, but no carry into sign bit. Overflow.
1001	−6	
0110	−8	
+1		
0111		

Following the reasoning of the previous section, it is a relatively straightforward matter to establish the correctness of the rules for one's-complement addition and to prove that the representation system is consistent. In particular, one's-complement representation is a representation in which the weight of the sign bit is $-(2^{m-1}-1)$.

One's-complement arithmetic operations can be programmed for the HP 2116 computer by implementing rule 2. The computers that have one's-complement representation built into their arithmetic hardware automatically follow rule 2, thereby relieving the programmer of a minor burden.

EXAMPLE 2·4

The following program illustrates how to implement rules 2 and 3 on the HP 2116 computer. If a carry out of the sign position occurs, the E register, a one-bit processing-unit register, is set to 1. The instruction clear E (code CLE) places a 0 in the E register prior to the addition operation. The E register is tested with the instruction skip if E is 0 (code SEZ).

LABEL	CODE	OPERAND	COMMENTS
1.	CLE		Clear E (carry out of sign bit).
2.	CLO		Clear overflow.
3.	LDB	ZERO	Clear B register to count carries.
4.	LDA	X	First operand to A register.
5.	ADA	Y	Add second operand.
6.	SOC		Skip if 0 or both carries occurred.
7.	ADB	ONE	Increment B if one carry occurred.
8.	CLO		Clear overflow, get ready for end-around carry.
9.	SEZ		Check for end-around carry.
10.	ADA	ONE	Increment A register if carryout occurred.
11.	SOC		Check for overflow on the previous instruction, skip if no overflow.
12.	ADB	ONE	Increase B to indicate another carry.
13.	CPB	ONE	Check for an odd number of carries.
14.	JMP	OFLOW	Jump to overflow program if exactly one carry occurred.
15.	. . .		

The instruction sequence can be shortened somewhat if overflow cannot occur or is not important. The following instruction sequence computes $X - Y$ without overflow checking:

CLE	Clear E register.
LDA Y	
CMA	One's complement of Y in A register.
ADA X	X—Y is in A register.
SEZ	Skip if E is 0.
ADA ONE	Add end-around carry.

Note that this instruction sequence is three instructions longer than the equivalent sequence for a two's-complement representation.

The range of representable numbers in the one's-complement system is of interest because it is slightly different from the range for two's-complement representation. Again, we let the first bit indicate the sign of a number and use the remaining $m - 1$ bits of an m-bit computer word to represent the magnitude of the number. The range of positive representable integers must be the same for both one's-complement and two's-complement representations, since the representation of positive integers is the same in both systems. The most negative representable number in the one's-complement system must be 1 greater than the most negative two's-complement number, because negative representations in the two systems differ by 1. Hence the range of representable numbers in the one's-complement system is $-2^{m-1}+1 \leq N \leq 2^{m-1}-1$. Notice that the range is symmetric with respect to zero, whereas for two's-complement representation the range is not symmetric with respect to zero. The significance of the symmetry is that in the one's-complement system, if N is representable, then so is $-N$. However, in the two's-complement system there is a representable integer N such that $-N$ is not representable. Which integer is this? What happens when we attempt to negate this integer with the CMA, INA instruction?

There is an interesting anomaly in the one's-complement system that can cause some frustration to the programmer. There are two different representations of zero in this system, since both $00 \cdot \cdot \cdot 0_2$ and $11 \cdot \cdot \cdot 1_2$ satisfy the usual rules that we reserve for zero. To differentiate between the two zeros we usually refer to $00 \cdot \cdot \cdot 0_2$ as *plus zero* and to $11 \cdot \cdot \cdot 1_2$ as *minus zero*. To verify that minus zero is truly a zero consider the following examples:

```
0101      5
1111    +(−0)
-----   -----
10100     5
    1           End-around carry.
-----
0101

0101      5
1010     −5
-----   -----
1111     −0
```

When the integer N is added to its negative, $-N$, in one's-complement notation the result is always minus zero rather than plus zero. In circumstances when it is necessary to check to see if a result of a computation is equal to zero, the result must be compared to *both* plus zero and minus zero, whereas only a single comparison is necessary for two's-complement notation, since the representation of zero is unique.

2·5·3 Signed-magnitude Representation

Each integer in this representation system is represented by m bits, of which the first is a *sign bit*. The remaining $m-1$ bits represent the magnitude of the integer in the conventional binary system. If $m = 4$, then representations of $+5$ and -5 are 0101 and 1101, respectively. Arithmetic in this system can be programmed on the HP 2116 computer, but with considerably more difficulty than either of the other two representations. The machines that use this representation have hardware that does arithmetic operations with signed-magnitude operands and produces signed-magnitude results without burdening the programmer with the details of representation. The range of representable numbers is identical to that for one's-complement representation, and both plus zero and minus zero are representable.

2·5·4 Excess-2^{m-1} Representation

In this number system the representation of the number N, where $-2^{m-1} \leq N \leq 2^{m-1}-1$, is the ordinary binary representation of $N+2^{m-1}$. Clearly $0 \leq N+2^{m-1} \leq 2^m-1$, so that $N+2^{m-1}$ is guaranteed to be a positive integer that is representable in m bits. It is rather interesting that this number representation system is identical to the two's-complement system, except that the sign bits are coded differently. A sign of 0 indicates a positive integer in the two's-complement system, whereas it indicates a negative integer in the excess-2^{m-1} system. Thus $1100000 = 32_{10}$ in the excess-64 system, whereas $0100000_2 = 32_{10}$ in the two's-complement system.

The relationship of the excess-2^{m-1} to the two's-complement system makes it particularly simple to derive the rules for detecting overflow. How can we use the overflow-sensing instructions to detect overflow in the system?

2·6 Floating-point Representation

In the number representations discussed thus far the computer hardware is insensitive to the location of the binary point. For example, suppose 0101110_2 and 0001011_2 are two operands; their sum is 0111001_2. If the binary point were to the right of the rightmost bit, then the two operands would be 46_{10} and 11_{10}, respectively, and their sum would be the representation of 57_{10}. However, if the binary point were between the fourth and fifth bits, counting from left to right, the operands would be the representations of 5.750_{10} and 1.375_{10}, respectively, and their sum would be the representation of 7.125_{10}. This example suggests that the programmer may establish a binary point in any position that he chooses. Of course, he must assure that the binary points of operands are aligned for addition and subtraction operations. Moreover, the position of the binary point of quotients and products depends on the position of the binary points of their operands. Hence for multiplication and division operations the programmer must adjust the results of the operation to account for a possible discrepancy between the actual position of the binary point and its desired position.

It is possible to simplify the bookkeeping related to binary-point locations by adopting the binary equivalent of scientific notation. In the usual scientific notation a number is represented by a mantissa and a power of 10—for example, $1.234 \cdot 10^7$. The exponent of 10 merely designates the true location of the decimal point, and the mantissa 1.234 contains the significant digits of the number, with a decimal point placed in a fixed position, usually to the right of the first digit. The representations that we have discussed thus far encode only the mantissas of numbers, and not the binary points. The location of binary points is implicit in the computer representation. Consequently, by appropriate scaling the programmer can fix the binary point in any location he desires. Number representations of data internal to computers in which the binary point is implicit are called *fixed-point representations*. Representations in which the location of the binary point is encoded separately from the mantissa are called *floating-point representations.* Scientific notation is an example of a floating-point representation.

A great many different kinds of floating-point representations are possible; in fact, there are at least a dozen different ones in use on commercial computers. A typical representation is as follows:

Sign	Sign of exponent	Exponent	Mantissa
0	0	001010	1000000000

The binary point of the mantissa is assumed to be between the first and second bits of the mantissa, and the exponent is assumed to be an integer. Thus the example represents the number $1.0 \cdot 2^{10} = 1024_{10}$. A positive exponent indicates that the binary point should be shifted to the right for a true representation, and a negative exponent indicates that a shift to the left is necessary. This convention is consistent with scientific notation.

The many variations possible for floating-point representations arise from the different possible representations for negative numbers and the possible locations for the implicit binary point in the mantissa. In yet another variation the exponent can be treated as an exponent of 8 or 16 instead of 2. In this case it is convenient to view the mantissa representation as a radix-8 or radix-16 representation in which the exponent describes the location of the octal point or the hexadecimal point, respectively. Most computers order the elements of the floating-point representation as shown above, although there are a few cases in which the exponent is located to the right of the mantissa.

Among the many representations that have been implemented, one's complement, two's complement, signed magnitude, and excess 2^{m-1} have all been used for the exponent. Similarly, the mantissa has been represented in one's-complement, two's-complement, and signed-magnitude schemes. The sign representation of the mantissa generally follows the usual practice of 0 for positive and 1 for negative. Radix points of mantissas are usually assumed to be just in front of the leading digit, after the rightmost digit, or between the first and second digits, where the digits are binary, octal, or hexadecimal.

The three examples in Table 2·1 illustrate the wide variety of representations. For purposes of comparison we assume that the bits in a computer word are numbered from left to right, starting at 0.

In any floating-point representation there are numbers that do not have a unique representation. This characteristic is due to representations that have different exponents with appropriately scaled man-

Table 2·1

	HP 2116 (TWO COMPUTER WORDS)	IBM SYSTEM/ 360-370	BURROUGHS B-5500 (BIT 0 NOT USED)
Exponent			
Sign position	31	1	2
Position	24 to 30	2 to 7	3 to 8
Representation	Two's complement	Excess 64	Signed magnitude
Mantissa			
Sign position	0	0	1
Position	1 to 23	8 to 31	9 to 47
Representation	Two's complement	Signed magnitude	Signed magnitude
Radix	2	16	8
Radix point	Before first digit	Before first digit	After last digit

tissas. Thus in scientific notation the numbers $1.00 \cdot 10^0$, $0.10 \cdot 10^1$, and $0.01 \cdot 10^2$ are all the same number, although they differ in the number of significant digits that follow the leading nonzero digit. In computers the usual practice is to choose a representation such that the leading digit of the mantissa is nonzero if the number is nonzero. This is called *normalized representation*. In radix-8 and radix-16 representations the leading octal digit or hexadecimal digit is nonzero, but the leading bit may be 0. Special hardware in some computers automatically produces results of floating-point operations in normalized form.

In spite of the variety of representations, the following rules for converting decimal numbers to floating-point numbers can be applied generally:

1. Convert the decimal number to binary in the system of representation used for the mantissa.

2. Compute the number of digits that the radix point must be shifted in order to obtain a normalized representation; this is the exponent.

3. Convert the exponent into the representation used for exponents.

4. Combine the exponent and the normalized mantissa.

EXAMPLE 2·5

Represent 1/32 in the IBM System/360 format.

1. $(1/32)_{10} = .00001_2$.

2. The representation is normalized by shifting the hexadecimal point one digit (four bits) right. Hence the exponent is -1.

3. The excess-64 representation of -1 is 0111111_2.

4. The full representation is

   0 0111111 1000 0000 0000 0000 0000 0000.

2·7 Representation of Instructions in Computer Memory

We have discussed various ways of representing numbers in a computer memory, but we have not yet discussed how to represent instructions. It is essential that instructions be encoded into sequences of bits, and design considerations suggest that they be encoded to occupy whole words or multiples thereof. In the HP 2116 computer, for example, each word has 16 bits, so that each memory fetch brings a group of sixteen 0's and 1's from memory to the T register. Hence the encoding used in this computer is such that instructions generally occupy one word, except for groups of special instructions that are combined in one word.

The 16-bit word shown in Figure 2·4 illustrates a typical pattern that might have been fetched from a word in the memory of an HP 2116 computer. The bits are numbered 0 to 15, from right to left, following the manufacturer's convention (this convention is exactly reversed for the IBM System/360 and System/370 computers). Suppose the computer reaches the point at which it has to find the next instruction.

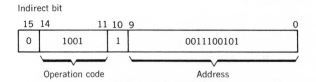

Figure 2·4 Instruction format for the HP 2116 computer

It initiates a READ operation to the word whose address is in the P register, and we shall assume that the result shown in Figure 2·4 appears in the T register at the end of the memory cycle.

The computer interprets the pattern in the register as an instruction in the following way. The four-bit segment of the word that extends from bit 14 to bit 11 is interpreted as the operation code according to the patterns shown in Table 2·2. The 10-bit word segment extending from bit 9 to bit 0 is interpreted as the binary representation of an integer lying in the range $0 \leq n \leq 1023$. The 10-bit number is the memory address of the operand of the instruction. We shall defer the explanation of the interpretation of bits 15 and 10 until Chapter 4.

Table 2·2

PATTERN	CODE
0101	JMP
0111	ISZ
1000	ADA
1001	ADB
1010	CPA
1011	CPB
1100	LDA
1101	LDB
1110	STA
1111	STB

An essential aspect of the instruction representation is that there is no inherent difference in the physical storage of instructions and data. When the computer fetches a datum from memory, the word obtained is interpreted as a number. When the computer fetches an instruction, the word obtained is interpreted as an instruction. Therefore two distinct memory cycles must occur during execution of the LDA instruction and similar instructions. The first memory fetch obtains the instruction; the second occurs when the instruction is obeyed.

In order to permit words fetched from memory to be interpreted in more than one way, the processor can assume one of three states during the execution of an instruction. This state determines how a word fetched from memory is to be interpreted. In particular, the two states FETCH and EXECUTE control the behavior described here. The third state, INDIRECT, controls another facet of the processor behavior that is described in Chapter 4.

If a word fetched from memory is to be interpreted as an instruction, it is placed in a processor register called the I register, which is shown in Figure 2·3. This is done when the processor is in the FETCH state. When the processor is in the EXECUTE state, the contents of the I register determine the operation that is performed. When, for example, the I register contains an LDA instruction, then another memory fetch occurs, but the next word fetched from memory is placed in the A register rather than the I register.

To be more precise, the computer obeys the following description (the notation I_{14-11} denotes bits 14 to 11 of the I register):

```
FETCH state      M ← P;
                 T ← MEMORY[M];
                 I ← T;
                 M ← T₉₋₀;
                 change state to EXECUTE state;

EXECUTE state    if I₁₄₋₁₁ = 1100 then
                     begin (LDA instruction execution)
                         T ← MEMORY[M];
                         A ← T;
                         P ← P+1;
                         change state to FETCH state;
                     end
                 else
                 if I₁₄₋₁₁ = 1110 then
                     begin (STA instruction execution)
                         T ← A;
                         MEMORY[M] ← T;
                         P ← P+1;
                         change state to FETCH state;
                     end
                 else
                 . . .
                 (other instructions)
```

When the processor completes its action in the FETCH state, it switches to the EXECUTE state. In the EXECUTE state, the contents of the I register are interpreted, the instruction is obeyed, and the P register is adjusted. On completion of instruction execution the state is changed back to the FETCH state, and the processor repeats the actions for obtaining a new instruction.

Since the instructions for a program and the data for a program reside in the same memory, it is possible to treat program instructions as data and to execute a datum as if it were a program instruction. In fact, we might write a program that replaces an STA instruction with an STB instruction, or replaces a JMP X with a JMP Y instruction. Such a program is said to be *self-modifying*. For many years it was fashionable to write self-modifying programs, and indeed, the design of early computers demanded that programs be self-modifying for the sake of efficiency. Although it has long been known that programs need not modify themselves, it has only recently been realized that programs that do not modify themselves enjoy certain advantages over self-modifying programs. In this text we shall generally adhere to the purist principle that programs never modify themselves, although some of the examples of programs for the Hewlett-Packard 2116 of necessity violate this dictum.

REFERENCES

In 1945 Eckert and Mauchly constructed what is generally said to be the first digital computer. Their computer, ENIAC, had instructions similar to those described in this chapter, but programs were not stored in computer memory. Programming for ENIAC was done by wiring plug boards.

The concept of the stored program is generally credited to Von Neumann, although Rosen (1969), in his historical survey of electronic computers, also credits Eckert and Mauchly for this idea. Burks, Goldstine, and Von Neumann (1946) proposed plans for the first electronic digital computer at the Institute for Advanced Study. Their proposal is rather remarkable in its detail and sophistication and reflects nearly all the concepts of present-day computer operation. Moreover, two decades of advances in computer technology have not changed computers materially from the original proposal.

Construction of the IAS computer was begun in the late 1940s, but it was not completed until 1952, by which time several other computers were also in operation. These early computers were quite similar to the computer described in this chapter, with the major differences attributable to the constraints on the memory organization imposed by the early memory technology.

For a detailed treatment of the history of the development of computers see Bell and Newell (1971).

EXERCISES

2·1 Verify the following equalities:

$$67_{10} = 74_9 = 103_8 = 124_7 = 151_6 = 232_5 = 1003_4 = 2111_3$$

2·2 Convert 13441_{10} to its radix-16 equivalent. Convert 7777_8 to radix 10 and $A3D2_{16}$ to radix 10.

2·3 State an algorithm for changing a number from radix-b representation to radix-d representation for any integers b and d greater than 1.

2·4 Prove that the radix-8 representation of any integer can be obtained from its radix-2 representation by partitioning the radix-2 representation into three-digit groups. (Note: Always partition from the binary point. $11011_2 = 11\ 011_2 = 33_8 \neq 110\ 11 = 63_8$.)

2·5 Find the binary representation of 5.3_{10}. Since 5.3_{10} can be represented exactly in radix-10 notation, why can it not be represented exactly in radix-2 representation? Find a number that cannot be represented exactly in radix-10 representation but can be represented exactly in some other radix.

2·6 Formulate algorithms for multiplication and division (*a*) when both operands are always positive and (*b*) when both operands are represented in two's-complement form. Assume that both operands are integers, and that the dividend is a multiple of the divisor.

2·7 Formulate algorithms for addition and multiplication when the operands are in floating-point format.

2·8 Let the integer 1 be represented as a single 1 bit preceded by as many 0's as necessary to occupy a word of computer memory. If, by mistake, this number is treated as a floating-point number by a B-5500 computer, what is its value? What is its value in System/360-370 format? (Note: The bits are assumed to be numbered from left to right in the formats given.) For the B-5500 and

System/360-370, which integers have a floating-point representation identical to their signed-magnitude representation?

2·9 Prove that two's-complement representation is the same as the radix-2 representation of integers, except that the sign bit has weight -2^{m-1}, where m is the number of bits per word. Prove that the sign bit has weight $-(2^{m-1}-1)$ in one's-complement representation.

3

IBM System/360 and System/370 Computer

The IBM System/360 and System/370 computers differ from the Hewlett-Packard 2116 in several ways that are significant to the programmer. In this chapter we shall consider the organization of these computers, and a few examples of instructions for them.

3·1 Memory Organization

In the Hewlett-Packard 2116 computer each word of memory is 16 bits. Moreover, all memory references cause a single 16-bit word to be transferred between the T register and memory. It is impossible to access more or fewer than 16 bits at a time. For added flexibility it is desirable to be able to access data of varying lengths, and System/360-370 computer memory is organized to give this flexibility.

A diagram of System/360-370 computer memory is shown in Figure 3·1. Each addressable cell in memory is eight bits long and is called a *byte*. Groups of bytes, as well as individual bytes, can be accessed during the execution of a single instruction. For example, Figure 3·1 indicates that a pair of adjacent bytes, the first of which is even numbered, can be accessed together as a group called a *halfword*. All the data lengths that can be accessed by a single instruction are as follows:

NAME	LENGTH	ADDRESS CONSTRAINT
Byte	8 bits	Any address.
Halfword	16 bits	First byte must have even address.
Full word	32 bits	First address must be divisible by 4.
Double word	64 bits	First address must be divisible by 8.

The constraints on addressing groups of bytes form natural boundaries within memory. The beginning of a byte with an even address is said to be a *halfword boundary* because a halfword may not cross this point. Full-word boundaries and double-word boundaries are defined similarly.

3·2 Organization of the Processing Unit

The processing unit of System/360-370 computers has substantially more registers than the HP 2116 computer. There are two different sets of registers, one for floating-point arithmetic operations and the other for general-purpose operations. These are shown in Fig. 3·2. There are four floating-point registers, each 32 bits in length. Instead of identifying the registers by different letters, as we have done for the HP 2116 computer, the usual convention is to use the integers 0, 2, 4, and 6. Figure 3·2 indicates that the four floating-point registers are used as four full-word or four double-word registers. There are 16 general-purpose registers in the processing unit, similar to the A and B registers of the HP 2116 computer, and these are numbered 0 to 15. These registers can be used as double-word registers, where the first register of a register pair is even numbered.

3·3 Arithmetic Instructions

To make use of the flexibility of the memory organization there is essentially a separate instruction repertoire for each datum length.

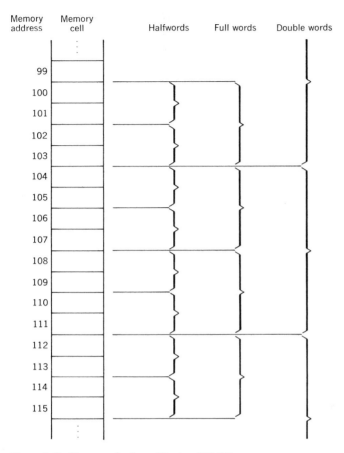

Figure 3·1 The organization of System/360–370 memory

We shall discuss in some detail the instructions that manipulate full word data and then consider briefly the classes of instructions that manipulate data of other lengths.

Full word data can be retrieved from memory and placed in one of the 16 general-purpose registers by using the load instruction (code L) as follows. The instruction

L   3,X

copies the full word, beginning at memory address X, into register 3. Of course, we assume that X is a memory address that lies on a full

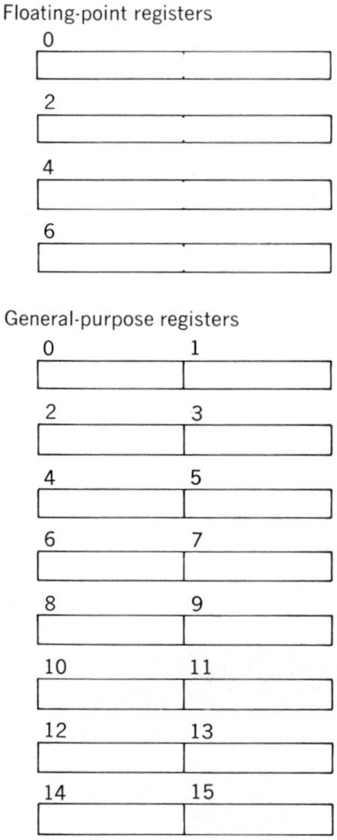

Floating-point registers

0

2

4

6

General-purpose registers

0	1
2	3
4	5
6	7
8	9
10	11
12	13
14	15

Figure 3·2 Data registers in the processing unit of a System/360–370 computer

word boundary. The action of the L instruction is then

REG[3] ← MEMORY[X;X+1;X+2;X+3];

The four subscripts of MEMORY separated by semicolons indicate that four bytes of memory are transferred. We also refer to general-purpose register 3 as REG[3], which exactly parallels the term MEMORY in reference to computer memory. The following table gives the full-word instructions for arithmetic operations:

INSTRUCTION	CODE	EXAMPLE	ACTION
Load full word	L	L 3,X	REG[3] ← MEMORY [X;X+1;X+2;X+3];
Store full word	ST	ST 3,Y	MEMORY[Y;Y+1;Y+2;Y+3] ← REG[3];

INSTRUCTION	CODE	EXAMPLE	ACTION
Add full word	A	A 7,Z	REG[7] ← REG[7]+MEMORY [Z;Z+1;Z+2;Z+3];
Subtract full word	S	S 7,W	REG[7] ← REG[7]−MEMORY [W;W+1;W+2;W+3];
Multiply full word	M	M 6,U	REG[6,7] ← REG[7]×MEMORY [U;U+1;U+2;U+3];
Divide full word	D	D 6,V	REG[7] ← REG[6;7]÷MEMORY [V;V+1;V+2;V+3]; REG[6] ← remainder of division;

The ST instruction is the inverse of the L instruction, and it is the counterpart of the STA and STB instructions for the HP 2116 computer. The A instruction adds two full-word operands and produces a full word result; its HP 2116 counterpart is the ADA instruction. The next three instructions are not similar to instructions in the HP 2116 computer.

The S instruction subtracts one full word operand from another and places the difference in a processing-unit register. As indicated in Chapter 2, the subtraction operations depend on the representation of negative numbers. System/360-370 uses two's-complement representation for the fixed-point full word arithmetic operations, and the subtraction, multiplication, and division processes are clearly sensitive to this choice. Consequently the programmer cannot choose the representation of negative numbers flexibly, but must use two's-complement representation to obtain maximum efficiency.

The M and D instructions require some discussion because of several characteristics not detailed in the table. In general, when two m-bit numbers are multiplied, the product can contain as many as $2m$ significant bits, but no more. For this reason the M instruction produces a double-word product from two full word operands. We recall that the first register of a double-word register pair must be even numbered, so that the result register—that is, the register addressed by the M instruction—must be even. This can be confusing, since the multiplier is not in the register addressed by the instruction, but in the register with an index one greater.

As an example of the use of the M instruction, suppose that the full word beginning at MEMORY[X] contains $2^{18}+1 = 0004\ 0001_{16}$, and suppose that REG[5] contains $2^{18}-1 = 0003\ FFFF_{16}$. Then, after the instruction

M   4,X

the double-word register REG[4;5] will contain

$$2^{36} - 1 = 0000\ 000F\ FFFF\ FFFF_{16}$$

Naturally the contents of REG[4] before the multiplication are lost, and they do not affect the result of the operation.

Division generally presents a problem in digital computers because a quotient may require an infinite number of digits in its representation even when the divisor and dividend both involve a finite number of digits. Hence division is usually truncated to a fixed number of digits in the quotient. System/360-370 full-word division is integer division. By this we mean that both the dividend and divisor are treated as integers, and an integer quotient is produced. Obviously the quotient cannot be exact except when the dividend is a multiple of the divisor. We indicate integer division in the description of the D instruction by using the symbol $\div$ instead of the symbol / as the division operator. Integer division is defined so that the remainder after division has the same sign as the dividend and is smaller in absolute value than the divisor. Thus $5 \div 3 = 1$ and $-5 \div 3 = -1$. In effect, positive quotients are truncated downward and negative quotients are truncated upward.

We noted that the product of two m-bit numbers will, in general, have $2m$ bits. By similar reasoning it is clear that the quotient of an integer division involving a $2m$-bit dividend and an m-bit divisor will have as many as m bits. Hence the D instruction operates on a double-word dividend and a full-word divisor to produce a full word result. For this reason the result register specified by the D instruction must be even. When the division operation is complete, the quotient is in the odd-numbered register and the remainder is in the even-numbered register of the same pair.

As an example of the D instruction, suppose that the full word beginning at MEMORY[X] contains the number $0000\ 0003_{16}$ and that the double-word register REG[8;9] contains the number

$$0000\ 0000\ 0000\ 0005_{16}$$

Then the instruction

D   8,X

produces the quotient $0000\ 0001_{16}$ in REG[9] and the remainder $0000\ 0002_{16}$ in REG[8].

If both operands of an arithmetic operation are available in the general-purpose registers, then it is possible to perform the arithmetic operation without fetching data from memory. The following full-word arithmetic instructions manipulate data stored only in the general-purpose registers:

INSTRUCTION	CODE	EXAMPLE	ACTION
Load (register)	LR	LR 3,4	REG[3] $\leftarrow$ REG[4];
Load complement (register)	LCR	LCR 3,6	REG[3] $\leftarrow$ $-$REG[6];
Add (register)	AR	AR 4,5	REG[4] $\leftarrow$ REG[4]+REG[5];
Subtract (register)	SR	SR 2,7	REG[2] $\leftarrow$ REG[2]$-$REG[7];
Multiply (register)	MR	MR 4,9	REG[4;5] $\leftarrow$ REG[5]$\times$REG[9];
Divide (register)	DR	DR 6,3	REG[7] $\leftarrow$ REG[6;7]$\div$REG[3]; REG[6] $\leftarrow$ remainder;

Except for LCR, all these instructions are identical to the corresponding instructions that reference memory for one operand. The LCR instruction forms the two's-complement of a number, so that it is used to compute the negative of a number. The two registers referenced in the LCR instruction may be the same register, in which case the LCR is essentially the same as the pair CMA,INA for the HP 2116 computers.

There is a small set of instructions for halfword data that is similar to the full-word instruction set. These instructions are given in the following table:

INSTRUCTION	CODE	EXAMPLE	ACTION
Load halfword	LH	LH 3,W	REG[3] $\leftarrow$ MEMORY[W;W+1];
Store halfword	STH	STH 5,X	MEMORY[X;X+1] $\leftarrow$ REG[5];
Add halfword	AH	AH 6,Y	REG[6] $\leftarrow$ REG[6]+MEMORY[Y;Y+1];
Subtract halfword	SH	SH 4,Z	REG[4] $\leftarrow$ REG[4]$-$MEMORY[Z;Z+1];

The AH and SH instructions perform 32-bit two's-complement addition and subtraction in the registers even though the operand fetched from memory is only 16 bits in length. This is done by treating the leading bit of a 16-bit operand as a sign bit and generating the 32-bit representation that represents the same number for use in the arithmetic operation. This means that if the sign bit is 0, the leading 16 bits of the 32-bit operand are cleared to 0, and if the sign is 1, the leading 16 bits of the 32-bit term are set to 1. Thus the sign bit is extended through the leading 16 bits. Similarly, the LH instruction either clears to 0 or sets to 1 the 16 leading bits of the result register.

As mentioned earlier, floating-point operations are performed in the floating-point registers. There are instructions for manipulating both full-word and double-word floating-point numbers. For example, the following instructions illustrate four ways of loading a floating-point register (FPREG denotes a floating-point register):

INSTRUCTION	CODE	EXAMPLE	ACTION
Load (floating-point full word)	LE	LE 4,X	FPREG[4] ← MEMORY[X; . . .];
Load (floating-point double word)	LD	LD 2,Y	FPREG[2;3] ← MEMORY[Y; . . .];
Load (floating-point full word, register)	LER	LER 2,4	FPREG[2] ← FPREG[4];
Load (floating-point double word, register)	LDR	LDR 4,6	FPREG[4;5] ← FPREG[6;7];

The table illustrates that the suffixes E, D, ER, and DR are used to distinguish the four floating-point load instructions. The same suffixes are used, together with A, S, M, and D, to generate four versions of each of the floating-point arithmetic instructions. Similarly, STE and STD are the two floating-point store instructions.

We shall not consider floating-point operations and several other forms of arithmetic operation in detail here. Instead we shall limit our attention exclusively to the full-word instructions, since they illustrate the salient characteristics of the System/360-370 computers.

3.4 Conditional and Unconditional Branching

Recall that the instruction repertoire for the HP 2116 computer includes instructions that change the sequence of execution of instructions. These instructions for the HP 2116 are called *jump instructions* if the instruction can change instruction sequence arbitrarily, or *skip instructions* if under certain conditions they cause an instruction to be skipped. The System/360-370 instruction repertoire includes instructions equivalent to the jump instructions which can cause jumps either conditionally or unconditionally. These instructions have come to be called *branch instructions*, but the terms "branch" and "jump" are synonymous in this context. There are no skip instructions or equivalent instructions in the System/360-370 repertoire.

Conditional branching is controlled by a two-bit register called the *condition code*. The value of the condition code is determined by data-dependent conditions that exist when the execution of an instruction is completed. Such conditions as overflow, the sign of a result, or the relative magnitude of two operands can cause the condition code to assume particular values. Unconditional branching is essentially the same as conditional branching, except that the condition code does not condition the branch.

The following instructions cause the condition code to be set to the values indicated:

INSTRUC-TION	CODE	EXAMPLE	CONDITION-CODE SETTING			
			0	**1**	**2**	**3**
Compare	C	C 3,X	REG[3] = MEMORY[X]	REG[3] < MEMORY[X]	REG[3] > MEMORY[X]	· · ·
Compare (register)	CR	CR 3,4	REG[3] = REG[4]	REG[3] < REG[4]	REG[3] > REG[4]	· · ·
Load and test (register)	LTR	LTR 3,4	REG[3] = 0	REG[3] < 0	REG[3] > 0	· · ·

The action of this example of LTR is to load REG[3] from REG[4] and then set the condition code. The LTR instruction is similar to the LR instruction in its execution; the only difference is that LTR sets the condition code and LR does not.

Many of the instructions that we have already discussed also set the condition code. For example, the A instruction leaves the condition code set to reflect the outcome of an addition. The settings for this instruction are the following:

CONDITION CODE	MEANING
0	Sum is 0.
1	Sum is negative.
2	Sum is positive.
3	Overflow.

A listing of the condition-code settings for all the instructions appears in the manual "Principles of Operation," form A22-6821 of the System 360 library. All our examples will use only the C, CR, and LTR instructions to control conditional branches.

Conditional branches are executed by means of an instruction that contains a four-bit field called a *mask*. The four bits correspond to the four possible states of the condition code, as given in the following table:

CONDITION CODE	MASK BIT
0	$1000_2 = 8_{16}$
1	$0100_2 = 4_{16}$
2	$0010_2 = 2_{16}$
3	$0001_2 = 1_{16}$

When a conditional branch instruction is executed, the sequence of instructions is as follows:

1. Find the value of the condition code.

2. Examine the corresponding bit of the mask.

3. If the mask bit is 1, then the branch is taken, otherwise no branch occurs and the instruction immediately following the current instruction is the next to be executed.

The branch instructions that make use of the condition code are the following:

INSTRUCTION	CODE	EXAMPLE	ACTION
Branch on condition	BC	BC MASK,X	Take next instruction from MEMORY[X] if value of condition code specifies a mask bit with value 1.
Branch on condition (register)	BCR	BCR MASK,2	Take next instruction from MEMORY[REG[2]] if value of condition code specifies a mask bit with value 1.

The difference between BC and BCR is that the second operand of the BC instruction is a memory address, whereas the second operand of the BCR instruction is a register that contains a memory address.

Now suppose the instruction that immediately precedes a branch instruction is the instruction

    CR   2,3

If the mask for the branch instruction is 8_{16}, then the branch instruction is taken only if registers 2 and 3 contain the same value. That is, the branch is essentially a branch if equal instruction. Therefore, instead of using the instruction

    BC   8,X

it is more informative to write

    BE   X

where the BE means branch if equal. Of course, there is no BE instruction in the repertoire. Wherever the BE instruction appears, it should be replaced by BC with a mask equal to 8_{16}. Similarly, BC with a mask set to all 1's always causes a branch. Thus we use B for this case and call it branch unconditionally. The following table gives all branches that are of use to us. They are arranged in two groups, one for use after the C and CR instructions and the other for use after the LTR or arithmetic instructions. The table includes only the various forms of the BC instruction. There is a similar set that are variants of the BCR instruction.

Following the usual convention, these have mnemonic codes that have the suffix R.

INSTRUCTION	CODE	MASK
Branch unconditionally	B	$F_{16} = 1111_2$
Branch on high	BH	$2_{16} = 0010_2$
Branch on low	BL	$4_{16} = 0100_2$
Branch on equal	BE	$8_{16} = 1000_2$
Branch on not high	BNH	$D_{16} = 1101_2$
Branch on not low	BNL	$B_{16} = 1011_2$
Branch on not equal	BNE	$7_{16} = 0111_2$
Branch on plus	BP	$2_{16} = 0010_2$
Branch on minus	BM	$4_{16} = 0100_2$
Branch on zero	BZ	$8_{16} = 1000_2$
Branch on not plus	BNP	$D_{16} = 1101_2$
Branch on not minus	BNM	$B_{16} = 1011_2$
Branch on not zero	BNZ	$7_{16} = 0111_2$
Branch on overflow	BO	$1_{16} = 0001_2$

There are two other classes of branch instructions that deserve mention here. One class, the BCT and BCTR instructions, controls iterations of a set of instructions and corresponds to the ISZ instruction of the HP2116 computer. The other class, the BAL and BALR instructions, causes the address of the instruction that immediately follows them to be saved before a branch is taken. The following table gives the special branch instructions (recall that the P register holds the address of the instruction being executed):

INSTRUCTION	CODE	EXAMPLE	ACTION
Branch on count	BCT	BCT 5,X	REG[5] ← REG[5]−1; if REG[5] $\neq$ 0 then P ← X;
Branch on count (register)	BCTR	BCTR 5,6	REG[5] ← REG[5]−1; if REG[5] $\neq$ 0 then P ← REG[6];
Branch and link	BAL	BAL 14,X	REG[14] ← P+1; P ← X;
Branch and link (register)	BALR	BALR 14,R	REG[14] ← P+1; if R $\neq$ 0 then P ← REG[R];

The comments in the ACTION column are not totally accurate, for reasons relating to the encoding of instructions. Where the phrase P+1 appears, it refers to the address of the instruction that follows. In reality the P register is increased by either 2 or 4, depending on the number of bytes occupied by an instruction. Similarly, it is not completely accurate to say that just the P register is saved during the execution of the BAL and BALR instructions, since the condition code and other items are also saved. We shall discuss both these points later.

One last point of great importance is that the BALR instruction need not cause a branch. The explanation of the instruction indicates that the instruction

BALR   14,0

does not cause a branch to be taken, whereas

BALR   14,15

causes the next instruction to be taken from the memory cell at the address that is contained in REG[15]. In either case the address of the instruction that follows the BALR instruction is placed in REG[14].

3·5 Instruction Encoding

All the instructions described thus far fall into one of two classes: instructions which specify a register and a memory cell or instructions which specify two registers. Since there are 16 general-purpose registers, only four bits are needed to specify a register. Clearly a four-bit memory address would be unduly restrictive. Consequently instructions that contain memory addresses require more bits for encoding than equivalent instructions that have register references in place of memory addresses.

The encodings for the two classes of instructions are shown in Figure 3·3. Instructions that specify two registers are generally called *RR instructions* (register-to-register), while the instructions that specify a register and a memory cell are called *RX instructions* (register-to-indexed-storage). The encodings shown in Figure 3·3 indicate that RR instructions occupy two bytes of memory and the RX instructions occupy four bytes because of the extra room required for memory addresses.

For all instructions the first byte is the *operation code*, which uniquely identifies the instruction. In RR instructions the next byte

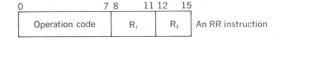

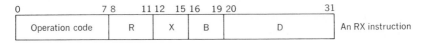

Figure 3·3 Instruction encoding for System/360–370 instructions

contains the identifiers of two registers, each four bits in length. The RX instructions use the second byte slightly differently from the RR instructions. The first four bits contain a register identifier, and the second four bits, labeled X in Figure 3·3, are used in conjunction with the remaining portion of the instruction to specify a memory address. The next two bytes contain a four-bit segment labeled B and a 12-bit segment labeled D. The contents of the B, D, and X fields specify a memory address according to an algorithm that will be described in detail in Chapter 4.

3·6 The Program Status Word

System/360-370 computers have a 64-bit register called the *Program Status Word* that holds information relating to the state of the computer. Obviously the address of the instruction currently being executed should be included in this register, and indeed, Figure 3·4 shows that the P register is the rightmost three-byte portion of the Program Status Word. Note also that the condition code resides in bits 34 and 35 of the Program Status Word. Other portions of the Program Status Word contain information that is not relevant to our discussion here.

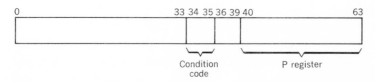

Figure 3·4 The Program Status Word. The unlabeled fields contain miscellaneous control information

The idea behind the Program Status Word is to concentrate all the information pertaining to the state of a program into one register. Then one program can be suspended and another can be initiated by changing the contents of the Program Status Word, provided that both programs can be resident in memory simultaneously. There are instructions both for storing and for reloading the Program Status Word that facilitate the process of changing from one program to another.

Any instruction that can modify the entire Program Status Word can be executed only by a program called the *operating system* or *executive program*, since this is the program that controls the allocation of the central processing unit among several programs. The mode of operation in which a computer can be shared by several programs that reside in memory simultaneously is generally known as *multiprogramming*.

Ordinary programs can access the rightmost four bytes of the Program Status Word by means of the BAL and BALR instructions. As indicated earlier, these instructions cause the P register to be copied into a designated register. Actually the entire four-byte group that contains the P register and the condition code is copied into the designated register. Our concern, however, is only in the ability to access the P register.

REFERENCES

The description of a large-scale computer such as the System/360-370 is inherently encumbered by myriad facts, any one of which may be essential for treating a pathological programming situation. The most complete source of all relevant facts is the IBM Systems Reference Library; however, its completeness interferes somewhat with efficient retrieval of pertinent information. Within this library, "Principles of Operation," form A22-6821, contains a complete description of the System/360 computer organization and of the instruction repertoire. It is a good reference document and serves well as a supplement to this text.

4

Address Modification and Logical Operations

Earlier chapters covered basic arithmetic instructions that are common to many computers. However, arithmetic computations represent a very small subset of the many types of computations for which computers are well suited. The Turing machine view of computers suggests that they are primarily symbol manipulators. Arithmetic computations are merely computations in which the symbols have meaning as numbers. Computers are also extremely valuable for such basically nonnumeric operations as information storage and retrieval, graphic arts, and simulation.

The logical operations and the addressing mechanisms described in this chapter significantly enhance the symbol-processing power of computers. Later chapters illustrate algorithms which make use of these processing capabilities.

4·1   Address Modification

Computers normally have facilities that permit the programmer to modify the operand address of an instruction when the instruction is executed. There are several applications for address-modification facilities that will come to light in later examples. One very important application is worth mentioning here. Address modification permits a single sequence of instructions to be used iteratively, acting upon different data in each iteration.

Several different address-modification facilities have been implemented in computers, and no single facility is common to all computers. Address modification in the HP 2116 computer is quite different from that in System/360-370 computers, for example, but the two types of computer together run the gamut of the most popular facilities.

Address modification, with few exceptions, is accomplished in the following way. The encoded form of an instruction includes an operand address and other data that indicate how the address is to be modified when the instruction is executed. When an instruction with a modifiable address is executed, the following actions occur:

1. The instruction is fetched from memory.

2. The operand address is extracted from the instruction, together with the address modification data.

3. The computer executes an algorithm that uses the address modification data and the operand address to produce a new operand address.

4. The new operand address is the address used for the execution of the instruction.

The address produced by the address-modification algorithm is called the *effective address* of the instruction. Address modification never alters the stored instruction in memory. It only modifies the interpretation of the instruction at the time of execution.

The sections that follow treat several different address-modification facilities that are available in the HP 2116 and System/360-370 computers.

4·1·1   Indirect Addressing   Let X be a memory address, and let MEMORY[X] contain a number which is the address of another word in memory. It is frequently advantageous to be able to obtain the operand whose address is stored in MEMORY[X] with one instruction, using

only the address X in the instruction. To accomplish this the HP 2116 computer can be instructed to act indirectly. We indicate indirection by the letter I after an address. The following list of instructions shows the effect of indirection:

INSTRUCTION	ACTION
LDA X,I	A ← MEMORY[MEMORY[X]]
LDB X,I	B ← MEMORY[MEMORY[X]]
ADA X,I	A ← A+MEMORY[MEMORY[X]]
ADB X,I	B ← B+MEMORY[MEMORY[X]]
STA X,I	MEMORY[MEMORY[X]] ← A
STB X,I	MEMORY[MEMORY[X]] ← B

Indirection is specified in an instruction by placing a 1 in bit 15. When bit 15 of an instruction is 0, the instruction is executed directly.

In Chapter 2 we noted that a word fetched from memory may be interpreted either as an instruction or as a datum. With indirection we see that a third interpretation is possible: A word may be interpreted as the address of another word in memory. Since interpretation is controlled by processor state, the HP 2116 computer has a state called INDIRECT that controls indirect addressing.

Our description of the HP 2116 processor given in Chapter 2 must be modified as shown below to include the indirect-addressing facility:

FETCH state	$M \leftarrow P$; $T \leftarrow MEMORY[M]$; $I \leftarrow T$; $M \leftarrow T_{9-0}$; **if** $I_{15} = 1$ **then** change state to INDIRECT **else** change state to EXECUTE;
INDIRECT state	$T \leftarrow MEMORY[M]$; $M \leftarrow T_{14-0}$; **if** $T_{15} = 0$ **then** change state to EXECUTE; (the INDIRECT state actions are repeated until $T_{15} = 0$)
EXECUTE state	. . .

If an instruction is a direct instruction, then the address left in the M register in the FETCH state is the effective address. If an instruction executes indirectly, then the M register is replaced by MEMORY[M] in the INDIRECT state. Notice that M contains an effective address when

EXECUTE state processing begins, regardless of whether the instruction is direct or indirect.

One important aspect of indirection is that it can be used to increase the number of words that are addressable by programs. The HP 2116 computer uses six bits of a 16-bit instruction for purposes other than specification of a particular memory address, leaving only 10 bits to specify the memory address. Hence the address portion of an instruction can specify addresses that lie in the range

$$0 \leq x \leq 2^{10}-1 = 1023_{10}.$$

This range of addresses is quite small, and it would severely hamper the construction of programs whose size exceeds 1024 words if the only addressing mechanism were direct addresses. With indirect addressing memory addresses in the range $0 \leq x \leq 2^{15}-1 = 32{,}767_{10}$ can be generated. In the FETCH mode a memory address 10 bits long is placed in the M register, reflecting the fact that this memory address is the address portion of an instruction. In the INDIRECT mode note that the address placed in the M register is 15 bits in length. Indirect address words do not have to respecify the operation code, which increases the number of bits that can be used to specify an address. There are interesting questions concerning the efficiency of memory utilization and the speed of computation in digital computers that use address-modification mechanisms such as indirect addressing. We shall discuss these questions in the next section.

Notice that an interesting repetitive behavior is possible in the INDIRECT state. For example, if the instruction LDA X,I is executed, and if the indirect bit of MEMORY[X] is 1, then the address in MEMORY[X] is treated as an indirect address rather than as a direct address. Thus if MEMORY[X] contains the address Y and the indirect bit is 1, the instruction will be executed as follows:

M $\leftarrow$ T$_{9-0}$;	The address of X is now in M.
M $\leftarrow$ MEMORY[M]$_{14-0}$;	The address of Y is now in M.
M $\leftarrow$ MEMORY[M]$_{14-0}$;	The address of the data is now in M.
T $\leftarrow$ MEMORY[M];	The data is now in T.
A $\leftarrow$ T;	T has been moved to A.

In this example indirection has occurred twice; that is, it has taken place at the *second level*. Obviously indirection can also occur at higher levels, but it is seldom employed beyond the second level. The various levels of addressing illustrated below for the LDA instruction in a shortened notation are:

ACTION	DESCRIPTION
A ← MEMORY[X];	Direct address
A ← MEMORY[MEMORY[X]];	Indirect address, first level
A ← MEMORY[MEMORY[MEMORY[X]]];	Indirect address, second level

Now, as an example of indirect addressing, let us simulate a Turing machine with the HP 2116 computer. The tape of the Turing machine will be simulated by computer memory such that successive words in memory represent successive squares on the Turing machine tape. In this simulation the tape alphabet is $\{0,1\}$.

Each Turing machine instruction is a five-tuple consisting of a state q_i, current symbol s_j, next state q_{ij}, written symbol s_{ij}, and head direction d_{ij}. For each state q_i in the Turing machine to be simulated we shall use addresses of the form QI, QIONE, QIZERO. QI is the address of the first instruction of a sequence of instructions that simulate the machine in state q_i. QIONE and QIZERO are the addresses of instructions that simulate the behavior of the machine in state q_i with a 1 input and a 0 input, respectively. The current position of the head is marked by a memory address placed at the symbolic address HEAD. The following instructions direct the simulation of a machine in state q_i to either QIONE or QIZERO, depending on the symbol that is currently being scanned by the head:

ADDRESS	CODE	OPERAND	COMMENTS
QI	LDA	HEAD,I	Put current symbol in A.
	CPA	ONE	Is it a 1?
	JMP	QIONE	If so, jump to QIONE, otherwise skip to QIZERO.
QIZERO	. . .		
QIONE	. . .		

At address QIONE and QIZERO the instructions simulate the action part of a five-tuple. There are three different actions to take. First we rewrite a symbol on the tape with

```
      LDA ONE
      STA HEAD,I
or
      LDA ZERO
      STA HEAD,I
```

where ZERO and ONE are the symbolic addresses of words in memory that contain the numbers 0 and 1, respectively. Next we move the tape head left or right with the following instructions:

```
      LDA HEAD          Move right.
      ADA ONE           A ←A+1
      STA HEAD

      . . .

      LDA HEAD          Move left.
      ADA MINUSONE      A ←A−1
      STA HEAD
```

Finally we enter a new state, q_j:

```
      JMP QJ
```

Example 4·1 is a simple simulation of the Turing machine program in Example 1·2.

4·1·2 **Paging**   As we have noted, in the HP 2116 computer there are 10 bits per instruction that are interpreted as a memory address, which permits any one of 1024 different memory locations to be specified. What happens when a program and its data occupy more than 1024 words of memory? If no address modification other than indirection were available, then all memory locations other than the first 1024 would be accessible only by indirect addressing.

Before describing the address modification mechanism, we might consider why the designers of the HP 2116 computer did not use longer addresses—say, 16 bits—which would increase the number of addressable words to 65,536. Clearly, if the address field of an instruction contained 16 bits, the instruction would contain 20 to 24 bits, and the size of the computer word would have to be increased to accommodate

EXAMPLE 4·1

ADDRESS	CODE	OPERAND	COMMENTS
Q1	LDA	HEAD,I	Find next symbol.
	CPA	ONE	
	JMP	Q1ONE	If it is a 1, jump.
Q1ZERO	LDA	ONE	If it is a 0, write a 1 and halt.
	STA	HEAD,I	
	JMP	HALT	
Q1ONE	LDA	ONE	Rewrite the 1.
	STA	HEAD,I	
	LDA	HEAD	Move head to right.
	ADA	ONE	
	STA	HEAD	
	JMP	Q1	Iterate.
HALT	HLT		HLT halts computer.

the longer instruction. The net effect, of course, would be to increase the cost of the memory. Hence we are tempted to seek alternative techniques for extending the addressable size of memory which are considerably less expensive to implement than large address fields in instructions. Indirection is a method in which increased flexibility is attained by increasing execution time.

The HP 2116 addressing behaves in the following way. The M register holds 15-bit memory addresses, not 10-bit addresses, in spite of the fact that addresses in instructions are 10 bits. Hence the M register can address $32,768 = 2^{15}$ different memory locations. The five bits not specified by an instruction address are obtained from one of two possible sources. In one case the five bits are forced to be 0, causing the address to become an address between 0 and 1023. In the other case the five bits are obtained from the corresponding five bits of the P register, so that the address becomes an address of an operand that is stored "near" the instruction whose address is found in the P register.

To be more precise, assume that the 10-bit address 0000000001_2 appears in an instruction. If five 0's are prefixed to this address in the M register, then the memory address specified is 1. If 00001_2 is prefixed, the address is increased by 1024, and the address becomes 1025. Obviously, if y is an operand address in an instruction, then the effective address could be any address of the form $1024 \cdot x + y$, where x satisfies $0 \le x \le 31$. Consider what region of memory can be addressed when the five high-order bits of the P register hold 6_{10}. Clearly, this is the region beginning at $6 \cdot 1024 = 6144_{10} = 14000_8$ and ending at $7 \cdot 1024 - 1 = 7167_{10} = 15777_8$. A different configuration of bits in the first five digits of the M register would permit a different set of 1024 contiguous words to be addressed. We call each such set of words a *memory page*, and we refer to the five-bit pattern which specifies a memory page as the *page number* for that page. The 15-bit address obtained after prefixing a page number to an address is sometimes called an *absolute address*. The page with page number 0 is frequently called the *base page*.

We have seen that a page number may be obtained in one of two ways. There is one bit per instruction, bit 10 (see Figure 2·4), which is used to specify how to obtain a page number. If the page-indicator bit is 0, then the page number is forced to all 0's, and the memory reference is made to the base page. If the page-indicator bit is 1, then the page number is obtained from the P register.

A complete algorithmic description of the FETCH state of the HP 2116 processor including the paging mechanism is as follows:

$M \leftarrow P$;

$T \leftarrow MEMORY[M]$;

$I \leftarrow T$;

$M_{9-0} \leftarrow T_{9-0}$;

if $I_{10} = 1$ **then** $M_{14-10} \leftarrow P_{14-10}$

else $M_{14-10} \leftarrow 0$;

if $I_{15} = 1$ **then** change state to INDIRECT

else change state to EXECUTE;

Paging affects only the operand address in an instruction; indirection and execution take place as described earlier.

EXAMPLE 4·2

The instruction LDA X is stored at location 03301_8, where X is the address 03425_8. Then the memory address in the instruction is 1425_8 (10 bits), and the page number at the time of execution is 01_8 (five bits). Figure 4·1 shows the effective-address calculation for this example.

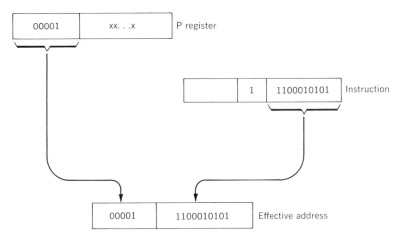

Figure 4·1 A paging computation for the HP 2116 computer

An interesting aspect of the page concept is that, given a program and data that fit entirely within a page of memory and in which there are no indirect references, that program will execute correctly when placed in any of the 32 pages of memory (for reasons to be discussed later, it may not execute correctly in the base page). Programs that contain indirect references can also be executed in any page, provided that the 15-bit memory addresses stored in the program are changed appropriately. Programs that can be executed in any page are said to be *page relocatable*. The ability to relocate programs facilitates the building of large programs from libraries of smaller ones.

The notion of pages and page relocatability has been implemented in greatly expanded form on several computers. The page indicator in each instruction can be many bits long, instead of just one bit, as in the HP 2116. For example, a three-bit page indicator can be used to select one of eight different registers as the source of the page number for a memory reference. Registers used for page numbers are frequently called *page registers*.

EXAMPLE 4·3

An instruction produces the address 0376_8 (10 bits) and has a three-bit page indicator containing the value 6. Page register 6 contains the value 24_8 (five bits). The memory address is computed to be 50376_8 (15 bits). Figure 4·2 shows the paging mechanism for this example.

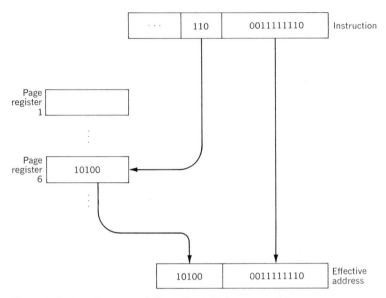

Figure 4·2 A paging computation with multiple page registers

4·1·3 **Index Registers and Base Registers** Instruction encoding for System/360-370 computers does not specify either paging or indirection. Address modification is accomplished instead by specifying general-purpose registers whose contents are to be added to the operand address to produce an effective address. Thus the effective address of an instruction can be modified by changing the contents of a general register.

The address-modification facilities pertain to the R X instructions, and not to the RR instructions, since the latter do not specify memory locations (System/360-370 instruction formats are discussed in Section 3·5). Consider the L instruction shown in Figure 4·3. We recall that the L instruction loads a register from a full word in memory. The first byte of the L instruction contains the operation code, which is 58_{16} for this case, and the R field contains the number of the result register. The fields labeled X, B, and D—for *index, base,* and *displacement*—enter into the effective address calculations as follows. The register labeled S is used to compute the effective address.

S ← D;

if X $\neq$ 0 **then** S ← S+REG[X];

if B $\neq$ 0 **then** S ← S+REG[B];   S now contains the effective address.

Operation code		R	X	B	D		
0101	1000	0010	0011	0101	0000	0001	0000

Figure 4·3   An example of the L instruction

When we write instructions in which we indicate the B, D, and X portions of an address explicitly, the convention normally followed is illustrated below for the L instruction

L   R,D(X,B)

EXAMPLE 4·4

Assume that REG[3] contains 1000_{10} and REG[5] contains 3000_{10}. Then the instructions below are executed as indicated:

INSTRUCTION	ACTION
L 2,16(0,5)	REG[2] ← MEMORY[3016; . . .];
L 2,16(3,5)	REG[2] ← MEMORY[4016; . . .];
L 2,16(5,0)	REG[2] ← MEMORY[3016; . . .];
L 2,0(0,3)	REG[2] ← MEMORY[1000; . . .];
L 2,100(0,0)	REG[2] ← MEMORY[100; . . .];

Notice that there is no intrinsic difference in processing the X field and the B field of an instruction. However, although the fields are treated identically, they are usually put to two different uses. When address modification is used so that an instruction can operate on different data each time it is executed, the address modification is said to be an *indexing operation*, and the register used for address modification is said to be an *index register*. Address modification can also be used to relocate a program in memory, so that it can be executed from more than one address. Address modification used in this manner is said to be a *program relocation*, and the register involved is called a *base register*. System/360-370 instructions permit indexing and relocation simultaneously. By convention, the X field usually specifies an index register and the B field usually specifies a base register.

Indexing is very much like indirection, because the contents of an index register are treated in almost the same way as an indirect address. In fact, if B and D are both specified to be 0, then the X register is identical to a one-level indirect address. The following example illustrates the similarity.

EXAMPLE 4·5

We wish to add the 10 words in memory, beginning at memory address 100_{10}. For the HP 2116 computer we use indirection and assume that MEMORY[TEN] and MEMORY[ZERO] contain 10 and 0, respectively, and MEMORY[ADDR] contains 100_{10}:

ADDRESS	CODE	OPERAND	COMMENTS
	LDA	TEN	Initialize COUNT to −10.
	CMA,INA		Form the two's complement.
	STA	COUNT	
	LDA	ZERO	Set A to 0.
LOOP	ADA	ADDR,I	The number added to the A register here is one of those stored in the region between MEMORY[100] and MEMORY[109].
	ISZ	ADDR	Increase indirect address by 1. Next iteration will obtain new number.
	ISZ	COUNT	Loop unless we reach 0.
	JMP	LOOP	Repeat, since COUNT $\neq 0$.
NEXT	. . .		A skip occurs for ISZ when COUNT $= 0$. Addition is complete when this point is reached.

In the following program for System/360-370 TEN, FOUR, ZERO, and HUNDRED are the symbolic addresses of memory cells that contain the values indicated:

ADDRESS	INSTRUCTION	OPERAND	COMMENTS
	L	COUNT,TEN	REG[COUNT] ← 10;
	L	SUM,ZERO	REG[SUM] ← 0;
	L	INDEX,HUNDRED	REG[INDEX] ← 100; REG[INDEX] now contains address of first addend.
LOOP	A	SUM,0(INDEX,0)	During each iteration a new effective address is produced here.
	A	INDEX,FOUR	Increase INDEX by 4 to find the address of the next full word.
	BCT	COUNT,LOOP	COUNT is decreased by 1. If it is not 0, branch to LOOP is taken.
NEXT	. . .		When this point is reached, the 10 numbers have been added.

Example 4·5 shows how address modification lets us use just one addition instruction to add 10 numbers. In one case we use indirection and modify the indirect address. In the other case we place an address in an index register and use it as an indirect address. However, index registers are more flexible than is indicated by Example 4·5 because there are uses for which we need not set the B and D fields to 0 when we use indexing.

Base registers have entirely different applications from index registers. When a general-purpose register is used as a base register, its contents remain constant for all instructions that use it as a base register. This is in contrast to index registers, where the power of indexing is achieved through the ability to change the contents of the register.

Base registers are similar to, but more general than, paging registers. The primary difference between base registers and paging registers is in the detail of address modification. Base registers produce effective addresses by an *addition* operation, whereas paging produces effective addresses by *prefixing* page numbers to operand addresses.

Earlier examples show how base registers produce effective addresses. A typical application of a base register is illustrated in Example 4·6.

EXAMPLE 4·6

Suppose that Z is the address of the first byte of a full word operand, and that Z is 100 bytes beyond the first byte of the instruction labeled LOOP. Then the following instructions can be executed from *any* address in memory for which LOOP begins on a full-word boundary (compare these instructions with their equivalents in Example 4.5):

ADDRESS	CODE	OPERAND	COMMENTS
	BALR	15,0	Places address of LOOP in REG[15], no branch taken.
LOOP	L	2,100(0,15)	Loads MEMORY[Z; . . .] into REG[2].
	. . .		
	BCT	6,0(0,15)	Branch on count. If REG[6] $\neq$ 0, then branch back to LOOP, the instruction addressed by REG[15].

The index- and base-register operations are shown separately in Examples 4·5 and 4·6 for clarity. The usual case, of course, is to combine the two operations, so that the L instruction would become

L 2,100(INDEX,15)

Notice in Example 4·6 that the BALR instruction establishes REG[15] to be a base register, so that both LOOP and Z are effective addresses produced by base-register computations. The effective address will be the correct effective address no matter where the program is placed in memory, provided that LOOP begins on a full-word boundary. The base-register facility of System/360-370 computers is somewhat more flexible than the paging facility of the HP 2116 computer. A base register can be used to relocate a program in memory by an essentially arbitrary amount rather than an amount equivalent to a page size. To be more specific, the D, or displacement, field is a 12-bit operand address. If page registers were used in place of base registers, then pages would be 2^{12} bytes long. However, a base register can relocate a program by amounts much less than 2^{12}, thereby affording many more possible places in memory from which a program can be executed. Strictly speaking, base registers cannot have arbitrary values, because relocation by amounts that are not divisible by 8 will place double words across double-word boundaries instead of within them. Thus allowable base-register values must be multiples of 8 for programs that have double-word operands. Similarly, multiples of 4 must be used for full words, and multiples of 2 must be used for halfwords.

4·2 Logic Operations

We have come to adopt the view that each word in a computer memory holds a single symbol. If the computer word contains n bits, then the alphabet of symbols that can be stored in a computer word has 2^n different symbols. We can adopt another view, however, in which each computer word is a collection of n symbols, and each symbol is drawn from the alphabet containing only 0 and 1. Each of these views is compatible with the operation of the computer, and each is useful in particular applications. Since it is usually necessary to represent a very large collection of distinct numbers, it is usually necessary to store one number per computer word. When the information stored in memory is a set of answers from a true-false quiz, then n answers per word can be stored by letting each bit represent the answer to a single true-false question. These two views are, moreover, not the only ones possible. A computer word can be partitioned into several subsets of bits, where each subset has its own interpretation. The mantissa and exponent of floating-point representation fall into this category.

Two advantages accrue from adopting a bit-oriented view of the contents of computer words instead of the one-symbol-per-word view. The first advantage is that memory can be used with great efficiency if many items are stored per word instead of just one item per word. Somewhat less important is the fact that parallel computation is possible because there are instructions that operate on all the bits of a word. When these bits are interpreted to represent many different symbols, we have a case in which several symbols can be manipulated simultaneously.

Among the bit-oriented instructions are the logical instructions which include the AND, OR, EXCLUSIVE OR, and the NOT operations. During execution of instructions from this group the several bits of a single computer word are manipulated identically and independently. The AND, OR, and EXCLUSIVE OR instructions each operate on a pair of operands, where the ith bits of each operand are combined to give the ith bit of the result. The following table gives the functional behavior of these instructions:

FIRST OPERAND	SECOND OPERAND	AND	OR	EXCLUSIVE OR
0	0	0	0	0
0	1	0	1	1
1	0	0	1	1
1	1	1	1	0

Note that the AND operation yields a 1 result if both the first *and* the second operands are 1. The OR operation gives a 1 if either the first *or* the second operand is 1; the EXCLUSIVE OR *excludes* the case when both operands are 1 from those conditions that yield a 1 output for the OR operation.

The NOT operation complements the bits of a computer word. As noted earlier, the CMA instruction performs this operation in the HP 2116 computer. The following table describes the logical instructions as they exist on the HP 2116 computer:

INSTRUCTION	CODE	EXAMPLE	ACTION
AND	AND	AND X	A ←A AND MEMORY[X]
(Inclusive) OR	IOR	IOR Y	A ← A OR MEMORY[Y]
EXCLUSIVE OR	XOR	XOR Z	A ←A EXCLUSIVE OR MEMORY[Z]
NOT	CMA	CMA	A ←NOT A

EXAMPLE 4·7

Let the A register contain the 16-bit quantity $A73E_{16}$, and let memory locations X, Y, and Z contain $3BB6_{16}$, 7111_{16}, and $9D01_{16}$, respectively. The successive states of the A register after executing the instructions listed in the table above become:

INSTRUCTION	RESULT
AND X	2336_{16}
IOR Y	7337_{16}
XOR Z	$EE36_{16}$
CMA	$11C9_{16}$

System/360-370 computers have full-word logical instructions that are essentially the same as those for the HP 2116 computer. These instructions are as follows:

INSTRUCTION	CODE	EXAMPLE	ACTION
AND	N	N 5,T	REG[5] ← REG[5] AND MEMORY[T: . . .];
AND (register)	NR	NR 5,6	REG[5] ← REG[5] AND REG[6];
OR	O	O 6,V	REG[6] ← REG[6] OR MEMORY[V; . . .];
OR (register)	OR	OR 6,8	REG[6] ← REG[6] OR REG[8];
EXCLUSIVE OR	X	X 3,W	REG[3] ← REG[3] EXCLUSIVE OR MEMORY[W; . . .];
EXCLUSIVE OR (register)	XR	XR 3,4	REG[3] ← REG[3] EXCLUSIVE OR REG[4];

There is no equivalent of the CMA instruction to form the logical complement of an operand. The complement can be computed, however, by using the X instruction with an operand that is

$$111 \cdot \cdot \cdot 1_2 = \text{FFFF FFFF}_{16}$$

EXAMPLE 4·8

Let REG[2] contain 0000 A73E$_{16}$, and let the full words in memory with addresses X, Y, Z, and W contain 0000 3BB6$_{16}$, 0000 7111$_{16}$, 0000 9D01$_{16}$, and FFFF FFFF$_{16}$, respectively. Compare the following instructions with those in Example 4·7:

INSTRUCTION	RESULT
N 2,X	0000 2336$_{16}$
O 2,Y	0000 7337$_{16}$
X 2,Z	0000 EE36$_{16}$
X 2,W	FFFF 11C9$_{16}$

4·3 Shift Operations

We noted the need for aligning operands in the discussion on arithmetic operations, where by alignment we mean the process of shifting bits left or right in a computer word. The operation is a simple one conceptually, but there are a number of variations that bear discussion.

Figure 4·4 diagrams several different shift operations that are commonly used. The cyclical shift is the operation in which bits shifted off one end of a register reappear at the other end. Although the figure shows a right shift of one bit, the effect is exactly the same as a left circular shift of 15 bits. Consequently instruction repertoires do not usually include both left and right cyclical shifts.

The arithmetic left shift and arithmetic right shift shown in the figure are shifts that leave the sign bit of an arithmetic operand unchanged. In this case, for two's-complement representation the left shift is the same as a multiplication by 2 and the right shift is the same as an integer division by 2. Bits that are shifted off the end of the

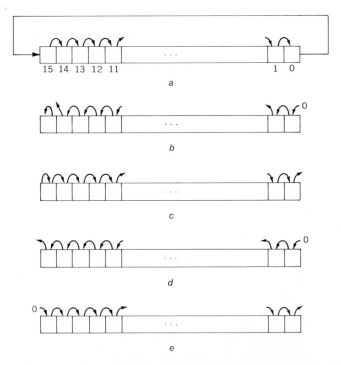

Figure 4·4 Shift operations: (a) right cyclic shift, (b) arithmetic left shift, (c) arithmetic right shift, (d) logical left shift, and (e) logical right shift

register are lost. Notice that the cyclical shift can be used to double and halve numbers in one's-complement representation, provided that the sign bit remains unchanged. What shift instructions will double and halve numbers in signed-magnitude representation?

Logical shifts are useful primarily for isolating fields within a word. The 0's that are shifted into a word displace unwanted information, which is shifted off the end of the word.

The following table gives the equivalent HP 2116 computer instructions for the shifts, where they exist:

INSTRUCTION	CODE	ACTION
Rotate A right	RAR	Right cyclical shift, one bit.
Rotate A left	RAL	Left cyclical shift, one bit.
A left four	ALF	Left cyclical shift, four bits.
A left shift	ALS	Arithmetic left shift, one bit.
A right shift	ARS	Arithmetic right shift, one bit.

The HP 2116 computer does not have the precise equivalent of a logical shift, although it does have other shift instructions which are not discussed here. In order to shift by amounts other than one bit or four bits, it is necessary to use combinations of the one-bit and four-bit shift instructions.

System/360-370 computers have arithmetic and logical shifts, but no cyclical shifts. The shift instructions have an interesting property that is not available for the HP 2116 computer. They use a format similar to the RX format, but the memory address is interpreted as a shift amount. Hence one instruction can be used to shift by any amount. Moreover, the shift amount is computed from the B and the D fields as if it were an effective address, so that shift amounts can be computed dynamically.

To be more explicit, Figure 4·5 shows the format for the logical right-shift instruction, SRL. The shift amount for the instruction is determined by extracting the least significant six bits from the quantity REG[B]+D. Register R is shifted when the instruction is executed, and

Operation code		R	X	B	D		
1000	1000	0010		0011	0000	0000	0001

Figure 4·5 The encoding for the logical right shift instruction SRL 2,1(3). The X field is not used for this instruction

if the shift amount is greater than 32, the 32-bit register will be cleared to 0 by the logical shift. There are double-register shift instructions as well as single register instructions, all of which are given in the following table:

INSTRUCTION	CODE	EXAMPLE	ACTION
Shift right	SRL	SRL 2,1	Logical right shift of REG[2], one bit.
Shift right (double)	SRDL	SRDL 2,1	Logical right shift of REG[2;3], one bit.
Shift left	SLL	SLL 3,17	Logical left shift of REG[3], 17 bits.
Shift left (double)	SLDL	SLDL 4,6	Logical left shift of REG[4;5], six bits.
Shift right arithmetic	SRA	SRA 2,1	Arithmetic right shift of REG[2], one bit.
Shift right arithmetic (double)	SRDA	SRDA 2,1	Arithmetic right shift of REG[2;3], one bit.
Shift left arithmetic	SLA	SLA 5,7	Arithmetic left shift of REG[5], seven bits.
Shift left arithmetic (double)	SLDA	SLDA 6,2	Arithmetic left shift of REG[6;7], two bits.

EXAMPLE 4·9

X, Y, and Z are the addresses of full words in memory. The following instructions leave Y÷Z in REG[7]. The SRDA instruction is used to extend the sign of the dividend through REG[6], producing a double-word representation of the full-word operand.

INSTRUCTION	OPERAND	COMMENTS
L	6,Y	REG[6] ← MEMORY[Y; . . .].
SRDA	6,32	Shift REG[6;7]. After shift, REG[7] contains previous contents of REG[6], and sign of operand has been extended through REG[6].
D	6,Z	REG[7] ← Y÷Z. REG[6] ← remainder.

EXAMPLE 4·10

Let Y be the address of a full word in memory which contains a positive integer less than 32. The following instructions shift REG[3] left arithmetically by MEMORY[Y; . . .]+1 places. Since the SLA instruction has no X field, we drop the X field from the operand address notation.

INSTRUCTION	OPERAND	COMMENTS
L	4,Y	REG[4] ← MEMORY[Y; . . .].
SLA	3,1(4)	Shift left REG[4]+1 places.

EXERCISES

4·1   Invent a method for using both indexing and indirection in an instruction repertoire. Describe the registers that take part in these operations, the encoding of instructions for specifying the operations, and the sequence of events that occur when an instruction is executed.

4·2   Show how paging can be implemented in the System/360-370 instruction repertoire as an address-modification mechanism in addition to base registers and indexing.

4·3   Write a sequence of instructions that adds two full-word operands, using only the logical and shift instructions to perform the processing. You may use the BCT instruction for System/360-370 or the ISZ instruction for the HP 2116, but the number of iterations counted by these instructions must not exceed the number of bits per word.

4·4   Write a sequence of instructions that multiplies two operands. The sequence may include logical, addition, and shift instructions, but not a multiplication instruction. Assume that the operands are positive integers less than $256 = 2^8$. You may use either the BCT or the ISZ instruction to control the iterations of a loop, but the number of iterations must not exceed 16.

5

Assemblers

In the stored-program computer, instructions
are held in memory in a binary encoding. We
can, in principle, put a program into a computer by placing each instruction of the program in encoded form at its proper place in
memory, one instruction at a time from the
console of the computer. The weaknesses of
this method become evident to any who try
it. Our program examples have stressed the
use of symbolic addresses and mnemonic instruction codes because these quantities are
much easier to use than binary codes.
Since instructions can be mechanically translated from symbolic form into a binary encoding, it is obvious that the translation
process can be performed by a computer
program. Consequently programs called *assemblers*, which perform these translations,
have been written for nearly every computer.
This chapter discusses assembly language as

a programming language and describes the translation process as it is performed by assemblers.

5·1 Assembly Language

The assembly process is one in which the binary encoding for each portion of an instruction is determined, and the several encodings are then combined to form a complete instruction. For example, the instruction LDA X, where X is a symbol representing address 767_8, is assembled by combining the code LDA with the encoding 767_8. The two codes are positioned in the correct places in a computer word, and that computer word is filed away. When an assembled program is put in the computer for execution, another program, called a *loader*, places each assembled instruction in the proper memory location for execution.

More specifically, for each instruction an assembler for HP 2116 computer instructions must determine the following quantities:

1. The address at which each instruction is to be assembled
2. The indirect bit
3. The instruction code
4. The page-indicator bit
5. The address specified by the instruction

The assembler determines these quantities from information in an assembly language program.

Assembly language for the HP 2116 computer has the following structure. Each instruction is described by one line of text, and each line has four fields named label, code, operand, and comments. The label field is often blank. If not, the symbol in that field represents the instruction address and may be used as a synonym for that location throughout the assembly language program. The code field contains mnemonics for the instruction codes, while the operand field contains addresses or symbols for addresses that are specified by the instruction. Descriptive remarks are placed in the comments field and are ignored by the assembler. Many examples of assembly language have already appeared in the text without identification as such.

In addition to mnemonics for instruction codes, assembly language also contains instructions that control the assembly process and do not have equivalent machine instruction codes. These codes are called *pseudo-instructions*. An important example of a pseudo-instruction for the HP 2116 computer is the origin instruction (code ORG), which specified the address at which the next instruction is to be assembled. The equate instruction (code EQU) specifies the numeric value of a symbolic address. The end instruction (code END) specifies that the end of the program has been reached.

Example 5·1 shows the use of the ORG, EQU, and END pseudo-instructions in an assembly language program. In this case, X, Y, and Z are the memory addresses 00300_8, 05126_8, and 05127_8, respectively. The codes for LDA, STA, ADA, CPA, and JMP are 1100_2, 1110_2, 1010_2, and 0101_2, respectively. HLT is encoded as the 16-bit instruction 102000_8.

Several important points are illustrated in Example 5·1. The ORG instruction forces assembly to begin at location 5000_8, where the suffix B in line 1 is interpreted by the assembler to mean radix 8. The operand field includes references to operands in both the base page and the present page. Hence in line 2 the page indicator bit is 0 in the assembled instruction, and in line 3 it is 1. Since the HLT instruction is assembled at location 5006_8, the symbol HALT represents the address 5006_8. In line 10 the 10 low-order bits of this address have been assembled in the instruction and the page-indicator bit has been set to 1.

Before we describe the pseudo-instructions in the assembly language for the HP 2116, it is necessary to consider a few details of the assembly process. The complete assembly process is described later. One of the essential tasks of the assembler is to replace symbolic names for memory addresses by their appropriate encodings. In order to perform this task the assembler constructs a table of symbolic names called the *symbol table*. In the symbol table each symbolic name is stored in the appropriate character representation, together with the memory address that it represents. Thus the symbol table for the program in Example 5·1 should be as follows:

SYMBOL	ADDRESS
HALT	5006_8
MOVE	5007_8
X	0300_8
Y	5126_8
Z	5127_8

Consider how the assembler builds a symbol table. Example 5·1 shows that the assembler can compute the addresses for HALT and MOVE by counting from 5000_8, incrementing the counter by 1 for each

EXAMPLE 5·1

	LABEL	CODE	OPERAND	COMMENTS
1.		ORG	5000B	Start assembly at 5000_8.
2.		LDA	X	Fetch X (in base page).
3.		CPA	Z	Compare to Z (in this page).
4.		JMP	MOVE	Jump if X = Z.
5.		LDA	Y	Fetch Y.
6.		ADA	Z	Add Z.
7.		STA	X	Store result in X.
8.	HALT	HLT	0	Halt.
9.	MOVE	STA	Y	Store X into Y.
10.		JMP	HALT	
11.	X	EQU	300B	X is address 300_8.
12.	Y	EQU	5126B	Y is address 5126_8.
13.	Z	EQU	5127B	Z is address 5127_8.
14.		END		

INDIRECT BIT	CODE	PAGE BIT	MEMORY ADDRESS	ASSEMBLED INSTRUCTION
. . .	. . .	. . .	. . .	None
0	1100_2	0	0 011 000 000_2	060300_8
0	1010	1	1 001 010 111	053127_8
0	0101	1	1 000 000 111	027007_8
0	1100	1	1 001 010 110	063126_8
0	1000	1	1 001 010 111	043127_8
0	1110	0	0 011 000 000	070300_8
1	0000	1	0 000 000 000	102000_8
0	1110	1	1 001 010 110	073126_8
0	0101	1	1 000 000 110	027006_8
. . .	. . .	. . .	. . .	None
. . .	. . .	. . .	. . .	None
. . .	. . .	. . .	. . .	None
. . .	. . .	. . .	. . .	None

instruction. The assembler uses an internal datum called the *program location counter* for this purpose. The ORG pseudo-instruction sets an initial value in the program location counter. Ordinary instructions cause the program location counter to be increased by 1 when their processing is completed. Hence when an assembler processes Example 5·1, the value of the program location counter will be 5006_8 at the point that HALT appears. Thus the normal action of the assembler when it processes an instruction with a symbol in its label field is as follows:

1. Place the symbol and the value of the program location counter in the symbol table.

2. Process the instruction.

3. Increase the program location counter by 1.

The symbolic addresses X, Y, and Z in Example 5·1 represent memory addresses for data rather than the addresses of instructions. There are several pseudo-instructions that are used for reserving space for data. A brief description of the important ones in the assembly language for the HP 2116 computer appear in the table below. Note that we use the abbreviation PLC for program location counter. Note also that the phrase Enter (R,PLC) in symbol table means that the symbol R and the current value of the program location counter are entered as a symbol and its corresponding memory address.

PSEUDO-INSTRUCTION	CODE	EXAMPLE	ASSEMBLER ACTION
Origin	ORG	ORG 1000B	$PLC \leftarrow 1000_8$.
Equate	EQU	X EQU 300B	Enter $(X,300_8)$ in symbol table.
Block storage start	BSS	R BSS 10	Enter (R,PLC) in symbol table. $PLC \leftarrow PLC+10_{10}$ (this reserves 10 memory cells).
Decimal convert	DEC	Z DEC 100	Enter (Z,PLC) in symbol table. Place 100_{10} in MEMORY[Z]. $PLC \leftarrow PLC+1$.

PSEUDO-INSTRUCTION	CODE	EXAMPLE	ASSEMBLER ACTION
Octal convert	OCT	Y OCT 100	Enter (Y,PLC) in symbol table. Place 100_8 in MEMORY[Y]. PLC ← PLC+1.
Define address	DEF	YNAME DEF Y	Enter (YNAME,PLC) in symbol table. Place memory address corresponding to Y in MEMORY[YNAME]. PLC ← PLC+1. YNAME is now the symbolic address of a memory cell that contains the address of Y.
Character convert	ASC	T ASC 2,ABCD	Enter (T,PLC) in symbol table. Place representations of characters A, B, C, and D in next two words of memory. PLC ← PLC+2.
End of program	END	END	End of processing.

Example 5·2 illustrates the use of these pseudo-instructions.

The EQU pseudo-instruction causes the assembler to enter a symbol and its address into the symbol table, and the program location counter is not changed. In Example 5·2 there is an EQU instruction that causes X to be placed in the symbol table. Note carefully that the program location counter is not changed by this instruction, so that Y is assembled at 5126_8, the same address at which it would be assembled if the EQU instruction were omitted.

The BSS instruction is used to reserve one or more memory cells for data. The symbol is given the address of the first cell reserved as indicated for SAVE3 in Example 5·2.

DEC and OCT are similar in action. Each causes its operand to be converted into a binary representation and placed in memory. The only difference is that DEC specifies that its operand is in radix-10 representation, whereas OCT specifies radix 8. The DEF instruction, like DEC and OCT, reserves a memory cell for a datum, but the datum is the address of another memory cell. Thus the DEF instruction of Example 5·2 puts the address of Y into the cell labeled YNAME.

The ASC instruction reserves n words of storage, where n is the integer in its operand field. The assembler places the encoded form of the characters that appear in the operand field in this storage area. Each character is represented by an eight-bit code, so that two charac-

EXAMPLE 5·2

ADDRESS	CONTENTS	LABEL	CODE	OPERAND	COMMENTS
			ORG	5126B	Assembly begins at 5126_8.
		X	EQU	300B	Place $(X,300_8)$ in symbol table.
5126_8	000000_8	Y	BSS	1	Save one word. This is MEMORY[5126_8].
5127_8	000000_8	Z	BSS	1	Save one word.
5130_8	000000_8	SAVE3	BSS	3	Save three words.
5131_8	000000_8				
5132_8	000000_8				
5133_8	000012_8	R	DEC	10	Assemble 10_{10}.
5134_8	000010_8	S	OCT	10	Assemble 10_8.
5135_8	005126_8	YNAME	DEF	Y	Assemble address of Y.
5136_8	052105_8	TEXT	ASC	2,TEXT	Assemble "TE" and "XT" in next two words. "TE" is in MEMORY[5136_8].
5137_8	054124_8				"XT" is here.
			END		End of assembly.

The symbol table for this example is:

SYMBOL	ADDRESS
X	0300_8
Y	5126_8
Z	5127_8
SAVE3	5130_8
R	5133_8
S	5134_8
YNAME	5135_8
TEXT	5136_8

ters can be placed in a single word. In Example 5·2 the codes for "T," "E," and "X" are 124_8, 105_8, and 130_8, respectively, and the data are assembled so that the first character of a pair occupies the high-order (left-hand) field of a word. The mnemonic ASC is drawn from the acronym ASCII, which is the name of the character-encoding scheme.

The operand of an instruction need not be a single symbol; it may be an expression involving constants and symbols. Although the allowable form of expressions is quite limited in the assembly language for the HP 2116 computer, most assemblers allow a large class of forms of arithmetic expressions to appear in the operand field. In particular, the HP 2116 assembly language allows an operand to be a constant, a symbol, or a sum or difference of constants and symbols. Some instructions, such as ASC, do not permit expressions in operands.

EXAMPLE 5·3

Let X, Y, and Z be symbols for the addresses 224_8, 537_8, and 172_8, respectively. Then the instructions below are assembled with the addresses as indicated:

CODE	OPERAND	ASSEMBLED ADDRESS
LDA	Y—X	313_8
ADA	Z+2	174_8
ADA	X—10B	214_8
STA	Y—10	525_8

The symbol * is used to indicate the current value of the program location counter. Thus the instruction

JMP   *+2

will be assembled with an address two greater than the address of the instruction. When the instruction is executed, the next instruction will be executed from MEMORY[P+2]. The instruction

JMP   *+1

is effectively a null instruction.

To simplify the task of dealing with constants most assemblers accept operands called *literals*. In assembly language for the HP 2116 computer the literals have a prefix =D if they are decimal and =B if they are octal. When the assembler detects a literal operand, it treats the operand as the memory address of a word in memory that contains the numeric value. The assembler allocates a memory word for the numeric value, initializes that word properly, and guarantees that all references to the same literal value specify the same address in memory when they are assembled. Literals are assigned to locations that follow the last memory location allocated to the program.

EXAMPLE 5·4

The following two sequences of instructions are equivalent:

	LABEL	CODE	OPERAND	LABEL	CODE	OPERAND
1.		LDA	ONE		LDA	=D1
2.	LOOP	ADA	TEN		ADA	=D10
3.		STA	X		STA	X
4.		CPA	D41		CPA	=D41
5.		HLT			HLT	
6.		JMP	LOOP		JMP	*—4
7.	X	BSS	1	X	BSS	1
8.	ONE	DEC	1		END	
9.	TEN	DEC	10			
10.	D41	DEC	41			
11.		END				

Indirection is specified by appending ,I to the operand field of instructions. Thus

LDA   X,I

is an indirect reference and will cause the instruction to be assembled with the indirect bit set to 1.

5·2 Assembly Language for System/360-370

The assembly language for System/360-370 computers is very similar to that for the HP 2116 computer. Instructions follow the same format of symbol, operation code, operand, and comments. Moreover, System/360-370 assembly language has equivalent pseudo-instructions for each of the pseudo-instructions that we have discussed. The following table lists the pseudo-instructions that are of prime importance. Example 5.5 illustrates how they are used.

PSEUDO-INSTRUCTION	CODE	EXAMPLE	ASSEMBLER ACTION
Origin	ORG	ORG X'100'	$PLC \leftarrow 100_{16}$.
Equate	EQU	X EQU 300	Enter $(X, 300_{10})$ in symbol table.
Define storage	DS	Y DS 3F	Move PLC to a full-word boundary if not already at one. Enter (Y,PLC) in symbol table. $PLC \leftarrow PLC+12$.
Define constant	DC	Z DC F'36'	Move PLC to a full-word boundary if not already at one. Enter (Z,PLC) in symbol table. MEMORY[Z; . . .] $\leftarrow 36_{10}$. $PLC \leftarrow PLC+4$.
Using base register	USING	USING *,15	REG[15] is now a base register and it contains the current value of the PLC.
Drop base register	DROP	DROP 15	REG[15] no longer is to be used as a base register.
End of program	END	END	End of processing.

The ORG and EQU instructions are identical to those for the HP 2116 computer. Example 5·5 shows how the EQU instruction is used to identify a register by a symbolic name. One reason for such usage of the EQU instruction is that the symbolic name COUNT is more descriptive and informative than the integer 7. The program in the example would be assembled identically if COUNT were replaced by the integer 7 in every reference. A second reason for using the EQU instruction in this manner is more subtle. Note that we can change the register named COUNT by changing the definition of COUNT in the EQU pseudo-instruction. In effect, one change by the programmer can be propagated through the

EXAMPLE 5·5

The following instructions add 10 full words beginning at memory address Z. The left-hand columns show the memory address at which each instruction is assembled and gives the operand encodings for the RX instructions. All numbers are given in radix 16.

ADDRESS R X B D	LABEL	CODE	OPERAND	COMMENTS
		ORG	X'10FE'	PLC ← $10FE_{16}$.
	COUNT	EQU	7	Add (COUNT,7) to symbol table. COUNT will be REG[7].
	INDEX	EQU	8	Similarly, add (INDEX,8) and (SUM,9) to symbol table.
	SUM	EQU	9	
10FE		BALR	15,0	REG[15] ← P+2.
		USING	*,15	Make REG[15] a base register.
1100	7 0 F 054	L	COUNT,TEN	Initialize value of COUNT.
1104	9 0 F 01C	L	SUM,ZERO	Start SUM at 0.
1108		LR	INDEX,SUM	Start INDEX at 0.
110A	9 8 F 024 LOOP	A	SUM,Z(INDEX)	Add next item to SUM.
110E	8 0 F 020	A	INDEX,FOUR	Increase INDEX to next full word.
1112	7 0 F 00A	BCT	COUNT,LOOP	Decrement COUNT and loop if not 0.
1116	F 0 F 058	B	NEXT	Branch around data.
111C	ZERO	DC	F'0'	
1120	FOUR	DC	F'4'	
1124	Z	DS	10F	
114C	ZNAME	DC	A(Z)	The address of Z.
1150	TEXT	DC	C'TEXT'	Four bytes reserved.
1154	TEN	DC	F'10'	
1158	NEXT	. . .		

program. If, however, we used the integer 7 in place of the symbol COUNT, then we would have to change several instructions in order to change the register to some other register. Moreover, in a large program there may be many references to REG[7], not all of which pertain to it in the same context. Reassignment of REG[7] in the COUNT context in such a program would require careful examination of every reference to REG[7]. Clearly the EQU instruction greatly assists in the task of reassigning registers when such changes must be made.

The DS and DC instructions reserve storage for data. Their HP 2116 counterparts are the OCT, DEC, DEF, ASC, and BSS instructions. The DS instruction merely reserves storage; it does not cause any values to be placed in the reserved area. The DC instruction both reserves areas and places initial values in these areas. Both these instructions are used for data of various lengths and representations. The following table gives the assembly language conventions for specifying the length and representation of data:

ASSEMBLY LANGUAGE CODE	DATA TYPE	EXAMPLE	INTERPRETATION
F	Full word, fixed point, radix 10	F'10'	A full word containing 10_{10}.
H	Halfword, fixed point, radix 10	H'20'	A halfword containing 20_{10}.
D	Double word, fixed point, radix 10	D'35'	A double word containing 35_{10}.
X	Digit, radix 16	X'A34E'	Two bytes containing $A34E_{16}$.
C	One-byte character	C'ABCD'	Four bytes containing the character codes for "A," "B," "C," and "D."
A	Full-word address	A(Y)	Full word containing address of Y.

The description of X-type data requires some clarification. Hexadecimal digits occupy four bits, but the assembler always allocates storage in multiples of eight bits. When an even number of digits is specified, as shown in the table, the storage is allocated with two digits per byte. If the constant contains an odd number of digits, the digit 0_{16} is prefixed to the constant to avoid the problem of allocating a portion of a byte. The various data lengths mentioned in the table were discussed in Section 3·1.

In Chapter 3 we saw that halfwords must begin on halfword boundaries, full words on full-word boundaries, etc. The assembler guarantees that data will be placed on proper boundaries. In Example 5·5 the B instruction assembled at 1116_{16} is four bytes long, so that the next item would normally be assembled at $111A_{16}$. However, this is not a full-word boundary. For this case the assembler reserves two extra bytes automatically, so that the full word ZERO will be assembled at $111C_{16}$ on a full-word boundary.

The USING instruction notifies the assembler that a register is to be used as a base register and indicates the address that is to be in it. In Example 5·5 the BALR instruction will place the address of the next instruction in REG[15]. Hence the USING instruction notifies the assembler that REG[15] contains the current value of the program location counter, 1100_{16}. The assembler automatically computes the base and displacement encodings for operands. For example, the instruction L COUNT,TEN must refer to an operand at memory address 1154_{16}. Since REG[15] contains 1100_{16}, the proper effective address can be obtained by using REG[15] as a base register with displacement 54, as indicated in the example. The assembler relieves the programmer of the tedious base-plus-displacement calculations because he may use symbolic names in referring to operands. Of course, he must establish the base registers properly, but this is much less tedious.

When the contents of a base register are changed, the programmer must notify the assembler. If the register is no longer to be a base register, then the pseudo-instruction DROP must be used. This merely tells the assembler to remove the indicated register from the list of base registers.

The instruction labeled LOOP shows the way to specify indexing of symbolic addresses. Our convention has been to specify index, base, and displacement in the form

displacement(index,base)

When we use symbolic addresses, we no longer specify both base and displacement. For this case we follow the convention

symbolic address(index)

97

as exemplified by Z(INDEX). Note that Z is the symbolic address that is encoded as REG[15]+24_{16}, and that INDEX is REG[8]. Hence the instruction is encoded as if its operand were written X'24'(8,15).

In this description of System/360-370 assembly language we have barely scratched the surface of the subject. For a full discussion see the System/360-370 reference manual "Assembler Language."

5·3 The Two-pass Assembler

The assembly process is an interesting example of a principally non-numeric application of computers. We shall study the assembly algorithm in this section for a better understanding of assembly language. All the elementary processes of an assembler are described in later chapters, so that it should be possible to write an assembler for a small instruction repertoire after completing this text.

The assembly process is shown by the flow charts in Figure 5·1 as a two-pass process. That is, a source program is scanned from start to finish twice during an assembly. Some assemblers are actually one-pass assemblers. For these assemblers the two phases of processing are performed during a single scan of the program by means of clever programming techniques. Before discussing the details of Figure 5·1, we should note the reason for two-pass processing. Consider the following excerpts from a typical program:

```
        . . .
        LDA   X
        . . .
X       DEC   7
Y       DEC   0
        . . .
        STA   Y
        . . .
```

The instruction STA Y can be assembled immediately in a single pass of the text because the memory address of Y has already been determined by the time the assembler encounters the STA Y instruction. For the LDA X instruction this is not the case, and assembly must be postponed until X is found in the label field. References to symbols to be defined later in a program are sometimes called *forward references*.

In general a two-pass assembler for HP 2116 assembly language behaves as follows. During the first pass the symbols found in the label field of a program are stored in the symbol table, together with their corresponding addresses. During the second pass the assembler finds the codes for address symbols by searching the symbol table. The codes are combined into words that are output as the assembled program.

Figure 5·1 shows the more important details of the assembly process. In the first pass a symbol appearing in the label field of an instruction is given the value of the location counter and is stored in the symbol table. If all instructions changed the location counter by 1, there would be no reason to inspect other fields of the assembly language instructions in the first pass. However, the EQU instruction leaves the location counter unchanged, and the ORG, ASC, and BSS pseudo-instructions change the location counter by amounts that are determined by their operands. Hence during the first pass the code field is inspected, and if the instruction is EQU, ORG, ASC, or BSS, special processing takes place. The END instruction terminates this phase of processing. If the instruction is none of these, the location counter is incremented by 1, and the same process is applied to the next instruction.

Special processing for pseudo-instructions in the first pass requires evaluation of the operand field to determine how much the location counter is to be changed. The increment is computed appropriately for each special pseudo-instruction, the location counter is changed, and the process is repeated for the next instruction.

The second pass is similar to the first pass in general flow of control. In this pass it is not necessary to examine the contents of the label field. In each case the code field is examined to determine whether the instruction is a normal instruction or a pseudo-instruction. If it is a normal instruction, then the code for that instruction is determined by a search through a table that associates each mnemonic code with its binary code. When the operand is evaluated, each symbol in that field is replaced by its binary code, which is obtained from the symbol table. Finally, all codes are assembled in the appropriate position in an instruction, and that instruction is transmitted to the output procedure. Pseudo-instructions encountered in the second pass are processed as special cases.

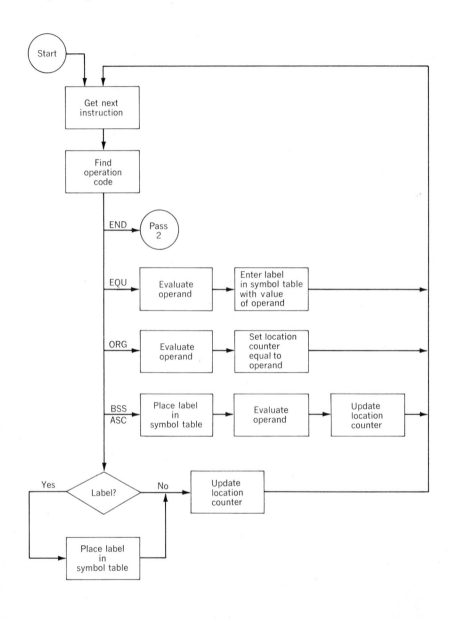

a

Figure 5·1 (a) Flowchart of first pass of assembly

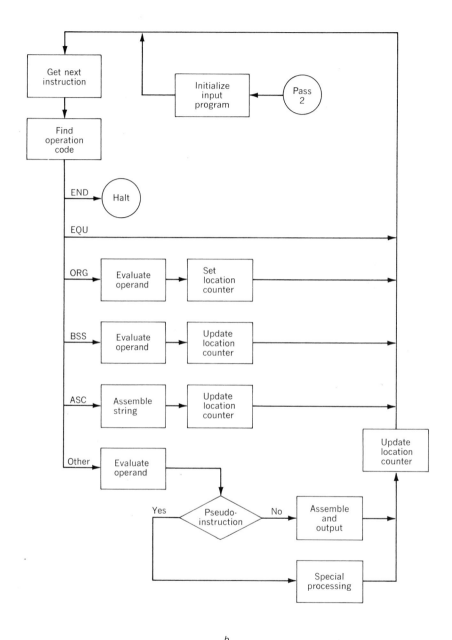

b

Figure 5·1 *(Continued)* *(b)* Flowchart of second pass of assembly

The assembly process for System/360-370 computers is essentially the same as that described for the HP 2116 computer, except for the following differences:

1. Instructions may be two, four, or six bytes long. During both passes of the program the assembler must determine the length of an instruction in order to update the program location counter correctly.

2. Halfword, full-word, and double-word data must be placed on the proper memory boundaries. The assembler reserves extra space, if necessary, to place data on the correct boundaries.

3. The assembler computes a base-register-plus-displacement encoding of a memory address. During the first pass of the program text, each symbol is stored in the symbol table with its memory address. During the second pass of the text, when the assembler computes the base-plus-displacement encoding for a memory address, it searches a list of base registers that are active at that point in the program and selects a base register which yields a displacement small enough to be encoded in the 12-bit displacement field. If none exists, the assembler notifies the programmer of an addressing error.

4. The assembler maintains a list of active base registers and their contents by taking note of USING and DROP pseudo-instructions.

5.4 Loaders and Program Relocation

As a program is assembled the assembler usually outputs the encoded program on some output medium such as punched cards, magnetic tape, paper tape, or a magnetic disk. Since the assembler is itself a program that occupies a portion of computer memory, it is usually impractical to place an assembled program in memory with the assembler. Conflicts can arise, for example, if the assembled program must reside in areas that contain portions of the assembler, so that the two cannot be in memory simultaneously. Another problem arises if the size of the assembled program, the assembler, and the symbol table combined are larger than available memory, even though the assembled program alone can reside in memory. Consequently assembled programs are usually recorded outside of computer memory after assembly and must be placed into memory in order to be executed.

For most computers there are programs called *loaders* that perform the task of loading an assembled program into its proper location in memory. In its most primitive form a loader only reads an assembled program from an external storage medium and places it in the proper area of memory. To facilitate this loading process assemblers partition the assembled program into blocks of words, and with each block they record information that controls how the block is to be loaded. Usually the information specifies the starting address of the block and the number of words in the block. During loading the loader examines the control information and places the block in memory at the specified address.

There is a somewhat more versatile type of loader called a *relocating loader*. This type of loader can be used to perform the following tasks, in addition to the basic loading operation:

1. A program can be displaced from its assembled address during loading, and the loader will automatically modify the addresses in the program so that the program executes properly in its displaced position.

2. Two or more separately assembled programs can be loaded together in nonconflicting areas of computer memory. Memory addresses in one program that refer to labels in another program can be filled in by the loader so that cross references among programs will be correct.

3. Programs can call on standard algorithms such as sine, cosine, or square root, and the loader will automatically search a library for them.

When relocation is performed by a loader, the result is essentially the same as would be obtained by modifying the ORG instruction at the beginning of the program. For example, if the first instruction were ORG 100, then the program could be displaced 200 memory cells by changing the instruction to ORG 300 and reassembling. The same result could be obtained by using a relocating loader to load the ORG 100 version of the program with a displacement of 200. The advantage of using a relocating loader is that the program need not be reassembled in order to relocate it, and relocation is considerably simpler than assembly.

To see what is involved in relocation consider the two assembly language programs below. The first is in HP 2116 assembly language and the second is in System/360-370 assembly language.

LABEL	CODE	OPERAND	COMMENTS
	ORG	100	
	LDA	X	Load X into A register.
	STA	Y	Store A register into Y.
	HLT		Halt.
X	DEC	5	
Y	DEC	0	
XNAME	DEF	X	The address of X.
	END		

LABEL	CODE	OPERAND	COMMENTS
	ORG	100	
TEMP	EQU	2	
	BALR	15,0	REG[15] ← P.
	USING	*,15	Establish REG[15] as base register.
	L	TEMP,X	REG[TEMP] ← X.
	ST	TEMP,Y	Y ← REG[TEMP].
	. . .		
X	DC	F'5'	
Y	DC	F'0'	
XNAME	DC	A(X)	The address of X.
	END		

If the first program were displaced 200 memory cells, what would change in the encoded instructions? Clearly the memory addresses X and Y would change in the LDA and STA instructions, as would the address of X in the DEF pseudo-instruction. The general rule for relocation is to add the amount of displacement to every memory address. Notice that the displacement must be added, not to every word in memory, but only to those words that contain memory addresses. The words labeled X and Y contain constants, and we must not alter these constants when the program is relocated.

Now we ask the same question about the second program. Do we have to change the encoding of memory address X in the L instruction? The answer to this question is negative. The address in the L instruction uses REG[15] as a base register, and the value in that register will always be the address of the L instruction, no matter where the program is relocated in memory. Hence the effective address for the L instruction will always be the correct memory address. Note that the address that is assembled in the cell labeled XNAME is affected by relocation. XNAME contains the true memory address of X, and not the address in base-register-plus-displacement form. The general rule for relocation in System/360-370 programs is to adjust all addresses appearing in DC pseudo-instructions by the amount of the relocation.

We see from the examples that relocation involves adding a constant to some, but not all, words in an assembled program. Unfortunately the loader cannot examine a word in an assembled program and decide whether it contains an instruction, a constant, or an address. If no other information were available to the loader, then it could not determine which words should be modified and which should not be when a program is relocated. Therefore the assembler inserts additional information in the assembled program that specifies which words contain addresses that must be modified. The loader uses this information when it performs relocation.

The relocation process may be slightly more complex than indicated above. For example, memory addresses in instructions for the HP 2116 computer may refer either to the base page or the current page. Relocation, therefore, involves treating the base page differently from other pages. When two or more programs are loaded together, their base-page addresses are relocated in the base page independently of the rest of the program. Therefore each program has two displacements associated with it: one for the base page and one for the rest of the program. For this reason the assembler identifies every relocatable memory address as either *base-page relocatable* or *program relocatable,* and the identification is included in the assembled program for use by the loader. When a relocatable program is loaded, the loader adds either the base-page displacement or the program displacement to relocatable addresses, depending on the type of address. To contend with many different program environments, assembly languages may have several different types of relocatable addresses in addition to the two mentioned here.

The second capability of relocating loaders concerns the loading of two separately assembled programs so that they can refer to each other. For example, if one program has the instruction LDA X and another has the instruction X DEC 0, the assembler cannot determine the memory address for the LDA instruction unless the second program is assembled with the first. By means of the relocating loader we can place such external references in programs and still assemble them separately. In essence we defer the assembly of external references until the programs are loaded.

We use two pseudo-instructions as follows for external references; the first pair is for the HP 2116 computer and the second pair is for System/360-370.

PSEUDO-INSTRUCTION	CODE	EXAMPLE	ACTION
External	EXT	EXT ABC	Mark ABC as a symbol defined in another program.
Entry	ENT	ENT ABC	Mark ABC as a symbol defined in this program that is used by another program.
External	EXTRN	EXTRN ABC	Same as EXT.
Entry	ENTRY	ENTRY ABC	Same as ENT.

Programs that refer to external memory addresses must use the EXT or EXTRN instructions to notify the assembler that the addresses are external to the program. The assembler will place this information in the assembled program along with other information that will permit the relocating loader to modify the memory addresses during loading. The information included in the assembled program is each external symbol and a list of the addresses of all instructions that refer to that symbol.

Similarly, if a program contains locations that are referenced by other programs, the program must notify the assembler by using the ENT or ENTRY pseudo-instruction. An assembler processes these instructions by placing the symbol and its address into the assembled program. Examples 5·6 and 5·7 show how EXT and ENT instructions are used in a program for the HP 2116 computer.

When a sequence of programs with external references is loaded, the loader places all ENT references in a symbol table, together with the addresses at which the ENT symbols are loaded. When all programs have been processed, the loader examines the list of EXT symbols. For each EXT symbol in a program the loader finds the corresponding address in the symbol table and places this address in every instruction that references the EXT symbol. The processing for the ENT and EXT is essentially the same as the processing that takes place during assembly. The loader uses the lists of EXT and ENT symbols only to construct

EXAMPLE 5·6

Symbols XYZ and ABC refer to locations that are not in the following program:

LABEL	CODE	OPERAND
	EXT	XYZ,ABC
	. . .	
	JMP	XYZ
	. . .	
	LDA	ABC
	. . .	

EXAMPLE 5·7

The following program is to be loaded along with the program of Example 5·6:

LABEL	CODE	OPERAND
	ENT	XYZ,ABC
	. . .	
XYZ	STA	TEMP
	. . .	
ABC	DEC	26
	. . .	

addresses for external references. None of the lists are loaded into memory with the program.

The third capability of relocating loaders is library searching and loading. A *program library* is a collection of frequently used programs that is stored externally to the computer on a magnetic disk, tape, or some equivalent storage medium. The programs in the library are stored in their assembled forms, as relocatable programs, so that it is not necessary to reassemble a library program each time it is used.

Since references to library programs are really no different from any other external references, library processing is a natural extension of external reference processing. The usual algorithm for relocating loaders is to match as many external references as possible with entry references. If any external references are left over, without corresponding entry references, the loader searches a library for programs that contain the missing references. Thus a programmer can call for an algorithm for computing the sine by using EXT SINE, provided that the sine program has been assembled for the library with the instruction ENT SINE.

We have discussed relocating loaders from a rather general point of view in this section. There are many loaders that differ somewhat from the description here. One notable example is the loader for System/360-370 computers. For these computers relocation, external reference processing, and library searching is performed by a program called a *link editor*. The System/360-370 link editor produces a version of the program which essentially needs only loading. The System/360-370 loader can do only loading and simple relocation. In effect, the processes that we have attributed here to a single program, the relocating loader, are split between the link editor and the loader for System/360-370.

5·5   Macro-instructions

There are many situations in which the programmer must tediously reproduce sequences of assembly language instructions at several different places in a program. For example, he may wish to increment a positive number in memory by 3. One way of doing this for the HP 2116 computer is to use the ISZ instruction repeatedly as follows:

```
 . . .
ISZ    X    Increment X by 1.
ISZ    X
ISZ    X
 . . .
```

Ideally the programmer wants to tell the assembler how to construct the sequence of instructions without specifying the instruction separately each time. In this example he ought to be able to tell the assembler to repeat the instruction ISZ X three times. Many assemblers have facilities for generating sequences of instructions under control of the programmer. Instructions that cause other instructions to be generated are commonly known as *macro-instructions*, or sometimes *macros*.

The HP 2116 assembly language has a very primitive macro-instruction capability for generating copies of a given instruction. The repeat instruction (code REP) tells the assembler to produce n copies of the next instruction, where n is the operand of the repeat instruction. Thus the following instruction sequence is equivalent to our earlier example:

```
. . .
REP     3      Repeat next instruction three times.
ISZ     X
. . .
```

Notice that the REP instruction causes assembler action to be taken, so that it is a pseudo-instruction, not an ordinary instruction.

System/360-370 assembly language contains a much more powerful macro facility. It permits a programmer to define a macro-instruction by giving a sequence of commands for that instruction. Then, whenever the macro-instruction is used, the assembler replaces the macro-instruction by the sequence of instructions used in its definition. For example, we saw earlier that the following sequence of instructions should be used for integer division with two full-word operands:

```
L       2,X     REG[2] ← X.
SRDA    2,32    Shift REG[2,3] right 32 bits.
D       2,Y     REG[3] ← X÷Y.
```

The SRDA instruction has to be inserted before the instruction for division in order to extend the sign of X through REG[2]. If we wish to perform integer division at several places in a program, it becomes convenient to define an integer-division macro-instruction which takes care of the SRDA instruction automatically. The following example shows how we define a macro-instruction DI for integer division:

```
MACRO              Beginning of macro definition.
DI       &DIV      The name of the macro is DI and it has one operand
                   named &DIV.
SRDA     2,32
D        2,&DIV    Use &DIV as a divisor.
MEND               End of macro definition.
```

After defining DI as shown the programmer can create the sequence of instructions for computing X ÷ Y by using the following instructions:

```
L    2,X    REG[2] ← X.
DI   Y      Integer-divide by Y.
```

When the assembler reaches the DI instruction, it will replace it by the definition of DI. In the original definition of DI the operand is named &DIV and is identified as an operand of the macro by the prefix &. Every reference to &DIV is changed to Y, because Y is specified as the operand for this use of the macro. Thus the DI Y instruction will produce both the SRDA and the D instructions, with the operand of the D instruction specified as Y.

The general format of a macro-instruction is as follows:

```
            MACRO
&LABEL      NAME      &OP1,&OP2, . . . ,&OPn
            INSTR1
            INSTR2
            INSTR3
            . . .
            INSTRm
            MEND
```

The definition begins with MACRO and ends with MEND. The first line after MACRO specifies the name by which the macro will be invoked (NAME), dummy names for the operands, and an optional dummy label name. The macro may be invoked by a call such as

```
LOOP    NAME    R1,R2,R3,R4.
```

This call causes all the instructions in the definition to be inserted into the program at the calling point, with &OP1 replaced by R1, &OP2 replaced by R2, etc., and &LABEL replaced by LOOP. Presumably &LABEL appears in the label field of exactly one instruction in the macro definition.

EXAMPLE 5·8

The following macro definition tests the full word operand &X to determine whether it is odd or even, leaving the result of the test in the condition code. A branch on zero instruction (code BZ) can be used after the EVEN macro-instruction, with the branch taken if the operand is even and no branch taken if the operand is odd.

LABEL	CODE	OPERAND	COMMENTS
	MACRO		
&START	EVEN	&X,&TEMP	EVEN is name of macro.
&START	L	&TEMP,&X	REG[&TEMP] ← MEMORY [&X; . . .]
	N	&TEMP,=F'1'	REG[&TEMP] ← REG[&TEMP] AND 1.
	LTR	&TEMP,&TEMP	Test REG[&TEMP] and set condition code.
	MEND		

If the macro is invoked by the instruction

TESTZ   EVEN   Z,5

then the following instructions are generated by the assembler:

LABEL	CODE	OPERAND
TESTZ	L	5,Z
	N	5,=F'1'
	LTR	5,5

The label TESTZ can be the target of a branch instruction elsewhere in the program. In this example the dummy label feature is used to distinguish this invocation of EVEN from all others.

Macro definitions may contain macro-instructions, as well as ordinary instructions or pseudo-instructions. For example, a programmer can define a macro-instruction which uses the macro EVEN, defined in Example 5·8. Macro-instructions embedded in other macro-definitions are known as *nested macros*.

REFERENCES

The System/360-370 assembly language contains several facilities in its macro language that are not treated here. One of the most useful of these is the set of instructions for conditional assembly which can be used to generate instructions selectively. These instructions can omit the generation of particular instructions or repeat particular instructions a variable number of times, with the generation controlled by the value of the operands of the macro at the point it is invoked. For a full discussion consult the System 360-370 reference manual, "Assembler Language," form C28-6514. A tutorial discussion of the macro-language appears in Kent (1969).

EXERCISES

5·1 If line 5 of Example 5·1 were deleted, what changes in the address portions of instructions would have to be made for the address references to remain correct? Assume that the storage addresses Y and Z do not change. The use of symbolic names frees the programmer from the task of changing instruction encoding when he adds or deletes instructions.

5·2 Explain why the pseudo-instructions EQU, ORG, and BSS do not allow forward references in their operand fields.

5·3 A programmer attempted to execute a program containing the instruction sequence

LABEL	CODE	OPERAND
	LDA	X
X	DEC	10
	STA	Y
	HLT	

What is incorrect in this sequence if the intent is to store the number 10 in MEMORY[Y]?

5·4 Determine the instruction encoding for the program in Example 5·4 under the assumption that the instruction in line 1 is immediately preceded by the pseudo-instruction ORG 40000B.

6

DATA STRUCTURES

The processing of data structures is of central importance in computer programming. *Data structures* are collections of data which are related. Vectors and matrices are examples of data structures in which the data have a positional relationship. A library card catalog is a data structure of a more complex type. A book listed in it may be cross referenced to other books on the basis of a related subject, a common author, or both. Moreover, a book may be included in several sets or groupings of books, each of which has a different basis of relationship.

Although there are many data structures that satisfy our vague definition, we shall confine this discussion to a few data structures of general importance. For computer programming purposes nearly every data structure of interest can be manipulated by casting it into one of the data structures that we shall describe.

The study of data structures is a fundamental part of the study of algorithms and programs. Just as numbers can be represented in several different systems, so can a set of related data be fitted into many different data structures. When a programmer creates an algorithm to solve a problem, he also creates a data structure that is manipulated by the algorithm. His choice of data structure can greatly affect the amount of storage required for processing, as well as the processing speed. It is common to find that memory requirements may vary by a factor of 2 to 10 for different structural representations of the same data. Moreover, because the data structure affects the processing of the data, computational speeds may vary by even larger factors. If N is some natural parameter of a problem, the computation time for one data structure may be proportional to N^2, while for another it may be only $N \log_2 N$. Clearly, as N becomes large, the differences in processing speed become extremely large. In some instances it is possible to exhibit computation times that vary from as high as $N!$ or 2^N to times that grow only algebraically in N, say N^5. The improvement in processing speed of efficient algorithms is often largely due to the use of appropriate data structures.

In this chapter we shall initiate the study of data structures by investigating some fundamental ones. Later chapters illustrate how these data structures can be used in practice. We shall also investigate, in Chapter 9, data structures that are somewhat more complex than those discussed in this chapter.

6·1 One-dimensional Arrays

The simplest data structure is the *one-dimensional array*. An array may be viewed as a list of items such that each item is identified uniquely by its index in the list. For example, let X be the label for an array with 100 elements whose indices range from 0 to 99. Then X[51] is an item near the middle of the array, X[0] is the first item, and X[99] is the last.

To take advantage of the characteristics of addresses in computers, it is customary to store array elements in sequence in memory so that the address of X[I] can be calculated by adding I to the address of X[0]. The following assembly code instruction creates an array with 100 elements and associates the name X with the first element, X[0], of the array

        X   BSS   100

Indexing through an array with the HP 2116 computer instruction set is most conveniently done by means of indirection. Example 6·1 illustrates one way of indexing through an array.

EXAMPLE 6·1

The program finds the maximum element of an array, leaving its index in A and its value in B. We make use of the fact that the A and B registers of the HP 2116 computer are treated as memory addresses 0 and 1.

	LABEL	CODE	OPERAND	COMMENTS
1.	A	EQU	0	
2.	B	EQU	1	
3.	XNAME	DEF	X	Address of X is placed in XNAME.
4.	LNGTH	DEC	100	Length of X is placed here.
5.	MAX	DEC	0	Address of largest element.
6.	LIMIT	DEC	0	One greater than address of X[99].
7.	X	BSS	100	
		. . .		
8.		LDA	XNAME	Initialize by setting MAX to address of X[0].
9.		STA	MAX	
10.		ADA	LNGTH	
11.		STA	LIMIT	Calculate and save limit address.
12.		LDA	XNAME	
13.	ROUND	INA		
14.		LDB	LIMIT	Increment address and compare with limit address.
15.		CMB,INB		
16.		ADB	A	
17.		SSB,RSS		Skip if A is less than limit address.
18.		JMP	OUT	

LABEL	CODE	OPERAND	COMMENTS
19.	LDB	A,I	Compare next element in X to MAX.
20.	CMB,INB		
21.	ADB	MAX,I	
22.	SSB		Skip if B $\geq$ 0.
23.	STA	MAX	New maximum found. Save address.
24.	JMP	ROUND	
25. OUT	LDB	MAX,I	Largest value is put in B.
26.	LDA	XNAME	
27.	CMA,INA		
28.	ADA	MAX	Index is computed, I = MAX—XNAME.

In this example the loop control variable is an indexed address, and the limit of the loop is an address one greater than the maximum allowable address. A more general form of solution is to use the running index as the control variable and calculate the indexed address from the base address and index each time in the loop. To modify the example for the more general case the value of LIMIT is set equal to the value of LENGTH and the A register is initialized to 0 before entering line 13. After line 18 it is necessary to insert the instructions

```
STA   TEMP
ADA   XNAME
```

to save the value of the index and to calculate an indexed address. After line 23 the instruction

```
LDA   TEMP
```

must be inserted to restore the A register to the value of the index.

Note carefully how the limit is tested in lines 14 to 17. The jump out of the loop is taken when A $\geq$ LIMIT. It would have been shorter and faster to replace lines 14 to 17 with the single instruction

```
CPA   LIMIT
```

However, in this case the jump out of the loop would be taken for A = LIMIT rather than for A $\geq$ LIMIT. If LNGTH is greater than zero, it makes no difference which test is used. However, suppose that LNGTH is zero. Then the value of the index when the first comparison occurs is 1, so that an equality test would cause 65,535 iterations to occur, while an inequality test would result in an immediate termination.

The lesson is that short cuts should not be used indiscriminately. The equality test is sensitive to bad data because it requires *exact* equality. It should be used only if a check is inserted at the beginning of the program to be sure that the data will not cause a loop to occur.

Example 6·2 is the same algorithm as Example 6·1, but written for System/360-370.

EXAMPLE 6·2

	LABEL	CODE	OPERAND	COMMENTS
1.	MAX	EQU	2	REG[MAX] will hold value of maximum.
2.	PLACE	EQU	3	REG[PLACE] will hold index of maximum element.
3.	TEMP	EQU	4	A temporary register.
4.	INDEX	EQU	5	The current index.
5.	XNAME	DC	A(X)	The memory address of X.
6.	LNGTH	DC	F'100'	The length of X.
7.	X	DS	100F'0'	Reserve 100 full words for X.
		. . .		
8.		L	MAX,X(0)	Initialize MAX and PLACE as if X[0] contained maximum.
9.		L	PLACE,=F'0'	
10.		L	INDEX,=F'1'	Start loop at X[1].
11.	ROUND	LR	TEMP,INDEX	Multiply the index by 4.
12.		SLA	TEMP,2	
13.		C	MAX,X(TEMP)	Is MAX < X[INDEX]?
14.		BNL	TEST	If so, continue, otherwise branch.
15.		L	MAX,X(TEMP)	Update maximum.
16.		LR	PLACE,INDEX	
17.	TEST	A	INDEX,=F'1'	Add 1 to index.
18.		C	INDEX,LNGTH	Is INDEX < LNGTH?
19.		BL	ROUND	If so, branch.
		. . .		

In Example 6·2 the index is in REG[INDEX] at line 11. To compute the address of X[INDEX] we have to multiply the index by 4, since each element of the full-word array X is four bytes long. The compare instruction in line 13 performs essentially the same test as lines 19 to 21 of Example 6·1. If a new maximum is found, then MAX and PLACE are updated.

Examples 6·1 and 6·2 illustrate the great similarities of indexing and indirection. The address calculations are virtually the same in both cases. The only difference of significance in the examples is due to the methods for comparing two numbers. The System/360-370 compare instructions lead to more compact programs than the skip instructions of the HP 2116 computer.

Examples 6·1 and 6·2 illustrate how to access elements of an array when the array has a lower bound of 0. It is common practice to give the first element of an array an index other than 0. For example, consider a program with an array named POPULATION that holds census data for the years 1950 to 1964. Since the data cover only 15 years, we want the array to be 15 words long. It may be desirable to index the elements of the array so that POPULATION[1950] holds the size of the population in 1950. However, we obviously do not want to leave 1950 memory cells blank in order to have the desired indexing. Hence we create the array so that POPULATION[1950] is the first element of the array or, equivalently, 1950 is the lower bound for POPULATION.

The FORTRAN programming language defines all arrays to have a lower bound of 1. Thus the FORTRAN statement

    DIMENSION   X(100)

creates an array named X with 100 elements such that the first has index 1 and the last has index 100. ALGOL permits the programmer to specify both the upper and lower bounds of the arrays he defines.

In general, then, every one-dimensional array has two integers associated with it: a lower bound and an upper bound. These are indices of the first and last elements of the array, respectively. The length of the array is

$$length = upper\ bound - lower\ bound + 1$$

It is frequently worthwhile to test indices to determine if they are in range before using them. Such tests expose a very common source of programming errors.

Example 6·3 shows two sequences of instructions for checking subscripts. The general rules to follow are:

1. Take error exit if index does *not* satisfy

   lower ≤ index ≤ upper bound

2. The indexed address is obtained by computing

   base + index − lower bound

EXAMPLE 6·3

The first sequence is for the HP 2116 computer and the second is for System/360-370.

	LABEL	CODE	OPERAND	COMMENTS
1.	INDEX	DEC	0	
2.	LOWER	DEC	1	Lower bound is index of first element.
3.	UPPER	DEC	100	Upper bound is index of last element.
4.	BASE	DEF	ARRAY	The address of first element.
5.	ARRAY	BSS	100	Array storage is reserved here.
		. . .		
6.		LDA	INDEX	Compute UPPER − INDEX.
7.		CMA,INA		
8.		ADA	UPPER	
9.		SSA		Skip if A ≥ 0.
10.		JMP	ERROR	A is negative if UPPER < INDEX.
11.		LDA	LOWER	Compute INDEX − LOWER.
12.		CMA,INA		
13.		ADA	INDEX	
14.		SSA		Skip if A ≥ 0.
15.		JMP	ERROR	A is negative if INDEX < LOWER.
16.		ADA	BASE	A register now contains the address of element BASE[INDEX].

The following sequence, for System/360-370, checks the index and then places 4·(index − lower bound) in REG[I] so that REG[I] can be used as an index register in another instruction.

	LABEL	CODE	OPERAND	COMMENTS
1.	INDEX	DC	F'0'	
2.	LOWER	DC	F'1'	Lower bound is index of first element.
3.	UPPER	DC	F'100'	Upper bound is index of last element.
4.	BASE	DC	A(ARRAY)	Address of first element.
5.	ARRAY	DS	100F	Reserve storage for array.
			. . .	
6.	I	EQU	2	Define I as REG[2].
7.		L	I,INDEX	Fetch value of index from memory.
8.		C	I,UPPER	Is INDEX > UPPER?
9.		BH	ERROR	If so, branch out.
10.		S	I,LOWER	Compute I − LOWER.
11.		LTR	I,I	Is INDEX < LOWER? (This instruction is redundant since previous instruction also sets condition code.)
12.		BL	ERROR	If so, branch out.
13.		SLA	I,2	Multiply by 4 by shifting twice.

In some cases the lower bound is known to be 0. For these cases it is not necessary to subtract a lower bound from the index. In the first sequence of Example 6·3 lines 11 and 12 can be deleted and line 13 can be replaced by

LDA   INDEX

6·2 Multidimensional Arrays

There are several ways to generalize the addressing of one-dimensional arrays to two or more dimensions. We shall consider two alternatives here.

6·2·1 The Address Polynomial Method of Indexing

Suppose that X is the name of an $M \times N$ matrix, and suppose that we consider the general problem of addressing X[I,J], the element of X in row I, column J. If we store X in a particular fashion, then we can compute the address of X[I,J] from the values of I and J by a multiplication and addition. A suitable storage format is to store X[1,1] at the base address of X, and at successive locations we store

X[1,2],X[1,3], ..., X[1,N], X[2,1], ..., X[2,N], ..., X[M,N]

Then the address of X[I,J] is given by

address = base + $[(I - 1)N + J - 1]$

The bracketed part of the expression is often called the *address polynomial*. In this example the elements of X are said to be stored in *row-major form*, because X is stored by rows in memory. It is equally acceptable to store X by columns (or *column-major form*) and to calculate the address of X[I,J] by use of the polynomial

address = base + $[(J - 1)M + I - 1]$

Addressing of this type is usually done in the machine language programs compiled by FORTRAN compilers (in fact the ANSI FORTRAN standard requires that arrays be stored in column-major form). If we permit arbitrary lower bounds and also require checking of indices before indexing an address, then the following general rules apply:

1. The index in each dimension must satisfy the relation

   lower bound $\leq$ index $\leq$ upper bound

2. For each dimension calculate an effective index by subtracting the lower bound for that dimension from the value of the index.

3. For each dimension compute a length from the formula

   length = upper bound − lower bound + 1

4. The address polynomial is computed for a k-dimensional array from the formula

   address polynomial
   $$= ((\cdots (E_1)L_2 + E_2)L_3 + \cdots + E_{k-1})(L_k + E_k)$$

   where the E_i are the effective indices and the L_i are the lengths.

6·2·2 Addressing by Indirection   Another form of addressing avoids the use of multiplications in the calculation of addresses within multi-dimensional arrays. It is best illustrated by an example in the two-dimensional case. Let X be an $M \times N$ array as before, and assume that X is stored in row-major form. To index into X we use an array named XROW of length M. The Ith entry of XROW contains the address of X[I,1], the first entry of the Ith row of X. Then the address of X[I,J] is given by

$$\text{address} = \text{MEMORY[base of XROW} + I] + J$$

The following example illustrates addressing into an array with indices I and J with $0 \leq I \leq 4$ and $0 \leq J \leq 2$.

EXAMPLE 6·4

The first of the two sequences is for the HP 2116 computer and the second is for System/360-370.

	LABEL	CODE	OPERAND	COMMENTS
1.	XROWN	DEF	XROW	
2.	XROW	DEF	X	
3.		DEF	X+3	
4.		DEF	X+6	
5.		DEF	X+9	
6.		DEF	X+12	
7.	X	BSS	15	
8.	A	EQU	0	
9.	I	DEC	0	
10.	J	DEC	0	
		. . .		
11.		LDA	XROWN	
12.		ADA	I	Calculate address of row I.
13.		LDA	A,I	Fetch address of row I to A.
14.		ADA	J	Address of element J in row.
15.		LDA	A,I	Load X[I,J].

In the following sequence for System/360-370 note the multiplication by four to compute addresses from indices:

	LABEL	CODE	OPERAND	COMMENTS
1.	XROW	DC	A(X)	
2.		DC	A(X+12)	Address of third full word beyond X.
3.		DC	A(X+24)	
4.		DC	A(X+36)	
5.		DC	A(X+48)	
6.	X	DS	15F	
7.	TEMP	EQU	3	A temporary register.
8.	JAY	EQU	4	REG[JAY] will hold value of J.
9.	I	DC	F'0'	
10.	J	DC	F'0'	
		. . .		
11.		L	TEMP,I	Fetch I to REG[TEMP].
12.		SLA	TEMP,2	Multiply by 4.
13.		L	TEMP,XROW(TEMP)	Fetch address of row I.
14.		L	JAY,J	
15.		SLA	JAY,2	Make J into an index.
16.		L	TEMP,0(JAY,TEMP)	Fetch X[I,J].

The programs in Example 6·4 can be expanded to include checks to ensure that the indices are in range, and they can be generalized to the case in which lower bounds are nonzero.

6·3 Push-down Stacks

Push-down stacks are one-dimensional arrays used for temporary storage of data. Items are entered and removed from stacks one at a time, such that the last item placed in the stack is the first one to be removed. The behavior of push-down stacks has often been compared to that of an ordinary stack of cafeteria trays.

The process of adding an item to a stack is called a *push-down*, and the process of removing an item is called a *pop-up*. Suppose that there are two subroutines, PUSH and POP, to perform stacking and unstacking operations, and suppose that PUSH stacks the contents of the A register, while POP unstacks one item and places it in the A register.

To stack the value of X we execute

```
LDA    X
JSB    PUSH
```

and to retrieve the current top of stack we execute

```
JSB    POP
```

To implement a push-down stack in machine language we use an array and a single variable that gives the index of the current top of the stack. The PUSH and POP routines would be written in the following way in an ALGOL-like language:

```
PUSH:    TOP ← TOP+1;
         if TOP ≤ UPPER BOUND then STACK[TOP] ← A
         else go to STACKOVERFLOW;
                . . .
POP:     if TOP < LOWER BOUND then go to STACKUNDERFLOW;
         A ← STACK[TOP];
         TOP ← TOP − 1;
                . . .
```

In some cases it is possible to dispense with the overflow and underflow checks. These checks are equivalent to the checks used for ordinary arrays to guarantee that indices are within range.

Stacks are useful data structures because many algorithms require that data be filed and retrieved on a last-in-first-out basis. Stacks are frequently used in compilers and in the compiled code of programs written in ALGOL and PL/I.

6·4 Queues

Queues are one-dimensional arrays that are like stacks in that items are entered and removed one at a time. The difference between queues and stacks is that the retrieval discipline for queues is first-in-first-out, and that for stacks is last-in-first-out. Two variables are associated with queues: the variable HEAD identifies the next item to be retrieved, and the variable TAIL identifies the place to put the next item to be added to the queue. The processes are called by many different names, such as QUEUE and DEQUEUE. We shall use the names PUT and GET.

Let us assume that the queue is implemented in an infinite array named QUEUE and that items are communicated to and from it through the A register, as before. The ALGOL-like descriptions of PUT and GET may be written as follows:

```
PUT:    TAIL ← TAIL+1;
        QUEUE[TAIL] ← A;
        . . .

GET:    if HEAD < TAIL then
            begin
                HEAD ← HEAD+1;
                A ← QUEUE[HEAD];
            end
        else
            go to QUEUE EMPTY;
            . . .
```

HEAD and TAIL are initialized to the same value. The routine GET retrieves an item from QUEUE, provided that there has been at least one more item stored in the queue than has been retrieved.

The routines are actually more complex than we have indicated. The array QUEUE is finite, so that the permissible values of HEAD and TAIL must be limited. Queueing is generally implemented by indexing from 0 to some maximum value designated MAX, and when either HEAD or TAIL surpasses the value of MAX, it is reset to 0. We have to be very careful that the indices HEAD and TAIL never pass each other. In the rough description above, the condition that HEAD increases beyond the value of TAIL indicates that the queue has been emptied and a special test ensures that this can never occur. If, however, TAIL increases beyond the value of HEAD (as it might, since it can be reset to 0), then MAX+1 successive PUTS have occurred without an intervening GET, and so the queue is full. The following examples illustrate queue processing in its full generality:

```
PUT:    TAIL ← TAIL+1;
        if TAIL > MAX then TAIL ← 0;
        if TAIL = HEAD then go to QUEUE FULL;
        QUEUE[TAIL] ← A;
        . . .

GET:    if HEAD = TAIL then go to QUEUE EMPTY;
        HEAD ← HEAD+1;
        if HEAD > MAX then HEAD ← 0;
        A ← QUEUE[HEAD];
        . . .
```

Note that the comparisons of HEAD and TAIL must be equality comparisons. The circular characteristics of the queue can produce situations in which HEAD > TAIL, for example, and therefore prevents a test of the form HEAD ≥ TAIL for queue emptiness.

Queues are used for buffering input/output data in many programming systems. For example, the process that calls PUT may be a program that reads characters from a teletype keyboard or from a paper-tape reader. The program that calls GET might be an application program that uses the input characters for data. Queueing is a natural method for permitting an input/output program to operate at the speed of the input/output device, while an application program requests data at a rate determined by the speed of computation of the application program. The input/output program must be prepared to suspend operation when the queue becomes filled until the application program catches up and empties one or more positions in the queue. Similarly, the application program must temporarily suspend operation when the queue becomes empty. This point is discussed more thoroughly in Chapter 8.

There are some algorithms for which it is convenient to generalize the notion of a queue to a data structure for which items may be inserted at either end or removed at either end. Such a data structure is called a *double-ended queue* or a *deque*. The routines for manipulating a double-ended queue are straightforward generalizations of PUT and GET. For convenience let us call these routines PUTHEAD, PUTTAIL, GETHEAD, and GETTAIL. Figure 6·1 illustrates how these routines function.

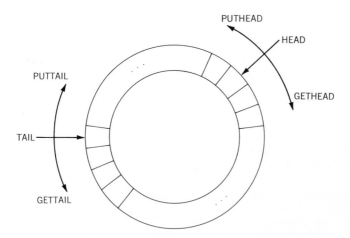

Figure 6·1 A double-ended queue

The double-ended queue is shown as a circular collection of data, with the pointers HEAD and TAIL specifying two elements. The curved arrows indicate the movement of the pointers when a routine is invoked. Figure 6·1 indicates that the double-ended queue is a generalization not only of a queue, but of a push-down stack as well. If we use only the routines PUTHEAD and GETHEAD, we have a push-down stack. If we use only the routines PUTTAIL and GETHEAD, we have an ordinary queue.

6·5 Packed Data Structures

In the previous discussions data structures have been formed in terms of multiples of machine words. They can also be formed from *data packets*, which are smaller than machine words. In such cases it is sometimes necessary to store two or more such packets in a single word in order to save memory space.

A good example of data packing in the HP 2116 computer is the use of a single word to store two 8-bit characters. Let the character that occupies the most significant bits of a word be called the *high character* and the character that occupies the low-order bits be called the *low character*. The following example illustrates two sequences of instructions, one for retrieving a high character and one for storing a low character.

EXAMPLE 6·5

At the label HGET we assume that the A register contains the address of the word to be accessed. The character is left in the A register, right justified. The high-order bits of the result word are all 0's.

	LABEL	CODE	OPERAND	COMMENTS
1.	HGET	LDA	A,I	Fetch word to A.
2.		ALF,ALF		Circularly shift eight places.
3.		AND	MASK	MASK out high-order bits.
		. . .		
4.	MASK	OCT	377	
5.	A	EQU	0	

At the label LPUT the A register contains the character to be stored in memory and the B register contains the address of the word to receive the character. The high-order character of the word in memory is left unchanged when its low-order character is updated.

LABEL	CODE	OPERAND	COMMENTS
1. LPUT	AND	MASK	Mask out high-order bits.
2.	STA	TEMP	
3.	LDA	MASK	Form a mask to mask out low-order
2.			bits.
4.	CMA		177400_8 is now in A.
5.	AND	B,I	Fetch word from memory and mask out low-order bits.
6.	IOR	TEMP	Insert new low-order character.
7.	STA	B,I	Restore in memory.
	. . .		
8. TEMP	DEC	0	
9. MASK	OCT	377	
10. A	EQU	0	
11. B	EQU	1	

The routines above illustrate the fundamentals of data packing and unpacking. The usual conventions are the following.

To retrieve packed data:

1. Fetch the word from memory.

2. Isolate the field, using AND or logical-shift operations or a combination of both.

3. Leave the isolated field right justified in the result register.

To insert a datum into a word packed data:

1. Fetch the word from memory.

2. Assume that the new datum is right justified. Using a combination of AND, OR, and logical-shift operations, place the new datum in the appropriate field of the word. Leave all other portions of the word unchanged.

3. Restore in memory.

Example 6·6 illustrates the use of AND and OR operations for packing new data into a word of memory.

EXAMPLE 6·6

Consider the action of a program that places a three-bit entry in bits 12 through 14 of a word in memory when the data have the following values:

Memory word: 167532_8

Data word: 000003_8

Mask: 107777_8

Mask memory word: 167532 AND 107777 = 107532

Shift data word: 000003 left shifted 12 bits = 030000

Complement mask: $\overline{107777}$ = 070000

Mask data word with new mask: 030000 AND 070000 = 030000

Form logical OR: 030000 OR 107532 = 137532

Example 6·6 can be coded directly in either the HP 2116 or the System/360-370 instruction repertoire. The System/360-370 logical-shift instructions also provide added flexibility in that the length and position of a field can be parameters of these instructions that are computed during program execution. Example 6·7 illustrates how to use logical shifts to isolate a specified data field.

Example 6·7

This instruction sequence accesses the word whose address is in REG[ADDR] and isolates the n-bit field of the word beginning at bit m. The values of n and m are held in REG[N] and REG[M], respectively. Since there are $m - 1$ bits to the left of the field to be isolated, the SLL instruction left-justifies this field in the odd register of an even-odd register pair. Then the SLDL instruction shifts the field into the previously cleared even register, leaving it right justified.

	LABEL	CODE	OPERAND	COMMENTS
1.	N	EQU	2	REG[N] contains field length.
2.	M	EQU	3	REG[M] contains position of the leftmost bit of field. Recall that bits in a word are numbered from 0 to 31, starting at left.
3.	EVEN	EQU	4	The even register of an even-odd register pair.
4.	ODD	EQU	EVEN+1	The odd register of a pair.
5.	ADDR	EQU	6	Address of datum is in REG[6].
6.		L	ODD,0(ADDR)	Fetch datum to REG[ODD].
7.		L	EVEN,=F'0'	Clear even register.
8.		S	M,=F'1'	Compute m − 1.
9.		SLL	ODD,0(M)	Left-shift m − 1 bits, leaving data left-adjusted in REG[ODD].
10.		SLDL	EVEN,0(N)	Left-shift REG[EVEN;ODD], leaving data right-adjusted in REG [EVEN] with high-order bits cleared.

Note in Example $6 \cdot 7$ how the logical-shift instructions have been used to force 0's into the high-order bits of a register in lieu of using an AND operation with a mask. In this particular instance the logical-shift instructions and the flexibility provided by single and double registers led to a more compact instruction sequence than we could have obtained with masking operations. This is not to be interpreted as a general rule, for there are some instances in which masking can be more efficient than shifting. Usually several different programming approaches must be tried for a few problems in order to gain a feel for techniques that are likely to make the most efficient use of instructions.

EXERCISES

$6 \cdot 1$ An upper triangular matrix is defined to be a square matrix with no entries below the main diagonal. That is, if X is a triangular matrix of dimension N, then X[I,J] = 0 for J < I, where $1 \leq I$, $J \leq N$. Find a way of storing triangular matrices so that no space is reserved for entries below the main diagonal. Indicate the layout of the array in memory and find a formula for the address of X[I,J] in terms of the values of I and J and the base address of X.

6·2 Write a sequence of instructions that generalizes Example 6·4 to nonzero lower bounds and performs checking of subscripts.

6·3 Write sequences of instructions that implement PUSH and POP procedures with underflow and overflow checks.

6·4 Write sequences of instructions that implement PUT and GET procedures.

6·5 Examine the PUT and GET routines and determine how many elements are in the queue when it is full.

6·6 Write routines for maintaining a double-ended queue. How many elements are in the queue when it is full?

6·7 Write an assembly language routine that either sets or clears the nth bit of a word. The value of n is assumed to be given to the routine in a machine register, and another register contains 0 if the bit is to be cleared or 1 if the bit is to be set.

6·8 Suppose that you are to create a packed data array in which each element is four bits long. Thus a 16-bit word in the HP 2116 computer holds four array elements, and the 32-bit word in the System/360-370 computers holds eight array elements. Assume that there are 64 array elements, held in contiguous words of memory. Write a pair of routines for respectively storing and retrieving the ith element of the array. Assume that the value of i is given in a machine register and that the routine for storing the ith element also receives the new value of the ith element in a machine register.

7

Subroutines, Coroutines, and Parameters

In the previous chapters the major emphasis has been directed to short sequences of instructions for primitive operations. In this chapter we shall discuss how to organize sequences of instructions into self-contained subprograms called *subroutines* and *coroutines*. The concepts embodied in subroutines and coroutines are fundamental to programming. Except for the most trivial programs, virtually every program is written as a collection of subroutines or coroutines, although in principle, no program has to be organized this way. As we investigate the mechanics of creating subroutines and coroutines, we shall also see more clearly the reasons for their importance to computer programming.

7·1 Subroutines

It is frequently necessary to execute a particular sequence of instructions at several different places in a program. For example, there may be several points at which the sine of an angle is calculated. By structuring programs as subroutines we need not duplicate instruction sequences in memory and consequently, we can use memory more efficiently.

Subroutines, then, are instruction sequences that can be entered from many different places in a program. When subroutine processing is complete, control returns to the point from which the branch to the subroutine occurred. To achieve this behavior, an address is supplied to a subroutine each time it is entered. The subroutine branches to this address when it completes its computation. Subroutine entries and exits are so common that all computers have special subroutine instructions. We shall first investigate these instructions for the HP 2116 and System/360-370 and then see how these instructions can be used to construct subroutines.

One of the branch instructions in the repertoire of the HP 2116 computer is the jump to subroutine (JSB) instruction. This is the only instruction that gives a program access to the P register. To be precise, recall that the action of the instruction JSB X is

MEMORY[X] ← P+1

P ← X+1

The second action causes a program branch in the usual way. The first action, the storing of the P register, is the unusual aspect of this instruction. Storing the value of P+1 in memory leaves a "trail marker," showing the branch point. The normal branch instruction, JMP X, leaves no such clue; after it is executed, there is no way to tell how instruction X was reached. After execution of JSB X−1, however, MEMORY[X−1] contains the address of the instruction following the JSB, and control can be returned to that instruction later. Note that the BAL and BALR instructions in the System/360-370 repertoire are roughly equivalent to JSB.

With the JSB instruction we can branch from a place in a program, execute a sequence of instructions, and then return to the instruction following the branch instruction. Example 7·1 shows how this is done.

Several aspects of Example 7·1 deserve comment. Assume that there are no instructions between NEXT and RETURN that branch out

---

EXAMPLE 7·1

The instructions labeled B1 and B2 pass control to the instruction labeled NEXT. When the label RETURN is reached, control returns either to C1 or to C2, depending on whether NEXT was entered from B1 or from B2.

	LABEL	CODE	OPERAND	COMMENTS
		. . .		
1.	B1	JSB	SUB	Call subroutine SUB.
2.	C1	LDA	X	Return point from SUB.
		. . .		
3.	B2	JSB	SUB	Call subroutine SUB.
4.	C2	LDA	Z	Return point from SUB.
		. . .		
5.	SUB	NOP		Save space for return address.
6.	NEXT	CLA		First instruction of SUB.
		. . .		
7.	RETURN	JMP	SUB,I	The next instruction will be executed from the address stored in MEMORY[SUB].

of that region. Then the program behaves as if the instructions labeled B1 and B2 had both been replaced by the sequence of instructions beginning at NEXT and ending at RETURN−1. In particular, notice that SUB holds the address of the instruction to which control is to be returned. The NOP instruction is inserted in the program solely to reserve space. During execution of the program the JSB instruction replaces the NOP by a memory address. To return control to the instruction following the JSB that branched to SUB, we jump indirectly through SUB.

The sequence of instructions beginning at SUB and ending at RETURN is called a *subroutine*. It can be invoked from many places in a program, and it will pass control back to the instruction following the one that invoked it. Instructions B1 and B2 are said to *call* the subroutine SUB when they are executed. The address stored at SUB is called the *return address*. In Example 7·1 the return address could be either C1 or C2, depending on which instruction calls the subroutine.

EXAMPLE 7·2

The following instructions illustrate how subroutine calls can be implemented in a System/360-370 program:

	LABEL	CODE	OPERAND	COMMENTS
1.	RETURN	EQU	14	REG[14] will hold return address.
2.	B1	BAL	RETURN,SUB	Branch to SUB and store return address in REG[RETURN].
3.	C1	L	2,X	
			. . .	
4.	B2	BAL	RETURN,SUB	Branch to SUB and store return address in REG[RETURN].
5.	C2	L	3,Y	
			. . .	
6.	SUB	LR	2,4	First instruction of subroutine.
			. . .	
7.	EXIT	BR	RETURN	Return to calling program.

The instructions labeled B1 and B2 in Example 7·2 branch to the instruction labeled SUB, which is the entry point of a subroutine. Note that the return address is stored in REG[RETURN] before the branch is taken. The instruction labeled EXIT returns to the point from which the subroutine is called by branching to the address that is stored in REG[RETURN].

Some of the important characteristics of subroutines are apparent from Examples 7·1 and 7·2. In particular, there can be a substantial saving of memory space by using subroutines. Each subroutine call takes only one instruction, but a subroutine call can invoke a very long sequence of instructions. Thus one copy of a subroutine called from many different places in a program can do the work of many copies of the same subroutine. We pay a small penalty for this space saving in that the subroutine call and subroutine return instructions take some execution time that would disappear if a subroutine call were replaced by the body of the subroutine.

Another disadvantage of subroutines is illustrated in Example 7·1 but is not present in Example 7·2. Since the return address of Example 7·1 is stored in the program area, the program area is modified by the

JSB instruction, and thus all programs that use the JSB instruction are self-modifying programs. On some computers, programs that do not modify themselves—that is, *reentrant programs*—can be protected from all attempts to write data into themselves, because all such attempts are surely errors. To facilitate the writing of reentrant programs the BAL and BALR instructions are designed to leave the return address in a machine register, instead of leaving it in a program area.

Some advantages mentioned previously for macro-instructions apply to subroutines. Programs that are written as collections of subroutines or macros can be easily modified because of their modularity. If a subroutine is changed in one place, the effect is to propagate that change to every place in a program that calls that subroutine. If the same program were written without subroutines or macros, a particular change might have to be made in 10 places, or in some extreme cases, several dozen places. Changes of this magnitude are very susceptible to human error.

Examination of Example 7·1 reveals that the subroutine SUB may call other subroutines. These can in turn call further subroutines. In fact subroutine calls can extend any number of levels. The important characteristic is that a subroutine is always entered from its entry point and always returns to its return address. Hence if subroutine SUB calls another subroutine—say, SUB1—SUB1 must eventually return to SUB, which in turn will eventually return to the program that called it. Figure 7·1 shows a typical sequence of subroutine calls.

7·2 Coroutines

Coroutines are subprograms that are related to, but more general than, subroutines. Certain computations are better suited to implementation in coroutine form rather than subroutine form, because the subroutine constraints lead to awkward and inefficient programs. In particular, input/output programs and programs that are structured as two or more interdependent processes are often best suited for coroutine implementation.

We can best understand coroutines by comparison to subroutines. A subroutine and the program that calls it behave in a relationship much like that of a supervisor and his subordinate. The calling routine stops momentarily and requests the subroutine to perform some process. When the subroutine completes operation, the calling routine resumes operation at the point of suspension. Each time a subroutine is called it begins execution from its beginning and terminates at its endpoint.

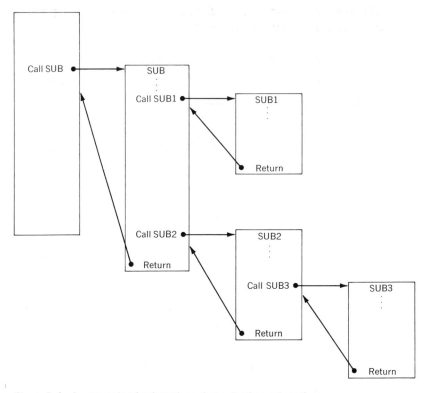

Figure 7·1 An example of subroutines that call other subroutines

A pair of coroutines behave more like a pair of coworkers. When coroutine X calls coroutine Y, X supplies a return address, just as in a subroutine call. The call to Y passes control, not to a beginning point, but to the address supplied by Y when it last called X. Thus coroutines are entered at the instruction that follows their last call, and they do not have a beginning and endpoint as subroutines do.

Figure 7·2 illustrates how the flow of control passes back and forth between coroutines. This behavior is quite different from the behavior of subroutines. Each time a subroutine is entered a new computation begins, and when the subroutine exit is reached, the computation terminates. A coroutine entry, in contrast, does not necessarily begin a new computation; rather, it resumes the computation that was in progress previously. Consequently the effect of a coroutine call by coroutine X is to temporarily suspend computation for X, rather than to terminate computation.

Specifically, a coroutine call consists of the following actions (assume coroutine X calls coroutine Y):

1. Save the value of P+1 as the return address for X.

2. Find the return address supplied by Y when it last called X.

3. Enter Y at its last return address.

Example 7·3 shows how to implement coroutines in machine language. We make use of special instructions to switch from one

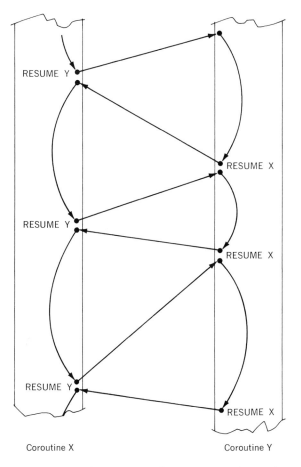

Coroutine X   Coroutine Y

Figure 7·2 The flow of control in a sequence of coroutine calls. RESUME denotes a coroutine call. The arrows show the flow of instruction execution

EXAMPLE 7·3

The first example is in HP 2116 assembly language and the second is in System/360-370 assembly language.

	LABEL	CODE	OPERAND	COMMENTS
1.		JSB	XSW	In coroutine Y a call on X.
		. . .		
2.		JSB	YSW	In coroutine X a call on Y.
		. . .		
3.	XSW	NOP		Return address for Y.
4.		JMP	YSW,I	Enter X through last return address.
5.	YSW	NOP		Return address for X.
6.		JMP	XSW,I	Enter Y through last return address.

For the System/360-370 program we place the return addresses in registers designated by the BALR instructions.

	LABEL	CODE	OPERAND	COMMENTS
1.	XRET	EQU	9	Return address for X.
2.	YRET	EQU	10	Return address for Y.
		. . .		
3.	CALLY	BALR	XRET,YRET	In coroutine X, a call on Y. Return address is left in XRET and branch is taken to address in REG[YRET].
		. . .		
4.	CALLX	BALR	YRET,XRET	In Y's program, a call on X.

coroutine to another in the program for the HP 2116 computer. The example for System/360-370 is much simpler because of the flexibility of the BALR instruction.

To illustrate the use of coroutines let us assume that a main program scans an array of characters from one end to the other and that each word contains 1 eight-bit character. To conserve space a string of blanks is stored as one blank followed by an eight-bit integer telling how many blanks are in the string. (If a string of blanks is longer than 255, it is represented as a sequence of strings, each shorter than 255.)

Example 7·4 shows two different programs that do the same computation. The first program uses a subroutine NEXTCHAR to find the next character for the main program. Since each call on NEXTCHAR depends on what happened previously, the first statement of NEXTCHAR determines which portion of NEXTCHAR should be executed. The second

---

EXAMPLE 7·4

We use an ALGOL-like language for the descriptions below. The symbol := is the ALGOL symbol for ← used above. Initialization and stopping conditions are not shown.

comment in this program the characters are stored in the array CHARS, the next item to examine in CHARS is CHARS[I], and subroutine NEXTCHAR places its output in the variable C for the main program to examine. The integer BLANKSREMAINING holds the number of blanks that have to be generated by NEXTCHAR before the next item in CHARS can be examined;

```
subroutine NEXTCHAR;
    begin comment check to see if NEXTCHAR is in the midst of generating a
    string of blanks;
    if BLANKSREMAINING = 0 then
        begin comment find the next item in CHARS and examine it;
            I: = I+1;
            if CHARS[I] ≠ BLANK then
                begin comment output the character to main program;
                    C := CHARS[I];
                end
            else
                begin comment start generating blanks;
                    I := I+1;
                    BLANKSREMAINING := CHARS[I]—1;
                    C := BLANK;
                end;
        end
    else
        begin comment at this point BLANKSREMAINING is not zero.
        Another blank has to be generated;
            C := BLANK;
            BLANKSREMAINING := BLANKSREMAINING—1;
        end
    end subroutine NEXTCHAR;
    . . .
```

comment the next statement in the main program calls NEXTCHAR to find the next character;

NEXTCHAR;

comment the next character is in C at this point and is available to the main program for use;

. . .

Following is the coroutine version of this program.

comment NEXTCHAR and the main program are coroutines. The variables are the same as in the subroutine version;

coroutine NEXTCHAR;
    begin comment this coroutine is written to loop forever. In real situations it should be written to halt when the last character is examined;
    LOOP: I := I+1;
      if CHARS[I] $\neq$ BLANK **then**
        begin comment the next character is not a blank. It is output to the main program;
          C:=CHARS[I];
          RESUME mainprog;
        end
      else
        begin comment generate a string of blanks and output them to the main program;
          I := I+1;
          comment CHARS[I] contains the number of blanks to output;
          for J := 1 **step** 1 **until** CHARS[I] **do**
            begin C := BLANK;
              RESUME mainprog;
            end
        end;
        go to LOOP;
    end coroutine NEXTCHAR;

coroutine mainprog;
    . . .
      comment the following statement calls NEXTCHAR for the next character;
      RESUME NEXTCHAR;
      comment the next character to process is now held in C;
    . . .

program employs coroutines to perform the same process. In this case NEXTCHAR is a coroutine of the main program, rather than a subroutine. Note that it is slightly shorter than the corresponding subroutine, and it is easier to comprehend.

Example 7·4 illustrates an important facet of coroutines. Note that the processing takes place in two phases. In the first phase NEXT-CHAR examines each input character and produces a modified version of the input. In the second phase the main program processes the modified input data. The computation alternates between these two phases, so that execution advances in both phases concurrently. The program could also have been structured with the two phases in sequence—that is, with second-phase processing initiated only after the input data had been completely processed by the first phase. In this form the program passes over all the input data twice. In the first pass the NEXTCHAR processing is performed, producing a modified version of the input. In the second pass the main program processes the modified input data. Thus Example 7·4 is equivalent to a two-pass algorithm even though the processing is done in a single pass.

It is usually more efficient to process data in a single pass rather than multiple passes, especially when there is a large amount of data. Consequently some multiple-pass algorithms can be transformed into more efficient one-pass algorithms in which the different phases of processing are structured as coroutines. Figure 7·3 illustrates this transformation. The horizontal axis is a time axis, so that Figure 7·3a depicts a case in which all first-phase processing is completed before second-phase processing is begun. Figure 7·3b shows a case in which processing alternates between the two phases. Consider how a typical datum, A, is processed in each program. In the first phase A is processed and the datum A′ is output, where A and A′ may be different. In the second phase A′ is changed to A″. Datum B illustrates a case in which new data are generated during a processing phase. The treatment of B in Figure 7·3 is the same as that of blank characters in Example 7·4.

Coroutines are commonly used for input/output processes as described in the next chapter. Assemblers also use coroutines to process macro-instructions. In principle an assembler could make one pass through a program to expand all macro-instructions, one pass to build a symbol table, and one pass to assemble instructions. The first two passes can be combined if the macro expansion process is a co-routine of the second-pass processor and if all macro-instructions are defined before they are invoked. The second and third passes of an assembler cannot be combined just by structuring them as coroutines because of forward references. When multiple passes are used, forward references can be placed in the symbol table during one pass, ready for use in the next pass. Unfortunately a coroutine structure causes these two passes to be done concurrently, which raises the difficulty of assembling an address for a symbolic name before the corresponding address is known for that name. In general multiple-pass processes

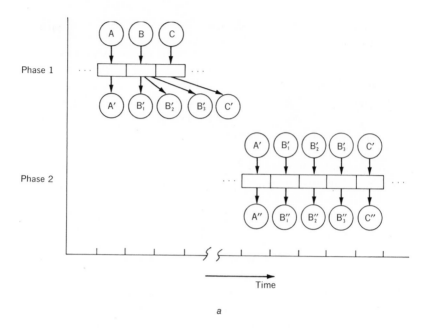

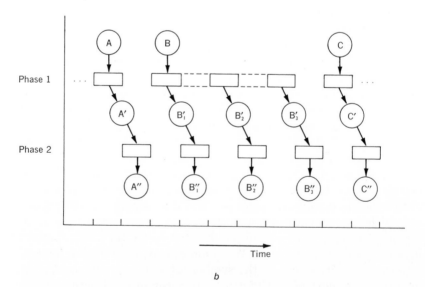

Figure 7·3 Two versions of a multiple-pass computation. Input/output data appear in circles, and each rectangle denotes the execution of a subprogram that processes a single datum. (*a*) The phases are executed in two separate passes of the data, and (*b*) program flow alternates between phases

can be collapsed into a single pass only if the resulting coroutine, structure does not create forward-reference problems.

7·3 Parameters

In most instances coroutine calls and subroutine calls include parameters. For example, a call to the sine subroutine is usually accompanied by a number, and the subroutine returns the sine of that number. The return address is also a parameter in a sense, so that subroutine and coroutine calls always transmit at least one parameter. Several techniques for dealing with parameters are in common use, and the characteristics of each should be thoroughly understood by the programmer.

Before we discuss the techniques themselves, let us introduce some terminology. We use the word *parameter* in two distinct contexts, as illustrated in Example 7·5.

EXAMPLE 7·5

The following subroutine is in an ALGOL-like language. The word **procedure** is synonymous with subroutine.

```
procedure QUADRATIC(ROOT,A,B,C);
    begin
        ROOT := (−B+SQRT(B↑2−4∗A∗C))/(2∗A);
    end;
```

A typical call on this subroutine is

```
QUADRATIC(ANSWER,1,W,Y);
```

After the call ANSWER will contain the result.

In this example ROOT, A, B, and C are dummy variables for the subroutine QUADRATIC. The processing within the subroutine is described in terms of ROOT, A, B, and C, but when the subroutine is executed, these variables will be replaced by other variables. ROOT is replaced by ANSWER, A by 1, etc. Parameters used as dummy variables are called *formal parameters*. The quantities that replace formal parameters when a subroutine is executed are called *actual parameters*. Thus ROOT is a formal parameter, and its corresponding actual parameter is ANSWER.

In considering the various methods of passing parameters between programs two fundamental questions are of concern:

1. Where do we place information that is transmitted to subroutines?

2. What information is transmitted during a subroutine call?

We shall discuss each of these questions in the following subsections.

7·3·1 The Mechanics of Passing Parameters

When we consider methods for transmitting parameters to a subroutine, we wish to minimize both execution time and memory requirements. Several different techniques have come into use, four of which are treated in this section. For any application and any computer at least one of these four should be adequate.

The first technique makes use of *common data*, sometimes known as *global data*. This is nothing more than using memory cells for communication, where the memory cells are accessible to both the subroutine and the program that calls it. For example, a program may include the instructions

```
    . . .
    STA   MAX   Store parameter in MAX.
    JSB   Y     Call subroutine Y.
    . . .
Y   NOP         Subroutine Y.
    . . .
    LDA   MAX   Fetch parameter within subroutine Y.
```

When subroutine Y and the main program are assembled together, both routines have access to the same symbolic names, and so both can refer to MAX. When the routines are assembled separately, they can both refer to MAX provided we treat MAX as an external symbol. However, external references for many parameters in a large program can become a great inconvenience.

A more fundamental disadvantage is the constraint on addressability imposed by the computer organization. For the HP 2116 computer MAX must be in the base page of memory or in the page containing all the references to MAX. For System/360-370 computers common data cells must be addressable by a base register available both to the main program and to the subroutine. Since the displacement field of a

System/360-370 instruction contains 12 bits, a region of memory addressable by a base register is $2^{12} = 4096$ bytes, or 1024 full words. These regions are relatively small, and common data areas are therefore a scarce resource. Another possibility is to use indirect references to MAX, but this solution wastes both memory and execution time.

The second obvious place to put parameters is in the processing-unit register. The A and B registers of the HP 2116 computer are natural places to put two parameters, and for many subroutines this is perfectly adequate. At first glance the System/360-370 computers seem to offer the luxury of using up to 16 general registers and eight floating-point registers for passing parameters. However, in reality only a few registers are actually available, because some must be allocated for base addresses, return addresses, frequently used temporary values, etc. In general the more registers we use for parameter passing, the more execution time we can expect to expend for subroutine entry and exit. This is because we often must save the original contents of the registers before we load them with parameters, and the original contents of the registers must be restored when the subroutine processing is completed. In short, processor registers are even more precious than common storage.

A third way of transmitting parameters makes use of special areas of memory called *parameter areas*. Before a subroutine is called, the parameters are placed in successive positions in a parameter area. Then the base address of the parameter area is transmitted to the subroutine in a processor register. The program below illustrates this technique.

In the subroutine the parameters are accessed as elements of the data array by means of techniques already discussed.

A variation of this technique makes use of what are called *in-line parameter areas*. The return address is used as the base address of the parameter area, eliminating the need to transmit an extra address to the subroutine. Naturally the parameter area must be embedded in the program to do this, and the program will therefore be self-modifying. Subroutine returns for this case are made to a point just beyond the parameter area. Example 7·7 illustrates this technique.

The last technique, which makes use of push-down stacks, has characteristics that make it desirable for use in the general case. Parameters are placed in a push-down stack prior to entry to a subroutine. After entry the subroutine accesses the top cells of the push-down stack for its parameters. Parameters are accessed by indexing relative to the stack pointer. Upon exit the stack is popped up and the parameters disappear, as they should. In the case of a nested sequence

EXAMPLE 7·6

An example of parameter passing for the HP 2116 computer:

	LABEL	CODE	OPERAND	COMMENTS
1.		LDA	ARG1	Pick up first parameter.
2.		STA	X	
3.		LDA	ARG2	Second parameter.
4.		STA	X+1	
		. . .		
5.		LDA	ARG9	Last parameter.
6.		STA	X+8	
7.		LDA	XNAME	Load address of parameter area.
8.		JSB	. . .	Enter subroutine.
		. . .		
9.	XNAME	DEF	X	
10.	X	BSS	9	Parameter area.

The same program written for System/360-370:

	LABEL	CODE	OPERAND	COMMENTS
1.	TEMP	EQU	1	A temporary register.
2.	PARAM	EQU	10	Register to hold address of parameter area.
3.		L	PARAM,PNAME	Load address of parameter area into REG[PARAM].
4.		L	TEMP,ARG1	Pick up first parameter.
5.		ST	0(PARAM)	Store in first word of parameter area.
6.		L	TEMP,ARG2	Second parameter.
7.		ST	4(PARAM)	Store in second word.
		. . .		
8.		L	TEMP,ARG9	Last parameter.
9.		ST	32(PARAM)	
10.		BAL	. . .	Enter subroutine.
		. . .		
11.	PAREA	DS	9F	Parameter area.
12.	PNAME	DC	A(PAREA)	Address of parameter area.

of subroutine calls the last set of parameters to be created is the first to be removed in a sequence of subroutine exits. The last-in-first-out characteristic of parameters matches precisely with the same characteristic of push-down stacks. Example 7·8 shows how arguments are passed in a push-down stack.

In the subroutine the first parameter is at the top of the stack, the second next to the top, etc. Hence the parameters are placed in the stack in reverse order. In the HP 2116 program, notice that the

---

EXAMPLE 7·7

The first sequence is written in HP 2116 assembly language and the second is in System/360-370 assembly language.

	LABEL	CODE	OPERAND	COMMENTS
1.		LDA	ARG1	
2.		STA	X	
		. . .		
3.		LDA	ARG9	
4.		STA	X+8	
5.		JSB	Y	
6.	X	BSS	9	Parameter area follows JSB.
7.		LDA	Z	First instruction executed after return.
		. . .		
8.	Y	NOP		Entry to Y.
		. . .		
9.		LDA	Y	Load third parameter into A.
10.		ADA	TWO	
11.		LDA	A,I	
		. . .		
12.		LDA	Y	Exit from Y.
13.		ADA	NINE	Compute actual return address.
14.		JMP	A,I	
15.	TWO	DEC	2	
16.	NINE	DEC	9	

The System/360-370 version of in-line parameter areas:

	LABEL	CODE	OPERAND	COMMENTS
1.	TEMP	EQU	1	A temporary register.
2.	PARAM	EQU	10	Register to hold address of parameter area.
3.	RET	EQU	14	Register for return address.
		. . .		
4.		L	PARAM,PNAME	Load address of parameter area into REG[PARAM].
5.		L	TEMP,ARG1	Load first parameter.
6.		ST	TEMP,0(PARAM)	Store in first word of parameter area.
		. . .		
7.		L	TEMP,ARG9	Load last parameter.
8.		ST	TEMP,32(PARAM)	Store in ninth word of parameter area.
9.		BAL	RET,Y	Call Y.
10.	PAREA	DS	9F	Reserve nine full words for parameter area.
11.	NEXT	. . .		The instruction to which Y will return.
12.	Y	. . .		
13.		L	TEMP,8(RET)	Load third parameter.
		. . .		
14.	YEXIT	A	RET,=F'36'	Compute return address (increase by nine full words).
15.		BR	RET	Return to calling program.
16.	PNAME	DC	A(PAREA)	Address of parameter area.

stack pointer is decremented rather than incremented in order to access parameters, and that the pointer is decremented to its previous state just prior to subroutine exit.

One of the major advantages of push-down stacks for parameters is the possibility of using less memory than with other methods. When we create parameter areas for each subroutine by reserving storage ahead of time, as illustrated in Example 7·6, then the total memory reserved for parameters is the total of the parameter areas in the entire program. However, when we use a stack, the total memory reserved in the stack need not exceed the maximum number of parameters that can occur in a nested sequence of subroutine calls. For some programs the memory savings is considerable.

EXAMPLE 7·8

The first sequence is written in HP 2116 assembly language and the second is in System/360-370 assembly language.

	LABEL	CODE	OPERAND	COMMENTS
1.	POINT	DEF	STACK	Current top of stack.
2.	STACK	BSS	100	
		. . .		
3.		ISZ	POINT	Push down second parameter.
4.		LDB	ARG2	
5.		STB	POINT,I	
6.		ISZ	POINT	Push down first parameter.
7.		LDB	ARG1	
8.		STB	POINT,I	
9.		JSB	Y	Call Y.
		. . .		
10.	Y	NOP		Entry to Y.
11.		LDA	POINT,I	Fetch first parameter.
		. . .		
12.		LDA	MINUS1	Fetch second parameter.
13.		ADA	POINT	The A register now contains address of second parameter. The value of POINT in memory is unchanged.
14.		LDA	A,I	
		. . .		
15.		LDA	MINUS2	Exit from Y. Prior to exit stack is popped up by two cells.
16.		ADA	POINT	
17.		STA	POINT	
18.		JMP	Y,I	

The System/360-370 version of the same program is as follows. Notice that the stack pointer is decremented rather than incremented to push down a new item, because decrementing is slightly more convenient here.

	LABEL	CODE	OPERAND	COMMENTS
1.	TEMP	EQU	11	A temporary register.
2.	POINT	EQU	12	Address of current top of stack.
		. . .		
3.		S	POINT,=F'4'	Push down second parameter.
4.		L	TEMP,ARG2	
5.		ST	TEMP,0(POINT)	
6.		S	POINT,=F'4'	Push down first parameter.
7.		L	TEMP,ARG1	
8.		ST	TEMP,0(POINT)	
9.		BAL	RETURN,Y	Call Y.
		. . .		
10.	YTEMP	EQU	7	A temporary register for Y.
11.	Y	L	YTEMP,0(POINT)	Entry to Y. Load first parameter.
		. . .		
12.		L	YTEMP,4(POINT)	Load second parameter.
		. . .		
13.		A	POINT,=F'8'	Pop up stack by two words.
14.		BR	RETURN	Return to calling routine.

7·3·2 Call by Name and Call by Value The previous section dealt with the problem of where to place parameters when they are passed to subroutines. In this section we focus attention on what information is actually transmitted. We shall also treat the problem of returning information from subroutines to the programs that call them.

Examination of Example 7·5 reveals that ROOT is used differently from A, B, and C. ROOT receives the output of the computation, whereas A, B, and C are unchanged by the computation. In an assembly-language version of Example 7·5 the memory address of the actual parameter that corresponds to ROOT must be supplied to the sub-routine, whereas the actual parameters for A, B, and C can be either the memory addresses or the values of the actual parameters. Obviously, if the calling routine transmits addresses to QUADRATIC, then QUADRATIC must be written to receive the addresses rather than the values of the actual parameters.

From this discussion we see that we have two choices for treating parameters A, B, and C, but we must transmit an address for parameter ROOT. Every variable has two attributes that can be used in a program: a memory address and the value contained in that memory address. These are generally referred to as the *name* and the *value* of the variable, respectively. In a high-level language program, when a variable appears in a statement in which it is assigned a value, the execution of the statement uses the name of the variable. Thus the subroutine in Example 7·5 uses the name of ROOT, not the value of ROOT. When a variable appears in an arithmetic expression, its value enters the calculation. If the name of a variable is given, it is possible to find its value. However, it is not possible, in general, to determine the name of a variable from its value.

We can implement subroutine calls by transmitting either the name or the value of a variable to the subroutine. Of course, we can transmit the value of a parameter only if the subroutine does not require its name. Let us refer to these two methods as *call by name* and *call by value*. Unfortunately, there is much confusion over these terms in the computer literature, because the programming languages ALGOL, FORTRAN, and PL/I all use slightly different definitions. The following discussion should clarify some of the confusion, and also bring to light the relative merits of the various methods.

There should be no confusion of terms when the actual parameter is a nonsubscripted variable, because the name and value of such a variable are well defined. The difficulty arises when the actual parameter is an expression or a subscript variable. Consider, for example, the following subroutine, which exchanges the values of R and S:

```
procedure SWAP(R,S);
   real R,S;
   begin TEMP := R;
      R := S;
      S := TEMP;
   end;
```

Suppose we call SWAP in the following way:

```
X[1] := 2;
X[2] := 5;
I    := 1;
SWAP(I,X[I]);
```

If we transmit the addresses of the actual parameters to SWAP, then the values of X[I] and I will be exchanged, which is the intent of the subroutine. However, another interpretation of call by name is possible in this case. In ALGOL the effect of call by name is precisely the same as would be obtained if the actual parameters were substituted for their corresponding formal parameters in the text of subroutine. This is known as the *replacement rule*. When we apply it to here, we obtain the following subroutine:

```
begin TEMP := I;
    I := X[I];
    X[I] := TEMP;
end;
```

Now the second line changes the value of I, so that X[I] in the third line is not the same as X[I] in the second line. For the example given above the old value of I is assigned to X[2], not to X[1].

The replacement rule adds an entirely new dimension to the notion of call by name. Note that there is no problem when simple variables are used as actual parameters, as in the call SWAP(I,J). The problem arises because the parameter X[I] is an element of an array. The particular element depends on the value of I; in fact both the name and value of X[I] depend on I.

The replacement rule can lead to difficulties of interpretation. For example, what is the meaning of the call SWAP(5+N,M)? If we adhere strictly to the replacement rule, we have to interpret the statement

```
5+N := M
```

This statement makes no sense as it stands. The effect during execution depends on the language in which the statement is embedded and can vary among different translators for the same language.

To begin our discussion of subroutine calls let us consider how to implement such calls in assembly language. First we deal with call by value:

ALGOL Call by Value   Place the value of the actual parameter in the parameter area. The subroutine accesses only the copy of the parameter in the parameter area. If the subroutine changes this value, the change is not transmitted to the calling routine.

We can use the techniques discussed in the previous section for transmitting parameters to a subroutine. When a parameter is called by value, the information transmitted is the value rather than the name of the parameter. Technically speaking, when an array is called by value, the contents of the array should be copied into a temporary array, which is then transmitted as a parameter. This permits the subroutine to modify the copy of the array without changing the original. Obviously value calls with array parameters can be grossly inefficient, and so some ALGOL compilers protect the programmer by forbidding such calls.

Some FORTRAN compilers, most notably the FORTRAN compilers for System/360-370 computers, use another method of passing parameters that is also known as call by value. In this method changes in parameters are transmitted back to the calling program at the completion of subroutine execution. Otherwise this method is identical to ALGOL call by value. Thus we have

FORTRAN Call by Value   Place the value of the actual parameter in the parameter area. The subroutine accesses only the copy of the parameter in the parameter area, possibly changing its value. When subroutine processing is complete, the value in the parameter area is copied back into the original parameter.

This type of call is implemented the same way as ALGOL call by value, except for processing at the return point in the calling program. At the return point the calling program copies the parameters back into their original locations, which is simply a reversal of the parameter-passing process.

Call by name is somewhat more complex than call by value, as indicated in the discussion of the ALGOL call-by-name replacement rule. Before we discuss the implementation of the replacement rule, let us consider a less general, but more efficient, variation of call by name, sometimes known as *call by reference*. This is used in many PL/1 and FORTRAN compilers. The actions for call by reference are as follows:

Call by Reference   If the actual parameter is an unsubscripted variable, then place the address of the variable in the parameter area. If the parameter is a subscripted variable, then compute its address and place this in the parameter area. If the parameter is an expression, then compute the value of the expression, store the value in a memory cell, and place the address of this cell in the parameter area.

In every case the subroutine receives the address of the value of the actual parameter. If the subroutine modifies a parameter called by reference, then the original parameter is modified automatically.

As an example, the subroutine call SWAP(I,J) is implemented by transmitting the address of I and J to SWAP. Clearly, when the actual parameter is an unsubscripted variable, call by reference and the ALGOL replacement rule produce identical results. Differences are observed when the actual parameter is a subscripted variable or an arithmetic expression, as we have mentioned earlier.

The implementation of the ALGOL replacement rule requires some discussion. We cannot transmit either the name or the value of an actual parameter to a subroutine for this type of call, because both can be altered during execution of the subroutine. Consequently we must be able to compute both the name and value of an actual parameter whenever its corresponding formal parameter is referenced. We use the following strategy:

ALGOL Call by Name (Replacement Rule) If the actual parameter is a variable, whether it is subscripted or not, construct a subroutine to compute the name of the parameter, and transmit the entry point of this subroutine as the actual parameter. If the parameter is an expression, construct a subroutine that computes the expression, stores it in a memory cell, and produces the name of the memory cell as its output. Transmit the entry point of this subroutine as the actual parameter.

Note that the parameter that is transferred is neither the name nor the value of an entity, but the address of a subroutine that can compute the parameter. To compute the name or value of the parameter we enter the appropriate subroutine, and upon exit we have the name of the parameter. Obviously we can find the value of an item when we are given its name.

The implementation of ALGOL call by name is shown in Example 7·9, which illustrates what happens for the call SWAP(I,X[I]). With this form of call, what happens during the call SWAP(5+N,I)? The first parameter for this call is a subroutine that computes 5+N and stores it in a memory cell—say, at MEMORY[XPRS]. Thus when the replace-

EXAMPLE 7·9

The following procedure for constructing the call SWAP(I,X[I]) employs ALGOL call-by-name conventions. The first program is in HP 2116 assembly language and the second is System/360-370 assembly language.

	LABEL	CODE	OPERAND	COMMENTS
		. . .		
1.	A	EQU	0	
2.	I	DEC	10	
3.	INAME	DEF	I	The name of I.
4.	XNAME	DEF	X	The name of X.
5.	X	BSS	100	The array X.
6.	IP	NOP		Entry point for subroutine that computes name of I.
7.		LDA	INAME	Put name of I in A register.
8.		JMP	IP,I	Return.
9.	XIP	NOP		Entry point for subroutine that computes name of X[I].
10.		LDA	XNAME	
11.		ADA	I	Name of X[I] is in A register.
12.		JMP	XIP,I	Return.
13.	IPN	DEF	IP	Address of entry point IP.
14.	XIPN	DEF	XIP	Address of entry point XIP.
		. . .		
15.	CALL	LDA	IPN	First parameter to A register.
16.		LDB	XIPN	Second parameter to B register.
17.		JSB	SWAP	Call SWAP.
		. . .		
18.	P1	BSS	1	Space for first parameter.
19.	P2	BSS	1	Space for second parameter.
20.	SWAP	NOP		Entry point of SWAP.
21.		STA	P1	Save parameters.
22.		STB	P2	
		. . .		

LABEL	CODE	OPERAND	COMMENTS
			The following four lines show the computation of R := S, where R and S are formal parameters.
23.	JSB	P2, I	Compute name of second parameter and leave in A register.
24.	LDB	A, I	Load value of second parameter into B register.
25.	JSB	P1, I	Compute name of first parameter and leave in A register.
26.	STB	A, I	R := S.
	. . .		
27.	JMP	SWAP, I	Return from SWAP.

In this program for System/360-370, the subroutines IP and XIP leave the value of the parameter in REG[VAL] and the name of the parameter in REG[NAM]. The instructions beginning at RS compute the statement R:=S in SWAP.

	LABEL	CODE	OPERAND	COMMENTS
		. . .		
1.	RET	EQU	14	Register for return address.
2.	RET1	EQU	13	Register for SWAP's return addresses.
3.	I	DS	F	Reserve a full word for I.
4.	INAME	DC	A(I)	The name of I.
5.	XNAME	DC	A(X)	The name of X.
6.	X	DS	100F	Reserve 100 full words for array X.
7.	S	EQU	9	A temporary register for S.
8.	TEM	EQU	10	A temporary register.
9.	NAM	EQU	11	Register for names.
10.	VAL	EQU	12	Register for values.
11.	IP	L	NAM, INAME	Load name of I into REG[NAM].
12.		L	VAL, 0(NAM)	Load value into REG[VAL].
13.		BR	RET	Return.
14.	XIP	L	TEM, I	Load I into REG(TEM).

	LABEL	CODE	OPERAND	COMMENTS
15.		SLA	TEM,2	Make into an index by multiplying by 4.
16.		L	NAM,XNAME	Load name of X into REG[NAM].
17.		AR	NAM,TEM	Compute name of X[I].
18.		L	VAL,0(NAM)	Compute value of X[I].
19.		BR	RET	Return.
20.	IPN	DC	A(IP)	The name of entry point IP.
21.	XIPN	DC	A(XIP)	The name of entry point XIP.
		. . .		
22.	CALL	L	0,IPN	First parameter to REG[0].
23.		L	1,XIPN	Second parameter to REG[1].
24.		BAL	RET1,SWAP	Call SWAP.
		. . .		
25.	P1	DS	F	Storage for first parameter.
26.	P2	DS	F	Storage for second parameter.
27.	SWAP	ST	0,P1	Save first parameter.
28.		ST	1,P2	Save second parameter.
		. . .		The next six instructions do R := S.
29.	RS	L	TEM,P2	Load address of second parameter subroutine.
30.		BALR	RET,TEM	Place value of S into REG[VAL].
31.		LR	S,VAL	Save this value in REG[S].
32.		L	TEM,P1	Load address of first parameter subroutine.
33.		BALR	RET,TEM	Place name of R into REG[NAM].
34.		ST	S,0(NAM)	R := S.
		. ...		
35.		BR	RET1	Return from SWAP.

ment rule places 5+N on the left-hand side of the assignment statement, its name is XPRS, and MEMORY[XPRS] receives the value of the assignment.

In ALGOL each formal parameter is separately specified as a name parameter or a value parameter. Thus an ALGOL program with both a name and a value parameter would appear as:

```
procedure SWAP(A,B);
    value A;
    real A,B;
    begin . . .
```

Note that A is explicitly specified as a value parameter; B, by default, is a name parameter.

Of the various methods available for transmitting parameters, call by reference is the one that usually requires the least execution time and is the most widely applicable. The ALGOL methodology probably encompasses the most general cases, but the cost in execution time and memory space can be excessive.

The different techniques for transmitting parameters to subroutines are essentially a set of tools for the computer programmer. A thorough knowledge of the techniques should provide greater understanding of the processes that take place during the execution of programs written in high-level languages. From the standpoint of program design, it is essential that the programmer be familiar with the various alternatives, that he know their relative merits, and that he is especially aware of their pitfalls.

REFERENCES

The concept of subroutines has been a part of the literature of algorithms for many years. Early Turing machine programs made much use of subroutines, as did instruction sequences for other abstract mathematical models of computers. Consequently instructions for implementing subroutine calls were part of the repertoire of all the early digital computers. The coroutine, however, is a later invention, an outgrowth of the notion of generators embodied in the list-processing languages of Simon, Newell, and Shaw (Newell, 1961). The term *coroutine* is credited to Conway, who has given a particularly lucid description of this concept (Conway, 1963). Techniques described here for parameter passing are representative of several compiler implementations and are in common use. The use of the push-down stacks as a parameter area appeared in the latter part of the 1950s, again in the languages designed by Simon, Newell, and Shaw. Much of the interest in push-down stacks was stimulated by ALGOL and by the list-processing languages, because the push-down stack is especially appropriate for these languages. The subroutines employed in the technique for implementing the ALGOL replacement rules are sometimes called "thunks" and have been described by Ingerman (1961).

EXERCISES

7·1 Show how an assembly language program can be written in which each subroutine call places its return address on a push-down stack. Indicate how the return address is placed on the stack and how it is used during a subroutine exit.

7·2 Suppose that during the execution of a program the subroutine SINE for some input data calls the subroutine COSINE, which in turn might call SINE. Show that no difficulty occurs if the return addresses are put into push-down stacks, but that if another non-equivalent method is used for return addresses, the program may loop forever.

7·3 Show the assembly language for the coroutine calls and exits for Example 7·4.

7·4 The program below is written in a nonstandard programming language. When it is executed, the printed output contains the number 5. Explain how this can happen.

```
begin comment the main program;
    i ← 3;
    call increase(i,2);
    i ← 2;
    print i;
end main program;
subroutine increase(a,b);
    begin b ← b+a;
    end;
```

7·5 In Example 7·8 the HP 2116 program increments the stack pointer for a push-down, whereas the System/360-370 program decrements the stack pointer. How do the programs change when the push-down convention is changed in each? Do you see why incrementing is more efficient for the HP 2116 and decrementing is better for the System/360-370?

8

Input/Output Operations

All computers have some mechanism for exchanging information with the outside world. The information may be a program, or input data for a program, or the results of a computation. The outside world might gain access to the computer through such peripheral devices as typewriters, line printers, punched-card readers, paper-tape readers and punches, or push-button telephones. If a computer has an external auxiliary memory, such as a magnetic tape or disk, the auxiliary memory may be considered to be part of the outside world, and information may be exchanged in the form of library programs or large data files. In any case input/output processing is one of the central problems of computer programming.

Input/output programs are among the most difficult to write, for a number of reasons. Because input/output actions are performed simultaneously with computation, timing factors can cause programs to fail in subtle ways. It is also typical of most computer systems that each peripheral device must be treated differently, so that there must be a program for each device, rather than one program for all devices.

In this chapter we shall discuss programming techniques for both the HP 2116 computer and the IBM System/360-370 computers. Normally the programmer does not prepare input/output programs for either of these computers. The program libraries contain a complete collection of the necessary input/output subroutines. In fact the programmer is specifically denied access to the input/output instructions of System/360-370 computers, and these instructions can be executed only by an executive program.

Unfortunately it is somewhat impractical to describe the input/output libraries for the HP 2116 or System/360-370 computers. Such libraries tend to be tailored to the specific requirements of each computer installation, with correspondingly tailored program conventions and parameters for library subroutines. Hence it is up to the individual programmer to inform himself of the characteristics of the input/output library for his particular installation. Nevertheless, a thorough understanding of the material discussed in this chapter should assist the programmer in making use of input/output libraries and enable him to obtain maximum performance from a computer.

8·1 Fundamentals

Each input/output operation involves the simultaneous operation of two different processors. One is the processing unit of the computer, and the other is a special control unit called an *interface* that transfers data between computer and peripheral device. Both these processors can operate simultaneously, but they must operate in a nonconflicting way.

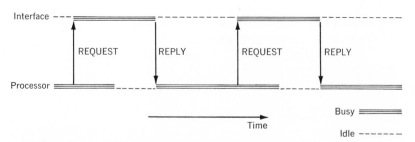

Figure 8·1 An example of REQUEST and REPLY signals for controlling input/outpu operations. Note that the interface and the processor can operate concurrently

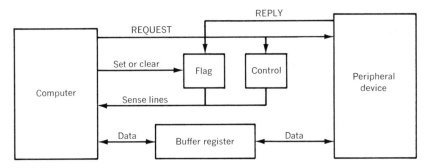

Figure 8·2 A block diagram of an input/output interface

The usual mode of operation is to use REQUEST and REPLY control signals. In this mode the computer sends a REQUEST to an input/output device and then proceeds with program computation. When the input/output operation is complete, a REPLY is returned to the computer. The computer, acting under program control, can sense the REPLY signal. If the computer reaches a point at which computation cannot continue until a REPLY is received, it can enter a loop, which it will exit only when the REPLY is received. This is shown graphically in Figure 8·1. The dashed portion of the processor activity line shows the period during which the processor loops while awaiting a REPLY. The dashed line for the interface unit indicates the time during which the interface is idle waiting for a new REQUEST. It is important to note that both the interface and the processor can be busy simultaneously.

In the HP 2116 computer there are two signal lines for each peripheral device to carry the REQUEST and REPLY signals. These are shown in Figure 8·2. The signal lines are connected to a pair of one-bit memory cells designated control and flag, respectively. Such memory cells are called *flip-flops*. Notice also in Figure 8·2 that an interface contains a data register called a *buffer* for holding information in transit between the processor and the peripheral device.

By convention, a flip-flop that has a 1 stored in it is said to be in the *set state*, and a flip-flop that has a 0 stored in it is said to be in the *reset*, or *clear*, *state*. The relation of the control and flag flip-flops to the REQUEST and REPLY signals is indicated by the following table:

SIGNAL	ACTION OF CONTROL SIGNAL
REQUEST	Set control flip-flop for peripheral device.
REPLY	Set flag flip-flop for peripheral device.

The REQUEST signal is generated by the processing unit and is a signal that will set the control flip-flop if it is not already set. For example, assume that a particular device is inactive. To initiate a new operation on this device we execute an instruction that sends a REQUEST to the device interface. The control flip-flop need not have been in the reset state before the REQUEST is issued, because it is the action of issuing the REQUEST that starts the device.

In normal operation, when a REQUEST is issued the computer also issues a signal that resets the flag flip-flop. Thus, when the REPLY is received from the device, the flag will change to the set state, and this change can be sensed by the computer.

Input operations are essentially the same as output operations, except that input data flow is in the opposite direction from output data flow. An input operation occurs when a REQUEST is transmitted to an input device. During input activity the device transmits data to the interface buffer. While this is going on the processor should not read from or write into the buffer. When the input operation is complete the device becomes inactive and issues a REPLY. At this point the processor can copy information from the buffer and initiate a new REQUEST. During an output operation the peripheral device reads data from the buffer register instead of writing into it. Similarly, the processor transmits data to the buffer to prepare for an output operation, which is just the reverse of the action for an input operation.

A list of the HP 2116 instructions that control the setting, resetting, and sensing the state of the input/output flip-flops appears below. Each instruction includes a six-bit operand which is used to identify a particular interface and its attached device. The operands are like memory addresses, but they are called *select codes* to reflect the notion that the operations involve selected devices rather than the contents of memory locations. Some examples for a device with the symbolic select code PUNCH are:

CODE	OPERAND	ACTION
STF	PUNCH	Set flag.
CLF	PUNCH	Clear (reset) flag.
CLC	PUNCH	Clear control.
CLC	PUNCH,C	Clear control and flag (,C means clear the flag).
STC	PUNCH	Set control (this is a REQUEST to start PUNCH).
STC	PUNCH,C	Set control and clear flag.
SFS	PUNCH	Skip if flag set.
SFC	PUNCH	Skip if flag clear.
CLC	0	Clear all controls.

The instructions that clear the flag flip-flop enable the computer to sense a REPLY when the flip-flop becomes set. The computer can test the state of the flag flip-flop with either the SFS or SFC instructions. It is quite common to use an instruction sequence of the form

```
. . .

SFS    DEVICE
JMP    *—1

. . .
```

to idle the computer until a REPLY sets the flag flip-flop. This type of loop is called a *wait loop*.

The instruction that sets the control flip-flop generates a RE-QUEST, which in turn initiates an operation. If an input/output operation is in progress, it can be terminated by issuing an instruction to clear the corresponding control flip-flop.

The following instructions control the transfer of data between the computer and the buffer registers. The symbolic select code PUNCH is assumed to be an output device, and READ is assumed to be an input device. The amount of data transmitted by each instruction depends on the device.

CODE	OPERAND	ACTION
LIA	READ	Load input to A. READ's buffer register transmitted to A register.
LIB	READ	Load input to B.
MIA	READ	Merge input to A. READ's buffer register logically OR'ed with contents of A register.
MIB	READ	Merge input to B.
OTA	PUNCH	Output from A. PUNCH's buffer register is loaded from A register.
OTB	PUNCH	Output from B.

The function of the control signals varies from one device to another, so that input/output operations must be described separately for each device. The succeeding sections show basic techniques for the paper-tape reader, the paper-tape punch, and the teletype.

8·1·1 **Paper-tape Reader**   A read operation is initiated by the instruction

```
STC    READ,C
```

which sets the control flip-flop and resets the flag. This generates a REQUEST signal to the paper-tape reader which causes it to read one character and place it into the buffer register. When the character is placed in the buffer, the flag will be set by the REPLY signal.

EXAMPLE 8·1

The following program will read one character from paper tape and place the result in the low-order character, bits 0 to 7, of the A register:

CODE	OPERAND	COMMENTS
STC	READ,C	Generate REQUEST to paper-tape reader.
. . .		
SFS	READ	Test for completion of READ operation, loop if not done.
JMP	*—1	
LIA	READ	Move data in buffer to A register.

We obtain maximum efficiency when the reading operation is overlapped with computation as much as possible. Hence a subroutine for reading paper tape should issue an STC READ,C instruction just before it exits. This will cause the next input operation to begin while computation proceeds in the main program. When the READ subroutine is reentered the next time, it should begin with the SFS instruction and wait for the READ operation to finish. Notice that for this case one read operation must be initiated before the READ subroutine is entered for the first time. The first read operation can be started by an initialization subroutine that is called only once during program execution.

8·1·2 **Paper-tape Punch**   The command STC PUNCH,C initiates an output operation. Before this command is executed, the data to be output must be transferred to the buffer in the input/output interface. The output operation is exactly analogous to the input operation described above. When the output operation is complete, the flag in the interface becomes set. Thus a typical sequence of output instructions is the following:

CODE	OPERAND	COMMENTS
SFS	PUNCH	Wait until unit is ready.
JMP	*—1	
OTA	PUNCH	Move data from A register to buffer in punch interface.
STC	PUNCH,C	

The low-order character, bits 0 to 7 of the A register, are transferred to the buffer by the OTA instruction.

For the maximum overlap of output activity with computation an output subroutine should initiate the output action just before exit. Upon entry to the output subroutine the first instruction should test the flag of the output device and wait for the operation to complete by looping as shown. Hence the sequence of instructions given above forms the body of an output subroutine.

8·1·3 Teletype Input/Output   The teletype is both an input and an output device. It consists of a keyboard and a printing mechanism. These two elements are not mechanically coupled, as they are in a typewriter. Striking a key on the keyboard sends a sequence of 11 bits to the computer, but it does not cause the print mechanism to operate. The teletype can function like a typewriter, however, if a computer program "listens" to the teletype keyboard and "echoes" the data back to the teletype printer.

Bits are transmitted serially between computer and teletypewriter. Each eight-bit character is preceded by a 0 bit and followed by two 1 bits in the stream of transmitted data. Input operation is started by executing a STC TTIN instruction, which initiates an 11-bit sequence. After each of the 11 bits reaches the buffer, a REPLY signal sets the flag flip-flop. This notifies the computer that the buffer can be accessed. As each bit is copied from the buffer, the computer resets the flag so that the next REPLY can be sensed. A typical teletype input program is shown in the following example.

In Example 8·2 notice that we must execute the instructions RAR and SFS TTIN while the flag is set and before the new bit is copied from the buffer into the A register. Although we can safely execute these two instructions, there is a limit on the elapsed time between the availability of a teletype input bit and the action of copying it into a

171

EXAMPLE 8·2

	LABEL	CODE	OPERAND	COMMENTS
1.		LDA	MIN11	11-bit counter.
2.		STA	COUNT	Stored for ISZ instruction.
3.		STC	TTIN	Initiate an input.
4.		CLA		Clear A register.
5.	LOOP	CLF	TTIN	Clear flag for next bit.
6.		RAR		Make room for new bit.
7.		SFS	TTIN	Wait for REPLY.
8.		JMP	*−1	
9.		MIA	TTIN	New bit is OR-ed into bit 7.
10.		ISZ	COUNT	Tally 1 and go around.
11.		JMP	LOOP	
12.		CLC	TTIN	Turn off teletype interface.
13.		RAL,RAL		Align eight bits in bits 0 to 7.
14.		AND	MASK	Mask out other bits.
		. . .		
15.	MIN11	DEC	−11	
16.	COUNT	DEC	0	
17.	MASK	OCT	000377	Mask for low-order eight bits.

processor register. Since each sequence of 11 teletype bits is transmitted to the computer in a fixed period of time (100 msec for the entire sequence, or 9.09 msec per bit), each bit in a sequence is in the interface buffer only during its allotted time slot. If a program fails to access a bit during the appropriate time slot, then the bit will disappear and will be replaced by the next bit in the sequence. In Example 8·2 the RAR and SFS instructions require only a few microseconds to execute, which is substantially shorter than the 9.09-msec time limit for accessing a bit. Although the teletype timing constraint is easily satisfied in this case, failure to satisfy timing constraints leads to unpredictable program malfunction. Timing constraints are the most difficult to satisfy when the elapsed time between critical instructions is unpredictable. Later in the chapter, when we discuss interrupt processing, we shall see that timing unpredictability in programs is the norm rather than the exception.

From the sample teletype input program of Example 8·2 it is straightforward to construct a teletype output program. For output the OTA and OTB instructions transmit bit 0 of the A and B registers, respectively, to the teletype interface buffer. Example 8·3 shows a typical output program.

EXAMPLE 8·3

The character is assumed to be right-adjusted in A.

	LABEL	CODE	OPERAND	COMMENTS
		. . .		
1.		AND	MASK	Mask high-order bits.
2.		RAL		Left-shift 1 bit for alignment.
3.		IOR	MASK1	MASK1 $= 003000_8$ (the two 1 bits are the last two transmitted).
4.		LDB	MIN11	Ready the counter.
5.		STB	COUNT	
6.		STC	TTOUT	Initiate an output. Flag is on at this point.
7.	LOOP	SFS	TTOUT	Wait for REPLY.
8.		JMP	$*-1$	
9.		OTA	TTOUT	Output next bit to teletype interface.
10.		CLF	TTOUT	Clear flag for next REPLY.
11.		RAR		Get next bit ready.
12.		ISZ	COUNT	Tally 1 and loop if not done.
13.		JMP	LOOP	
14.		CLC	TTOUT	Turn off teletype interface.

The length of the instruction sequences and the rather arbitrary requirements for data transmission illustrate some of the difficulties encountered in input/output programming. The next section describes additional complications of interrupt processing.

8·2 Interrupts

The programs in the previous section generally take the following form:

1. Initiate an operation.
2. Compute as long as possible.
3. Wait for operation-complete signal with an SFS instruction.
4. When ready, go to step 1 and repeat.

However, the third step in this process, the loop containing an SFS instruction, is often undesirable. While the computer is waiting, it might be capable of performing other operations. When two or more devices are active, it is essential that the computer be capable of reacting to the first device that becomes ready, instead of idling in a wait loop associated with a single device. Consequently most computers use a special mechanism called an *interrupt system* for efficient input/output.

The purpose of the interrupt system is to provide for useful computation in place of wait loops. The interrupt system permits the computer to respond to REPLY signals from devices as soon as they are received, without having to enter a wait loop. Specifically, a REPLY from a device can *interrupt* normal processing and force the computer to execute instructions that control that device. The previous input/output examples show input/output operations when the interrupt system is turned off, since the only effect of the REPLY signals in these cases is to set the corresponding flag flip-flop. In this section we shall see how to do input/output operations under interrupt control.

First we note that the following instructions are used, for the HP 2116, to turn the interrupt system on and off:

CODE	OPERAND	ACTION
CLF	0	Turn off interrupt system.
STF	0	Turn on interrupt system.

When the interrupt system is on, an interrupt occurs when a flag bit is set by an external device and the corresponding control flip-flop is in the set state. The interrupt causes the computer to execute a single instruction located at an address in memory which is equal to

174

the select code for the interrupting device. For example, an interrupt by the device with select code 11_8 causes the instruction at MEMORY[11_8] to be executed. If the instruction executed at the interrupt location is a JSB, then the return address stored in memory is not the address of the location immediately following the interrupt location, but the address of the next instruction to be executed after the interrupted instruction. Obviously the return address can be used to reenter the interrupted program at the point of interruption when the input/output processing program relinquishes control.

Consider how the return address is computed. If the interrupted instruction is not a jump or a skip instruction, then the return address is the value of P+1. If the interrupted instruction modifies the P register in some way other than incrementing it by 1, then the new value of the P register is stored as the return address. If the interrupted instruction is an indirect jump, for example, then the return address must be the ultimate target address of the jump instruction. In determining the return address one or more memory accesses might occur after the interrupt is recognized and before control passes to the interrupt location.

Since a return address is generated by the process described above, we can treat interrupts just like subroutine and coroutine calls. For example, assume that a matrix-inversion program is in execution when an interrupt occurs. At this point the control branches to the subprogram for the input/output device that generated the interrupt. The input/output program presumably initiates a new operation and then uses the return address to branch back to the matrix-inversion program. This input/output program is essentially a subroutine or coroutine of the matrix-inversion program. However, the matrix-inversion program contains no instructions that call the input/output program explicitly, since the input/output program is called by an interrupt.

An interrupt-driven input/output program may be structured as either a coroutine or subroutine, depending on the characteristics of the program. When an interrupt occurs, if the input/output program ought to resume at the point of the previous exit, then it should be a coroutine. If the program is always entered at a unique beginning point, then it can be a subroutine. Since the coroutine structure is the more general structure, we shall focus on coroutines exclusively in the remainder of this discussion.

To see how coroutines can be used for interrupt processing, consider the steps taken by a typical input/output program. When a program suspends itself we say it "goes to sleep," and when it is reentered we say it is "awakened." In these terms a typical sequence of steps for an input/output program is:

1. Initiate the input/output action.

2. Return to the main program, and thereby go to sleep.

3. When awakened by an interrupt, continue from the point of suspension.

4. Perform postprocessing if necessary.

5. Return to step 1 for another iteration if more is to be done, otherwise exit.

Example 8·4 shows a typical input/output program.

In actuality Example 8·4 is not quite correct, for the following reason. The input/output program cannot disturb the state of the computer during the period of time in which the main routine is interrupted unless it restores the original state before the main routine is reentered. A trivial example of a disruption such as that implied by Example 8·4 is the destruction of the contents of the A register by the input/output program. It is generally not possible to predict beforehand whether the main program will be interrupted at a point in which the A register contains data to be used subsequently, or whether, in fact, the contents of the A register can be destroyed. Consequently, if an input/output program makes use of the A register, it must save the contents of the A register when it is entered from the main program and restore the contents of the A register when it exits to the main program.

Somewhat more subtle problems are caused by disturbing the state of memory cells or of control registers. For example, an input/output program can alter the state of the overflow indicator inadvertently during an arithmetic operation. If the main program is sensitive to the state of the overflow indicator because of specific overflow tests, interrupt processing can cause spurious overflows to occur in the main program unless the interrupt program specifically stores the state of the overflow indicator on entry and restores the state on exit.

We assume that there is a subroutine called SAVE which stores everything that might be disturbed by an input/output program, and that a subroutine UNSAVE restores the saved items to their original state. The subroutine UNSAVE can be programmed to preserve the state of the input/output program (such as the A and B registers) at the same time that it restores the state of the interrupted program. The subroutine SAVE in this case performs the inverse operation and

---

EXAMPLE 8·4

The following set of instructions illustrates the coroutine linkage of an interrupt-driven input/output program:

	LABEL	CODE	OPERAND	COMMENTS
		. . .		
1.	PUNCH	EQU	14B	Define select code of output device.
2.		ORG	PUNCH	
3.		JSB	SLEEP	Instruction in interrupt location.
		. . .		
4.	SLEEP	NOP		Return address for interrupted program.
5.		JMP	AWAKE,I	Enter output program at point of suspension.
6.	AWAKE	NOP		Return address for output program.
7.	NEXTN	DEF	NEXT	The address of one entry point for output program
8.	NEXTM	DEF	NEXT1	The address of another entry point for output program.
		. . .		
9.		OTA	PUNCH	In output program, transfer data to output buffer.
10.		LDA	NEXTN	Store new return address in coroutine switch area.
11.		STA	AWAKE	
12.		STC	PUNCH,C	Initiate new output operation.
13.		JMP	SLEEP,I	Return to interrupted program.
14.	NEXT	ISZ	COUNT	The entry point when an interrupt for PUNCH is recognized.
		. . .		
15.		OTA	PUNCH	Another output instruction in output program.
16.		LDA	NEXTM	Store another return address in coroutine switch area.
17.		STA	AWAKE	
18.		STC	PUNCH,C	Initiate new output operation.
19.		JMP	SLEEP,I	Return to interrupted program.
20.	NEXT1	ISZ	ADDR	The entry point when an interrupt for PUNCH is recognized.
		. . .		

restores the state of the input/output program while saving the state of the interrupted program. The coroutine call that suspends the input/output program in Example 8·4 ought to be placed in the context shown in Example 8·5 when SAVE and UNSAVE subroutines must be used.

Programs for input devices differ from Example 8·5 only in that the OTA instruction is removed and an LIA or MIA instruction follows the subroutine call to SAVE.

EXAMPLE 8·5

The following program follows the same conventions as Example 8·4, except that it includes the calls on the SAVE and UNSAVE subroutines:

	LABEL	CODE	OPERAND	COMMENTS
1.		ORG	PUNCH	
2.		JSB	SLEEP	Instruction in interrupt location.
		. . .		
3.	SLEEP	NOP		Return address for interrupted program.
4.		JMP	AWAKE,I	Enter output program at point of suspension.
5.	AWAKE	NOP		Return address for output program.
		. . .		
6.		OTA	PUNCH	Transfer data to output buffer.
7.		LDA	NEXTM	Store new return address in coroutine switch area.
8.		STA	AWAKE	
9.		JSB	UNSAVE	Restore state of interrupted program and preserve state of this program.
10.		STC	PUNCH,C	Initiate new output operation.
11.		JMP	SLEEP,I	Return to interrupted program.
12.	NEXTM	DEF	NEXT1	Address of entry point to output program.
13.	NEXT1	JSB	SAVE	Save state of interrupted program and restore state of this program.
		. . .		

In Example 8·5 the call on the subroutine UNSAVE occurs *before* the output operation is initiated, rather than after it is initiated. If the example had been written with the instructions in the order

```
. . .
STC     PUNCH,C     Initiate new output operation.
JSB     UNSAVE
JMP     SLEEP,I
. . .
```

then under certain conditions the program would fail to execute correctly. Specifically, suppose that the output device is so fast that it completes its operation while the UNSAVE subroutine is in process and before the JMP SLEEP,I instruction is executed. Then, when the interrupt is recognized, the instruction JSB SLEEP in the interrupt location will be executed and will store a *new* return address at location SLEEP. This return address is the address of an instruction in UNSAVE. When the new return address is stored, it destroys the return address that should be taken by the JMP SLEEP,I instruction, and with the old return address destroyed, the output program has no way of returning to the main program. The JMP SLEEP,I instruction returns control back into the UNSAVE subroutine, forcing the output program into a loop from which it cannot exit.

From this discussion we see that when an operation for a particular device has been initiated, an interrupt for that device cannot be recognized until *after* the JMP SLEEP,I is executed. Otherwise the return address to the interrupted program will be lost. However, in this case, is Example 8·5 correct? If we were to use a hypothetical ultrafast output device, it might generate an interrupt immediately after the STC instruction initiated a new operation and before the JMP SLEEP,I instruction was executed. In fact, in the next section we shall discover that the interrupt is quite likely to occur there when two or more devices are operating simultaneously. Fortunately the HP 2116 has been designed to prevent an error when this occurs. The HP 2116 will not honor any interrupts in the interval between an input/output instruction and an indirect jump instruction when they occur successively. If an interrupt would otherwise occur in this interval, it is held in abeyance until the indirect jump instruction has completed execution. Therefore in Example 8·5 no interrupts can occur between the STC instruction and the JMP SLEEP,I instruction, so that this example is indeed correct.

The preceding discussion explains another unusual aspect of Example 8·5. The instructions

```
LDA    NEXTM
STA    AWAKE
```

store the return address for the output program in the coroutine switch area. We have usually used the JSB instruction to generate a return address. Thus we might execute the instructions

```
        STC    PUNCH,C    Initiate new output operation.
        JSB    AWAKE      Coroutine call to interrupted program.
        . . .
AWAKE   NOP               Return address for output program.
        JMP    SLEEP,I    Return to interrupted program.
```

However, this sequence of instructions can fail, because an interrupt can occur after JSB AWAKE and before JMP SLEEP,I.

The type of failure discussed here is characteristic of all interrupt programs. The crux of the problem is sensitivity to timing, which greatly increases the difficulty of writing interrupt programs correctly and of analyzing their behavior. An incorrect interrupt program may seem to work properly, but time dependencies can cause it to fail on rare occasions. Interrupt programs require careful design to ensure that all the nuances of timing have been taken into consideration.

8·3 Control of Multiple Devices

The previous section focused on the problem of controlling a single device in an input/output environment. Usually, however, many different input/output devices are in operation simultaneously. In fact a computer system usually operates at peak efficiency when input/output operations are simultaneous instead of sequential. Suppose, for example, that devices READ and PUNCH operate simultaneously. Examination of Example 8·5 reveals that the subroutines SAVE and UNSAVE must be private to the device PUNCH in the sense that they maintain the status for the PUNCH program and must not confuse its status with that of the READ program. Hence the READ program should follow the format of Example 8·5, except that it should use different status-changing routines. It might use routines called SAVE1 and UNSAVE1, for example, to distinguish them from SAVE and UNSAVE.

When two or more input/output devices are active simultaneously, what happens if more than one interrupt occurs at the same time? Clearly the computer cannot respond to more than one interrupt at a time. Therefore, interrupts are usually ordered by a priority weighting scheme, and the computer responds to the interrupt of highest priority. All lower-priority interrupts are held in abeyance until the high-priority interrupt has been executed, and then the interrupt with the next highest priority is processed. If a high-priority interrupt occurs during the processing of a lower-priority interrupt, it is recognized immediately, and control transfers to the appropriate interrupt location.

The HP 2116 computer uses the device select codes to determine priority, and it uses the flag and control flip-flops to control interrupt intervention. Lower-numbered devices have priority over higher-numbered devices. For even greater flexibility, control flip-flops can be used to disable interrupts for the corresponding devices even when they would otherwise have priority. The HP 2116 computer always recognizes the interrupt for the device with highest priority which has its control flip-flop set. If an interrupt occurs for a device for which the control flip-flop is reset, or if the interrupt is not recognized immediately because another device has priority, then that interrupt is saved. It can be recognized later, provided the control flip-flop becomes set, and the device has priority over all other devices that have interrupts pending. Any program can force an interrupt that simulates a normal peripheral device interrupt by executing a set flag instruction (code STF).

When two or more devices are operating simultaneously under interrupt control, interrupts for one device can occur while the program for the other device is in execution. If the input/output programs use the conventions shown in Example 8·5, then they can operate without interactions that lead to failure. In this way a high-priority device can interrupt the program for a low-priority device without failing, and a low-priority interrupt can be held in abeyance while a program for a high-priority device is in execution.

To illustrate, suppose that a low-priority device is being processed when a high-priority interrupt occurs. The interrupt generates a return address, and the computer enters the program for the high-priority device. The first action of the high-priority program is to preserve the status of the low-priority program. When high-priority processing is complete, the status of the low-priority program is restored, and control returns to the low-priority program at the point of interruption. Thus the high-priority interrupt processing causes a delay between some pair of instructions in the low-priority program. A problem arises only when such a time delay occurs after a low-priority operation is initiated and before the low-priority program reaches its exit. In this case the low-priority operation may be completed before the low-priority-program exit is taken, and the program will fail, as described earlier. However, if the low-priority program follows the conventions of Example 8·5, the time delay can lead to program failure only if it occurs between the STC instruction and the JMP SLEEP,I instruction. The design of the HP 2116 precludes this possibility, so that no failures can occur when a high-priority device interrupts a low-priority program.

Now suppose that a low-priority interrupt occurs during the processing of a high-priority device. By assumption, the high-priority flag flip-flop is set when the high-priority program is entered, and it remains set until it is cleared for initiation of a new operation. Hence the low-priority interrupt is held in abeyance until a new high-priority operation is initiated. Because no interrupts can occur between the STC and JMP SLEEP,I instructions, the low-priority interrupt cannot be honored until after the high-priority program has executed the JMP SLEEP,I instruction. As a result the effect is the same as if the low-priority interrupt had occurred immediately after completion of the high-priority processing. Thus one input/output program does not interrupt another in this case, and no timing failures are introduced.

Although the conventions in Example 8·5 are completely general, some programmers prefer to turn off the interrupt system as the first action in an input/output program and to turn it on as the last action. An interrupt that occurs while the interrupt system is off is thus held in abeyance until the interrupt system is turned on again, so that no interrupts are lost. A typical sequence of instructions that follows this convention is shown in Example 8·6.

As in Example 8·5, no interrupts can occur between the STF 0 and JMP SLEEP,I instructions. Hence an interrupt that is pending when the interrupt system is turned on by the STF 0 instruction can be honored only after the JMP SLEEP,I instruction has been executed. From our previous reasoning we see that this technique cannot lead to program failure. However, this method is less desirable when high-priority devices should truly be given priority over low-priority devices. When the interrupt system is turned off, high-priority processing waits until low-priority processing has terminated. When the interrupt system remains on during input/output processing, low-priority processing is interrupted in favor of high-priority processing.

EXAMPLE 8·6

The following input program processes interrupts with the interrupt system off:

	LABEL	CODE	OPERAND	COMMENTS
		. . .		
1.	ENTRY	CLF	0	This is the entry point to the input program. Turn off interrupt system.
2.		JSB	SAVE	Save status of interrupted program and restore status of this program.
3.		LIA	READ	Load new data into A register.
		. . .		
4.		STC	READ,C	Initiate new operation.
		. . .		
5.		STF	0	Turn on interrupt system.
6.		JMP	SLEEP,I	Coroutine call back to interrupted program.
		. . .		

8·4 Data-channel Input/ Output

The input/output mechanism described in the previous sections requires the use of the A or B register for temporary data storage. Thus during input/output operations the central processor is in the data flow path between main memory and the outside world. As a consequence the central processor must be interrupted as each datum is transferred between main memory and the outside world.

System/360-370 computers, as well as many others, use a somewhat different input/output mechanism, which removes the central processor from the input/output data flow path. This increases the potential computation speed of the computer system by decreasing the load on the central processor. The input/output mechanism makes use of a special input/output processor called a *data channel* or *direct-memory-access channel*, which can access main memory independently of the central processor. A typical computer system with two data channels is shown in Figure 8·3. Note that three different data flows

183

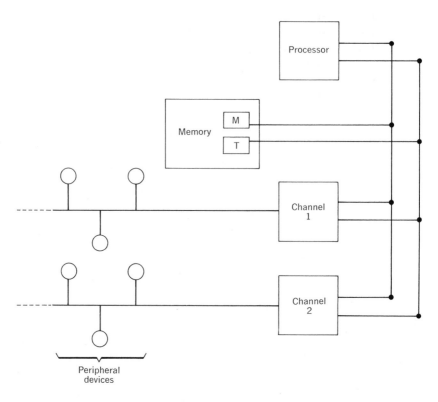

Figure 8·3 A computer system with two data channels for input/output operations

can be supported concurrently in the computer system: one between the central processor and memory, and one through each data channel between memory and peripheral devices. Because the memory shown in Figure 8·3 has only one M and T register pair, only one datum can be fetched or stored at a time. Hence conflicts can arise when two independent requests reach memory simultaneously.

There are several ways of resolving memory-access conflicts. A straightforward method is to establish priorities for access and to defer a low-priority memory access in favor of high-priority memory access. Usually the data channels are given priority over the central processor, because the channels operate in a mode in which timing is critical, whereas the central processor can be delayed without ill effect. In any event, this method essentially time-shares the memory by interleaving the memory requests of the data channels and the central processor. As a result the computational speed of the central processor tends to decrease when input/output activity increases, but the decrease is much less than that in a system without data channels.

High-performance computers are often organized with modular memories in order to reduce the performance degradation due to memory-access conflicts. Figure 8·4 shows a computer system in which main memory consists of four memory modules, each with its own M and T register. Each word in this memory has a unique address, just as in the memory shown in Figure 8·3, and each memory module contains one-fourth of the memory addresses. The advantage of the modular memory is that all modules can honor memory requests simultaneously. Thus if the data channels and the processor request data from different modules simultaneously, no memory conflict occurs. Memory conflicts can still occur in this computer system, so that the processor performance will tend to be degraded during periods of high input/output activity. However, conflicts will tend to be much less frequent than in the system shown in Figure 8·3, and therefore processor performance is much less sensitive to input/output activity.

Since data channels are essentially processors, in many computers channels are controlled by programs analogous to those which control the actions of a central processor. The major difference between channel programs and ordinary programs is that data channels do not perform the same operations as a central processor, and they therefore require a different instruction set. Some of the System/360-370 channel

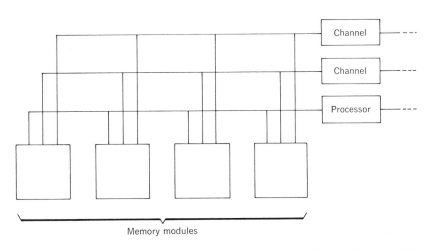

Figure 8·4 A modular memory system. Each line represents both the address and the data lines shown in Figure 8·3

commands are listed in the following table:

CHANNEL COMMAND	PARAMETERS	ACTION
READ	BUFFER,N	Read N bytes into successive bytes of memory, starting at address BUFFER.
WRITE	BUFFER,N	Write N bytes from successive bytes of memory, starting at address BUFFER.
TRANSFER IN CHANNEL	NEXTCOMMAND	Take next channel command from address NEXTCOMMAND.

Figure 8·5 shows how the control information is stored in a channel command word. The shaded areas hold data whose function is very specialized and is not discussed in this text.

In normal operation an input/output program constructs a sequence of channel commands and then issues an instruction that causes a channel to execute the channel program. Each channel command has a bit called a *chain command bit*, which is used like a HALT instruction. If the chain command bit of a channel command is 0, then the channel terminates operation when that channel command has been executed. If the chain command bit is 1, the channel executes the next command in the channel program. When a channel operation

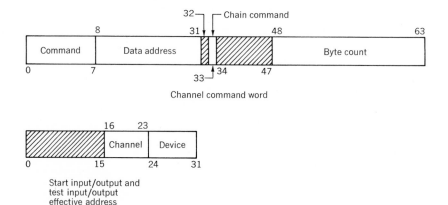

Channel command word

Start input/output and
test input/output
effective address

Figure 8·5 System/360-370 input/output control-word representation

186

terminates, the end of operation is signaled by an interrupt. Thus input/output operations with data channels can be controlled by interrupt programs similar to those discussed in the previous section.

Since the channel commands above do not specify which device or channel is involved in an input/output operation, this information is specified in the instruction that initiates a channel operation. Hence the System/360-370 input/output instructions include the following:

INSTRUCTION	CODE	PARAMETERS	ACTION
START I/O	SIO	CHANNEL,DEVICE	Initiate an input/output operation on specified channel and device.
TEST I/O	TIO	CHANNEL,DEVICE	Set condition code to indicate present status of channel and device.

The base and displacement fields of these instructions encode the channel and device. Execution begins with the computation of the effective address by adding the contents of a base register to a displacement. Then the effective address is interpreted as a channel number and device number, as shown in Figure 8·5.

When the START I/O instruction is issued, the specified channel begins executing a channel program. By convention the address of the first channel command is stored in memory address 72. Execution of START I/O also sets the condition code to indicate whether the operation has been successfully initiated. The condition code setting of 0 denotes the normal case, and other settings indicate unusual conditions such as a busy channel, which require special processing. The TEST I/O instruction is equivalent to the HP 2116 instruction that tests the state of the flag bit. The action of the TEST I/O instruction is to set the condition code to indicate the state of the channel and device. In Example 8·7 the condition code setting of 0 indicates that the channel and device are inactive.

Example 8·7 is intended as a sketch of techniques for performing data-channel input/output. Many details have been omitted by necessity. The System/360-370 interrupt system has not been discussed here, but of course it is of central importance for input/output programming. This interrupt system functions much like the HP 2116 interrupt system, but it differs considerably in its details. When an interrupt occurs at the completion of an operation, the computer branches to a location in memory that is reserved for that interrupt. As in the HP 2116

EXAMPLE 8·7

The following program for System/360-370 reads a punched card with 80 characters into memory. The program uses a data channel for input/output and a wait loop to test for the end of an operation. We assume that interrupts cannot occur.

LABEL	CODE	OPERAND	COMMENTS
	. . .		
1. CCW	DS	D'0'	Reserve double word for a channel command word.
2. CCWN	DC	A(CCW)	Address of channel command word.
3. READCMD	DC	F'2'	Code for a READ operation in channel command word.
4. BUFFN	DC	A(BUFF)	Address of buffer storage area.
5. BUFF	DS	80C' '	Reserve 80 bytes for storing data on one punched card.
6. COUNT	DC	F'80'	Number of characters to be read.
7. CHANNEL	DC	F'1'	The channel number.
8. READER	DC	F'3'	Device number for card reader.
9. TEMP	EQU	2	A temporary register, the even register of a double register.
	. . .		
10.	L	TEMP,CCWN	Move address of channel command word to location 72.
11.	ST	TEMP,72	
12.	L	TEMP,READCMD	Begin construction of channel command word. Load code for READ operation.
13.	SLL	TEMP,24	Align this command into leftmost byte.

LABEL	CODE	OPERAND	COMMENTS
14.	A	TEMP,BUFFN	Add address of buffer.
15.	L	TEMP+1,COUNT	Load byte count into right end of double register. The chain command bit is 0.
16.	STM	TEMP,TEMP+1, CCW	Store REG[TEMP; TEMP+1] as a channel command word.
17.	L	TEMP,CHANNEL	Construct channel and device information for SIO instruction. Load channel number.
18.	SLL	TEMP,8	Shift left one byte.
19.	A	TEMP,READER	Add device number.
20.	SIO	0(TEMP)	Start operation.
21.	BC	2+4+8,ERROR	Branch to ERROR on any condition code except 0.
22. TEST	TIO	0(TEMP)	Test for input/output completion.
23.	BC	2+4+8,TEST	Loop until operation is done.
24.	L	. . .	At this point 80 bytes have been read into the buffer.

. . .

program, a return address is generated and stored, and then control passes to an input/output program.

Very few programmers ever write input/output instructions for System/360-370 computers. Instead, these computers normally operate under the control of an executive program. One of the primary functions of the executive program is to do all of the input/output processing and thus to relieve the ordinary programmer of the problems related to input/output programs. To perform input/output the user programs have to call standard input/output subroutines which are part of the executive program. System/360-370 designers were particularly careful to prevent ordinary users from executing input/output instructions directly. When a user program is in process, the input/output instructions are not executable, and any attempt to execute such an instruction causes an interrupt that branches to an error program.

8·5 Asynchronous Control of Input/Output

We have seen that input/output operations in the HP 2116 and System/360-370 computers can be executed concurrently with computation in the processor. Most peripheral devices operate at data transmission rates much lower than those a computer can sustain, because peripheral devices normally have mechanical motion of some kind, whereas computers do not. During input/output operations the computer is constrained to transmit information at a rate sustainable by the peripheral devices, which can result in a significant decrease in computation rate. For maximum efficiency during an input/output action we wish to compute at the fastest possible rate within the constraints imposed by the peripheral device, and we can do this only if the computation and input/output actions are correctly synchronized.

Consider, for example, the following outline, which is typical of many programs:

1. Read a set of input data.

2. Compute with these data, producing a collection of results.

3. Output the results.

4. If there are more input data, return to step 1, otherwise halt.

The least efficient use of the computer for this program is illustrated in Figure 8·6a, where we see that there are no concurrent operations. In this example processing is suspended immediately after the computer issues an input or output operation, and processing resumes when the corresponding REPLY signal is received. The behavior here is typical of programs that use wait loops for input/output operations.

In Figure 8.6b we see an example of an interrupt driven program that is somewhat more efficient than the previous example. Here computation continues after input/output operations have been initiated. The periods of no computation occur because the input device is a bottleneck. When computation reaches a point at which new input data are required, processing is suspended until the input device completes its operation. The output device also is suspended for periods of time while waiting for the computation to generate new output data. Immediately after each input operation terminates, a new input operation is initiated so that the input device runs continuously.

Figure 8·6c is similar to Figure 8·6b except that the bottleneck is the output program instead of the input program. Now computation must be suspended while the output device performs an operation, and

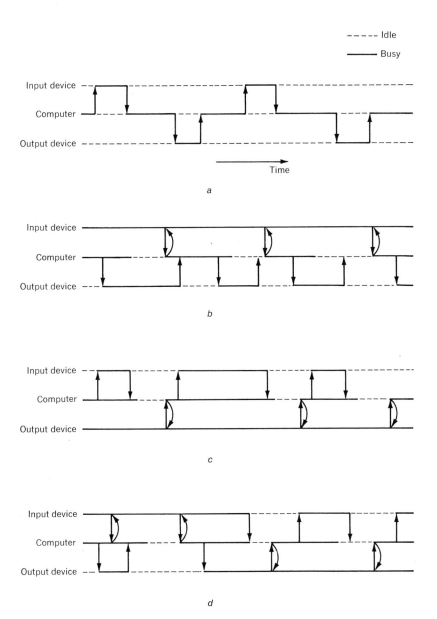

Figure 8·6 A study of the activity of a typical program. The arrows that leave a line marked COMPUTER are input/output requests, and those that enter are replies. (a) No interrupts; (b) with interrupts, computation limited by input; (c) computation limited by output; (d) computation limited by both input and output

the input device, in turn, is suspended periodically until program processing reaches a point at which it can accept new data. As in the previous example, input/output operations can proceed concurrently with computation, but the effective computation rate is determined by the speed of the output device.

We wish to write our programs so that they automatically adopt the behavior shown in Figure 8·6b and c depending on which device is slower. That is, the slowest device should be made to run continuously by initiating a new operation on that device immediately after an operation terminates. Moreover, concurrent operation of input/output devices and processor should occur as much as possible. Automatic suspension of activity should occur whenever one part of the system has to wait for another. The behavior we desire should also be able to adapt to complex situations such as the one shown in Figure 8·6d. Here we see a case where the input device is a system bottleneck periodically, and should run continuously at such times. At other times the output device is the bottleneck, so it should be controlled to run continuously. In either case, the processor should perform computation until it reaches a point at which it must suspend activity pending completion of an input or output operation.

To perform input/output operations with high efficiency we construct the input/output programs as coroutines and use the interrupt system to generate calls on these coroutines from the main program. We avoid the inefficient behavior shown in Figure 8·6a, by allowing the input/output coroutines to operate slightly out of step with the main program. Thus an input coroutine might work ahead of the main program by initiating new input operations during periods when the input device might otherwise be idle, and before the input data have been requested by the main program. Conversely, the main program might work ahead of a slower output coroutine, instead of waiting in order to remain in step.

To produce this behavior all data are exchanged between the input/output coroutines through queues, rather than by the usual methods for passing parameters. Figure 8·7 shows how queues are placed between the input/output coroutines and the main program. Consider, for example, a short time interval in which the input device transmits data faster than the main program can accept data. The input coroutine places the first item in the queue and immediately initiates a new input operation. When this operation is complete, the new data are queued, and another operation is initiated. This process is repeated as each input operation is completed. The queueing process places the data where they can be retrieved by the main program in

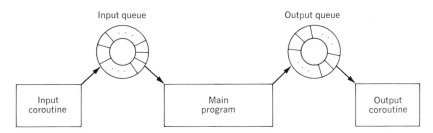

Figure 8·7 A program that uses input/output coroutines and queues

the same order that they were processed by the input coroutine. The advantage of the queue is that for brief periods the main program can process data at a different rate from that at which they are processed by the input coroutine.

The input coroutine reads information from a peripheral device and places it in the input queue. Similarly, the output coroutine picks up information from the output queue and transmits it to the output device. The input and output queues permit us to do computation concurrently with input/output, as shown in Figure 8·6b and c, instead of as shown in Figure 8·6a. Moreover, the queues can smooth variations in input or output data rates of the type shown in Figure 8·6d. In Figure 8·6b, the computation speed is determined by the input device, and the input queue is empty in the steady state. Whenever the input coroutine places new information in the input queue, the main program removes it immediately. In Figure 8·6c the output queue is normally empty. In Figure 8·6d neither queue may be empty in the steady state. For this case the queue tends to permit computation at a rate limited by the average input/output rate rather than by the instantaneous minimum of input and output rates.

The size of the queue has no effect on the computation rate in Figure 8·6b and c, provided that it contains at least two elements. When variations in input/output rates can occur, as in Figure 8·6d, the computation rate will tend to increase as the queues get larger, until the queues are large enough to smooth out the peak variations. When queue sizes are increased beyond this point, the computation rate will not increase.

While Figures 8·6 and 8·7 illustrate the principles of programming with queues, there are significant details that warrant explanation. The main queue operation is rather straightforward. For example, the input coroutine places new data at the tail of the input queue, and the main program removes data from the head of the input queue.

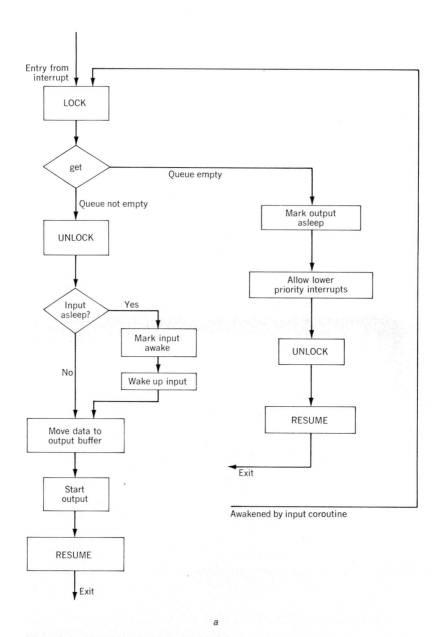

Figure 8·8 (a) Flowchart of output coroutine

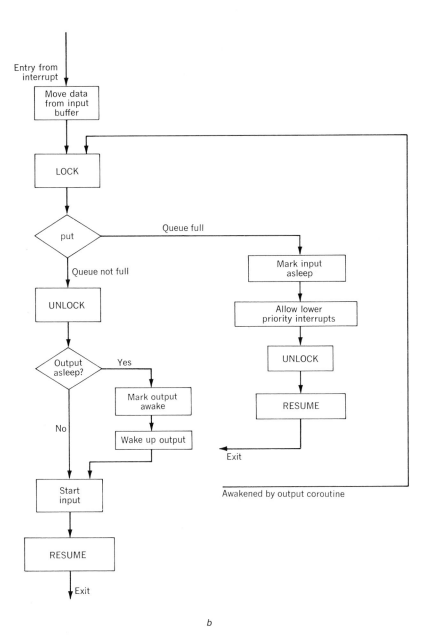

b

Figure 8·8 *(Continued)* (*b*) Flowchart of input coroutine

Output coroutine activity is analogous. The problems arise when we consider what happens when a queue becomes full or empty.

Specifically, when the input queue is full, the input coroutine must suspend further input operation until one or more items are removed from the queue. The input coroutine then sets a variable to indicate that it has suspended operation and returns from interrupt processing without initiating a new READ operation. Since the input coroutine can be restarted if, and only if, the main program removes something from the input queue, every time the main program removes an item it checks to see if the input coroutine is in a suspended state. If so, the main program forces an interrupt for the READ program to occur and then proceeds with its usual processing.

An analogous situation arises when the input queue becomes empty. However, in this case it is the main program that has to be suspended. When the input program places new data in the queue, it also checks to see if the main program is suspended. If so, it awakens the main program and continues processing.

There are many different ways of implementing this behavior. It is usually necessary to have at least one instruction that branches to itself in a wait loop. This is because the main program may be suspended and both input and output coroutines may be asleep while waiting for input or output operation to complete. The wait loop is broken when an interrupt occurs. Example 8·8 shows a pair of input/output coroutines that communicate with each other through a queue. A flowchart for the coroutines appears in Figure 8·8.

Example 8·8 contains the statements LOCK and UNLOCK, which turn the interrupt system off and on, respectively. In previous exam-

---

EXAMPLE 8·8

The queueing conventions in the following coroutines are the same as those for input/output coroutines communicating with a main program. The coroutines are written in an ALGOL-like language, with comments indicating the equivalent machine instructions. In this example the calls to SAVE and UNSAVE have been omitted for simplicity.

```
coroutine output;
    begin real data;
        comment entry point for output interrupt;
    LOOP: comment interrupts off;
```

```
        LOCK;
        comment get item from queue, branch to QEMPTY if queue is empty;
        get(data,QEMPTY);
        comment interrupts on;
        UNLOCK;
        comment wake up input coroutine if it is suspended;
        if inputasleep = 1 then
            begin inputasleep := 0;
                comment force an input interrupt;
                wakeup(input);
            end;
        comment move data to output buffer;
        bufferout(data);
        startoutput;
        comment coroutine call to return from interrupt program;
        RESUME;
        go to LOOP;
QEMPTY: comment mark this program suspended;
        outputasleep := 1;
        comment allow lower-priority interrupts to occur;
        clearflag(outputdevice);
        comment interrupts on;
        UNLOCK;
        comment coroutine call to return from interrupt program;
        RESUME;
        comment entry point when awakened by input coroutine;
        go to LOOP;

end coroutine output;

coroutine input;
    begin real data;
        comment entry point for input interrupt;
LOOP: comment load data from input buffer;
        bufferin (data);
QUEUEUP: comment interrupts off;
        LOCK;
        comment attempt to place data in queue.
        Branch to QFULL if queue is full;
        put(data,QFULL);
        comment interrupts on;
        UNLOCK;
        comment wake up output program if it is suspended;
        if outputasleep := 1 then
            begin outputasleep := 0;
                comment force an output interrupt;
                wakeup(output);
            end;
        startinput;
        comment coroutine call to return from input program;
        RESUME;
        go to LOOP;
```

```
        QFULL: comment mark this program suspended;
               inputasleep := 1;
               comment allow lower-priority interrupts;
               clearflag(inputdevice);
        comment interrupts on;
        UNLOCK;
        comment coroutine call to return from interrupt program;
        RESUME;
        comment entry point when input coroutine is awakened by output
               coroutine;
        go to QUEUEUP;
    end coroutine input;
    comment main program begins here;
        startinput;
        comment loop waiting for interrupt;
    ROUND: go to ROUND;
```

ples of interrupt-driven input/output programs the interrupt system was always on. However, in this case it is absolutely necessary to turn the interrupt system off when the queue routines are entered. We have a situation in which two different programs inspect the HEAD and TAIL pointers of the queue and take actions conditioned on their values. The LOCK and UNLOCK actions guarantee that one program cannot be interrupted by the other while the queue pointers are being inspected.

To see that a program failure can occur without the LOCK and UNLOCK, consider the following situation.

1. The input coroutine inspects the queue pointers and finds that the queue is full.

2. The higher-priority output coroutine interrupts the input coroutine.

3. The output coroutine inspects the queue pointers and finds that the queue is full.

4. The output coroutine removes one item from the queue.

5. The output coroutine checks to see if the input coroutine is suspended and finds that the input coroutine is active.

6. The output coroutine initiates a new output operation and returns.

7. The return passes control back to the input coroutine.

8. Before the input coroutine can proceed, a high priority output interrupt is recognized and control passes to the output coroutine. (This is quite possible if there are many different devices active

simultaneously, and interrupts from these devices prevent the input coroutine from continuing execution.)

9. The output coroutine repeats steps 3 through 6, possibly several times until it empties the queue.

10. Control returns to the input coroutine which, having found the queue full, marks itself suspended and exits.

11. An output interrupt reactivates the output coroutine.

12. The output coroutine inspects the queue pointers and finds that the queue is empty.

13. The output coroutine suspends itself.

When the last condition arises, both the input and the output coroutines are suspended, and neither can be awakened. The program has failed.

In the situation above both the input and the output coroutines observed particular data (the queue pointers) and took actions based on the values of the pointers. The failure occurred because the values of the pointers can change at unexpected times in an interrupt environment. Once again we see that subtle timing problems can lead to unpredictable behavior of input/output programs. The techniques discussed in this chapter will work correctly for a large class of problems on a large number of different computers. Nevertheless, careful and thorough analysis is essential for constructing input/output programs, because a situation may present special problems that do not fit the framework of our discussion.

REFERENCES

Nearly all the earliest computers had some capacity for performing input/output concurrently with computation. Leiner (1952), for example, wrote an early article describing the hardware in an interface in great depth, but he was by no means the first designer to conceive of concurrent input/output. Burks, Goldstine, and Von Neumann (1946), in their proposal to build a computer, mentioned the value of concurrent input/output and the fact that it could be achieved with buffer storage and synchronization logic. They elected to leave it out of their initial designs because of the relatively high cost of hardware at that time. However, four years after their proposal computers with concurrent input/output ability were under construction.

Interrupts and interrupt-driven input/output programs must also be credited jointly to many of the pioneers in computing. Much of the development of sophisticated interrupt-driven input/output programming techniques was spurred by the wide acceptance of the IBM 704 (later the IBM 709) in the middle and late 1950s. An outgrowth of a project initiated by the SHARE users' group for this computer was an input/output subroutine library that used interrupts and queues similar to those described here. A description appears in Mock and Swift (1969). In Europe, Dijkstra (1958) developed comparable programs for which he deserves equal credit. A recent study of the control of concurrent input-output operations in the context of multiprocessing systems appears in Lampson (1968).

EXERCISES

8·1   Write a program in assembly language for the four processes below. Use four different entry points to the program and employ a common collection of input/output subroutines. The interrupt system need not be used in this program.

a.   Simple teletype echo. Characters keyed on the teletype are echoed by the computer and printed on the keyboard.

b.   Queued teletype. Characters keyed on the teletype are queued and not echoed. Each time the character Z (332_8 or 132_8) is received, it is queued and the five characters at the head of the queue are printed. If fewer than five characters are in the queue, then just these characters are printed.

c.   Push-down stack echo. Characters are keyed on the teletype and entered into a push-down stack. When the character Z is struck the stack is emptied, in last-in-first-out order.

d.   Coroutine echo program. Use coroutine to expand number-letter pairs to n occurrences of the letter, where n is the value of the number. That is, "4F" becomes "FFFF." Use the coroutine in a simple teletype echo program, so that the echoed characters are expanded forms of the keyed-in characters. Only the numbers 2 to 5 should cause expansion. The least significant seven bits of the code for these numbers are 062_8 to 065_8.

8·2   Write an assembly language program for the SAVE and UNSAVE operations. Assume that the A register and the overflow indicator of the main program must be saved, and that the **A** register of the input/output program must be saved.

8·3 Write a program that uses the interrupt system on the HP 2116 computer and does the following:

a. Characters are read from the paper-tape reader and queued.

b. Characters are removed from the queue and output to teletype.

c. The main program (after initialization) is a single instruction, SELF JMP SELF.

8·4 Show that the coroutines of Example 8·8 can never both be suspended simultaneously.

9

Linked Data Structures

Possibly the most important factor in the construction of efficient algorithms is the representation of data. Computer instruction repertoires are biased to perform some processes very efficiently and some inefficiently. For example, compare the difficulty of the following two computations:

1. Find the value of A[I], given the value of I.

2. Given the value of X, find a value of I for which A[I] = X, if there is such an I (if there is more than one such I, pick any).

Clearly the first computation requires only a simple index operation, but the second might require that the entire array A be searched. Consequently we should expect that the second computation will be considerably longer than the first.

The conclusion is not necessarily correct, however, because it presupposes that the A array is represented as a linear array as described in Chapter 6. Under certain conditions we can use a different representation for A[I] and perform the second computation with practically the same efficiency as the first. Suppose, for example, that X is an integer with a value constrained to lie in the interval $0 \leq X \leq N$, where N is not too large. Then we can use an array IVALUE, indexed from 0 to N, with the property that

If IVALUE[X] = I, then A[I] = X

and

If IVALUE[X] = $\emptyset$, then there is no I such that A[I] = X

Here the symbol $\emptyset$ is a special sentinel. We can choose $\emptyset$ to be an integer that is out of bounds for A. Note that IVALUE is another representation of the array A, but that some information about A is lost in this representation. If, for example A[I1] = A[I2], then the representation we have permits us to deduce the value of at most one of the pair A[I1] and A[I2].

We need not keep A in its usual array representation if the only processing to be performed on it is the search described in the second computation above. Thus we see that it is possible to obtain rather large increases in processing speed by adapting the representation of a data structure to the processing to be performed on it. In this chapter and the next we shall explore some of the alternatives to the representations discussed earlier. Chapter 11 discusses several uses of these representations in algorithms for searching and sorting.

9·1 Simple Lists

The programmer frequently finds that he must organize his data into lists that are linearly ordered. If new items are added to one end of a list and no items are ever deleted, then the list can be implemented as a one-dimensional array, where the first element is A[1], the second is A[2], etc. When items are added to or removed from the list, and it is known that all operations must be performed at either end of the list, the appropriate implementation of the list is a push-down stack, a queue, or a double-ended queue, depending on the case at hand. If items are to be inserted or deleted somewhere in the interior of the list, then it is often best to abandon the notion of contiguous storage of items in the list. The difficulties in inserting and deleting items in the interior of lists are illustrated by the following example. Suppose that a list with MAX items is to be stored in a one-dimensional array named A. Then to delete the tenth item in the list we might execute the program

```
for i := 10 step 1 until MAX−1 do
    A[i] := A[i+1];
```

Similarly, to insert an item as the new tenth element of the list we might execute the program

```
for i := MAX step −1 until 10 do
    A[i+1] := A[i];
A[10] := newitem;
```

The time penalty for executing the insert and delete programs becomes excessive when MAX is large. Moreover, a great deal of memory can be wasted if the list that is actually stored in A contains relatively few elements in comparison to the size of the array. The difficulty in inserting and deleting is a result of contiguous storage of elements in the list. It is possible to improve matters substantially by using non-contiguous storage.

To see how list items can be held in noncontiguous storage we shall make use of two arrays: one to hold the items in the list and the other to point to the next items in the list. Suppose the item array is called V for value and the pointer array is called NEXT. We let NEXT[I] be the index in V of the item that follows V[I]. The pointer value 0 can be used to denote the end of a list, provided that V has lower bound 1— that is, that V[0] is not an element of V. The following program can be used to scan a list from V[start] to the end of the list, where the procedure LOOKAT is assumed to process an item in a list:

```
I := start;
loop: LOOKAT(V[I]);
    I := NEXT[I];
    if I ≠ 0 then go to loop;
```

We call this representation a *linked list,* and we sometimes use *link* interchangeably with *pointer.* The program demonstrates that a linked list can be scanned from one end to another as easily as a simple array can be scanned. We now show that items can be inserted and deleted

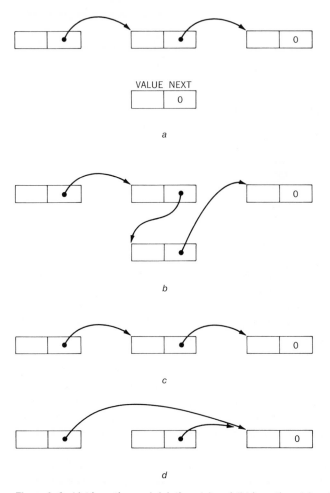

VALUE NEXT

a

b

c

d

Figure 9·1 List insertion and deletion: *(a)* and *(b)* insertion; *(c)* and *(d)* deletion

in linked lists rather easily. The two procedures in Example 9·1 illustrate the processes; Figure 9·1 shows the processes graphically.

It is somewhat redundant to use the array V as a parameter for the procedures in Example 9·1, because it is never referenced. The reason for placing it in a prominent position is to emphasize its relation to the array NEXT. In actual practice the arrays V and NEXT are often one and the same. Data packing is used to place a pointer to a successor element in the same word that contains the value of an element of the list.

206

EXAMPLE 9·1

```
procedure insert (item,V,NEXT,place);
array V, NEXT; integer item, place;
comment V[item] to be inserted into the list as the successor of V[place];
    begin
        NEXT[item] := NEXT[place];
        NEXT[place] := item;
    end procedure insert;

procedure delete (place,V,NEXT);
    array V, NEXT; integer place;
    comment the successor of V[place] is deleted from the list;
    begin NEXT[place] := NEXT[NEXT[place]];
    end procedure delete;
```

To illustrate applications of linked lists let us consider the use of the queue for input/output. For computers such as System/360-370, which use data channels for input/output, the input/output requests for particular channels have to be queued, since the data channels can be busy when a request is made. If a first-in-first-out policy for honoring requests is in effect, then a queue of the type described in Chapter 6 is adequate. In many cases performance is significantly better if the queue is ordered on the basis of priority or some other attribute instead of on a first-in-first-out basis. The performance improvement is usually related to the ability to schedule requests to minimize the rotational delay of moving magnetic memories such as drums and disks.

For this problem let us compare the efficiency of the linked-list representation of a queue with that of the array representation in Chapter 6. Assume that a request is received which belongs in the queue between items I and I+1 and that the queue contains N items. The REQUEST processing algorithm breaks naturally into two parts: search for the place to enter the item, then item entry. If we use the array representation of the queue and search the queue sequentially, beginning at the tail, then the search time will be approximately the same as the time required to search a linked-list representation of the queue, beginning at the tail. How do we make an insertion in the middle of the array representation of a queue? We do this by moving the items in the queue to make space for the new request. We may have to move as much as half the queue to do this. However, with a linked-list representation the insertion can be made by moving a few pointers. The time required for this is independent of the length of the list. Thus the linked-list representation of the queue is more efficient for inserting requests than the array representation. We shall have more to say about this later.

Another important application of the linked list is text editing. Processing of ordinary text by computers has become rather common as computers have become larger, faster, and more economical to operate. Consider the representation of a moderate-sized document in a computer memory, and assume that we wish to change all occurrences of beta in the text to alpha. If we store the text in an array representation, with each array element packed with characters, then we cannot replace the four characters in beta by the five characters in alpha without moving some text to create space. Notice that we have to scan the array from beginning to end to find all occurrences of beta, and so we cannot take advantage of the efficient indexing that is characteristic of array representations.

Consider the same problem when the representation is a linked list, with each item in the list a character of text. The search for each occurrence of beta takes about the same amount of time in each representation, but when a text replacement is made, the linked list leads to considerably more efficient processing. Of course, the linked list requires extra memory for the pointers, but we do not have to use one pointer per character. For efficient storage the value field of a typical item in our linked-list representation might contain, say, up to 256 characters, and it would also contain an integer that gives the number of characters in the value field. In this representation we can replace beta by alpha everywhere and never have to move more than 255 characters for any replacement. As we increase the number of characters that we permit in a single value field, the memory used for pointers decreases and the processing time for a replacement increases. We clearly have a trade off here in which we can exchange memory space for processing time.

The simple lists described here are frequently called *one-way linked lists*, because they can be scanned only from beginning to end. Given a pointer to an element in the list, it is not possible, in general, to find the predecessor of the element. A simple generalization of the one-way linked list is the circular list shown in Figure 9·2. The last link in the list points back to the beginning of the list, instead of indicating no link as the 0 link does. It is usual practice in the implementation of circular lists to use a special tag bit in each link to identify the end of a list. If this bit is 0, for example, then the link is a true link to the next element. A tag bit of 1 indicates there are no more elements on the list, and the link points to the beginning of the list.

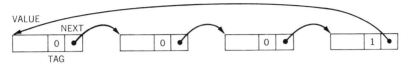

VALUE

NEXT

TAG

Figure 9·2 A circular list

9·2 Two-way Linked Lists

When lists are manipulated in such a manner that they must be scanned in both directions, the one-way linked-list structure is unsuitable, and the circular-list structure requires excessive processing to find the predecessor of an element in a list. The concept of linked lists is easily generalized to data structures that have bidirectional links. An example of such a structure is shown in Figure 9·3. Elements in such a data structure can be inserted or deleted by generalizing the basic procedures for scanning linked lists. The insertion process, for example, generalizes to the procedure of Example 9·2.

For application of the two-way linked list let us look again at the queue. We have already noted that one-way linked lists are useful when items are to be inserted into the interiors of queues. Suppose that the insertion process requires that the insertion point be found by a *tail-to-head search,* and that each deletion requires that an item be found by searching the queue from *head to tail.* That is, we have to be able to search a queue in both directions. Since a one-way linked list cannot be scanned efficiently from head to tail, the one-way linked-list representation of a queue is inherently inefficient for this problem. However, the two-way linked list can be scanned in both directions efficiently, and thus it is satisfactory for this case.

Although two-way linked lists afford certain advantages in processing, we cannot disregard their disadvantages. Insertion and deletion is twice as costly as with one-way lists, because twice as many pointers must be altered to perform each operation. Moreover, the extra set of linkages in two-way linked lists occupies a significant amount of storage. Therefore the usual practice is to use two-way lists only if list manipulation requires two-way scanning. Otherwise one-way pointers are used.

PRED   SUC

VALUE

Figure 9·3 A two-way linked list

EXAMPLE 9·2

The following program shows how to insert into a two-way linked list:

```
procedure insert(item,V,SUC,PRED,place);
array V,SUC,PRED;
integer item, place;
comment V[item] is to be inserted into the list as the successor of V[place],
SUC[place] is the link to the successor of V[place] in the list and PRED[place]
is the link to the predecessor of V[place] in the list;
begin SUC[item] := SUC[place];
    PRED[SUC[place]] := item;
    comment the two preceding statements changed the links that establish
    the correct successor to V[item], the next two statements establish the
    links for the predecessor of V[item];
    SUC[place] := item;
    PRED[item] := place;
end procedure insert;
```

There is an interesting case in which two pointers can be stored in the same number of bits that one pointer would normally occupy. This case is characterized by the fact that whenever an item is accessed, it is accessed by scanning the doubly linked list in one direction or the other. Thus when we reach a cell in the list, we know the address either of its predecessor or of its successor. The link in the cell need only contain the value SUC+PRED, where SUC and PRED are the addresses of the successor and the predecessor, respectively. When we scan from the front of the list to the end, the value of PRED is known at each step, and the value of SUC can be determined by subtracting PRED from the link contained in the cell. Similarly, PRED can be computed if SUC is known. Thus we have the essentials of a doubly linked list.

Note that the link stored in each cell in this case must be one bit longer than the link for either PRED or SUC, because the maximum value for this link is twice the maximum value of PRED or SUC. We can even eliminate that bit if we choose to store the EXCLUSIVE OR of SUC and PRED instead of this arithmetic sum. If we let $\oplus$ denote the EXCLUSIVE OR operation, then we have the identities

$$SUC = PRED \oplus (PRED \oplus SUC)$$
$$PRED = SUC \oplus (PRED \oplus SUC)$$

Obviously we can recover the value of SUC if we know the value of PRED and of PRED⊕SUC.

9·3 Threaded Lists

The various types of linked-list structures discussed thus far are primitive examples of linked data structures. Data structures of arbitrary complexity can be created merely by adding additional pointers to items on a list. The two-way list uses two pointers, one for successor and one for predecessor. This can be generalized, for example, to the representation of items in a two-dimensional matrix by using pointers to each of the four neighbors for each element in the matrix. In this case each item has four links associated with it, each of which "threads" the list elements in a particular direction—whence the name *threaded list.*

To illustrate this concept, suppose that we want to construct a list of people in several generations of a family so that we can deduce a number of family relationships from the data structure. To do this we can use the data structure shown in Figure 9·4. The name of each person has five pointers associated with it: father, mother, next oldest brother (or sister), oldest son, and oldest daughter. Figure 9·5 shows a family tree and its representation in this data structure. The sons of any person can be found by tracing the link from that person to the oldest son to find the first son; all other sons are then found by con-

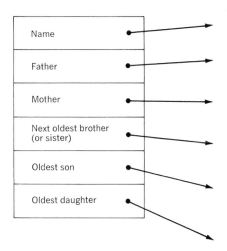

Figure 9·4 A threaded-list representation of a person and his family relationship

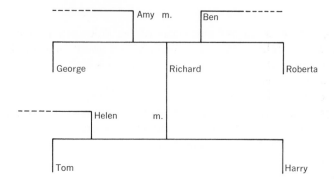

a

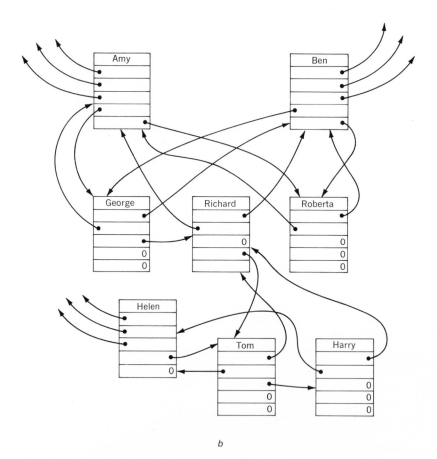

b

Figure 9·5 (a) A portion of a family tree and (b) its threaded-list representation

tinuing to trace along the next oldest brother link until an empty link is found. How might we find the nephew, the grandchild, or the cousin of a person in the list? Note that we cannot find a person's spouse when he has no children.

Compare this example of a threaded-list representation to the other representations we have discussed. Can we represent a family tree in an array without pointers and still process the data efficiently? Suppose, for example, that we use a representation in which the data for each person are stored in a group of memory cells. In the first cell we put the person's name—say, JOHN SMITH. In the next cell we put his father's name, HENRY SMITH. The cells that follow then contain the names of his mother, his next oldest brother, etc. To identify his paternal grandfather, we look for his father's name and find HENRY SMITH. Now we have to look for the father of HENRY SMITH. However, this necessitates searching the entire array, since, by assumption, we have no pointers in the data structure. Obviously we want to keep the index to the data for HENRY SMITH, but this index is a pointer, and the use of such pointers creates the data structure shown in Figure 9·5.

There are many practical applications of threaded lists. One that arises frequently has to do with data that are ordered in two different ways. For example, organization membership lists are ordered alphabetically by name of subscriber, so that membership directories can be constructed efficiently, and by ZIP code because of Post Office requirements on organization mailings. We can use a threaded-list representation that satisfies both requirements. We use two threads, one that links members in alphabetical order and another that links members in order by ZIP code. For our processing requirements each thread can be a one-way linked list. Other aspects of the problem could lead us to consider circular and two-way linked lists instead of or in combination with one-way linked lists.

The many variations possible for threaded-list data structures are limited only by the imagination. Linkages can be placed in a data structure freely, but they should be included only if they increase the efficiency of computation. The gain in computation speed must always be balanced against the increased use of memory and the added cost of inserting and deleting items. In Chapter 11 we shall discuss some tools for analysis and design of linked data structures.

9·4 Memory Allocation and Garbage Collection

In the discussion of linked data structures the assumption has been implicit that unused memory is always readily available for new items to be linked into lists. However, when we delete an item from a list, the memory in which the deleted item had been stored is lost unless we take measures to reuse it. In practice we can seldom afford to cast away memory for deleted items. Available memory is usually far too small to hold all the active data lists plus all the items that have ever been deleted from them.

Early list-processing programs utilized the list mechanism itself to control available memory and to recover memory made available by deletions. All available memory was linked to a list known as the *free-storage list*. When items were deleted from active lists, the unused memory was inserted at the beginning of the free-storage list. Recovery of memory in such programs was nearly always specified explicitly by the programmer.

In more recent programming systems, such as LISP, a method known as *garbage collection* is used. All active lists declared in these languages are linked together, so that at any point an executive program can trace links and determine all active memory locations. Then, when available space is exhausted, a garbage-collection program is called to do the link tracing. As this program scans the links, it tags each memory location with a special bit if it is an element of an active list. All untagged locations are then known to be garbage and are reclaimed into a free-storage list. The garbage-collection process is invisible to the programmer.

REFERENCES

Although many of the early computer scientists deserve to share credit for linked data structures, the most extensive work was done by Simon, Newell, and Shaw. They originated a novel programming language called IPL-V, in which the only data structures available were linked lists and push-down stacks (cf. Newell and Shaw, 1957; Shaw et al., 1958; Newell, 1961). This language greatly influenced subsequent languages invented for manipulating nonnumerical information. Current trends in language development suggest that the notion of linked data structures is too fundamental to be compartmentalized in the field of nonnumeric processing. Recent languages, such as PL/I and the proposed successors to ALGOL, include capabilities for building linked lists and presume an underlying garbage-collection processor for storage reclamation (Wirth and Hoare, 1966; Van Wijngaarden et al., 1968). Ross's article on data structures, which he called *plexes*, marks one of the early references to threaded lists (Ross, 1961).

Techniques for storage management and garbage collection in programming systems that use linked data structures have been developed in parallel with the linked data structures. Simon, Newell, and Shaw are usually credited with the idea of placing all unused memory on a list from which cells can be allocated as needed. IPL-V did not have an automatic garbage-collection algorithm, but depended on the programmer to return each cell to the free-storage list as it became available. An excellent description of garbage-collection algorithms, the subtle constraints on them, and the history of their development appears in Knuth (1968).

EXERCISES

9·1 Let X be a large two-dimensional array—say, 1000×1000—and assume that it is sparse in the sense that very few of its elements are not 0. Construct a data structure for X that requires an amount of memory proportional to the number of nonzero elements of X. Write a subroutine in an ALGOL-like language for finding the value of X[I,J], given I and J.

9·2 Let X be a given number, and let L be a list of numbers, one of which is X. If L is represented as a one-way linked list, and it is equally likely that X is any one of the elements of L, then what is the average number of elements that must be scanned to find which one is X? Find the average when X has probability p of being on the list and probability $1 - p$ of not being on the list. Assume that if X is on the list, it has equal probability of being anywhere on the list.

9·3 Let L be a one-way linked list. Write subroutines in an ALGOL-like language for appending a new element to the end of the list and for creating a new one-way linked list that contains the elements of L in reverse order.

9·4 Construct a linked-list representation of a queue. Write subroutines in an ALGOL-like language for PUT and GET processes for the queue.

9·5 Let L be a list such that each element of L is itself a list. We call the second-level lists *sublists* of L. Write a subroutine in an ALGOL-like language that constructs a new list which contains a copy of every item that is on two or more sublists of L.

9·6 Repeat Exercise 9·5, but instead of creating a new list, use threaded links to link together every reference to the same item.

9·7 Suppose it is necessary to be able to add items efficiently to the head of a list, as well as to the end. Show that this can be done efficiently with one-way linked lists by maintaining two pointers to the list, one to the head and one to the tail.

9·8 Let L be a list, and let each of its elements be a list that contains numbers from the set $\{1, 2, \ldots, N\}$. Assume that no number appears on more than one sublist of L.

    a. Write a subroutine in an ALGOL-like program that merges two specified sublists of L into a single sublist of L (L should have one less sublist after the merge operation).

    b. Write a subroutine that can determine, for a specified pair of sublists, if there exists an integer I on one sublist and an integer I+1 on the other.

    c. Write a subroutine that adds a threaded link to L, beginning with the number 1 and tracing through the integers in numerical order.

10

Rooted Trees, Recursive Programs, and Push-down Stack Machines

The title of this chapter suggests a composite discussion of three widely separated topics. Actually these three topics are quite closely related. The rooted tree is a graphic flow diagram of a recursive program, and the stack machine is the natural vehicle for executing the recursive program.

10·1 Rooted Trees

Rooted-tree data structures are generalizations of linear arrays and linear linked lists. Rooted trees are useful in many algorithms for which the linear data structures do not support efficient processing. In this section we shall examine some of the properties of such trees and discuss methods for using them in data structures.

Figure 10·1 exemplifies the class of graphs called *rooted trees*, informally defined as follows:

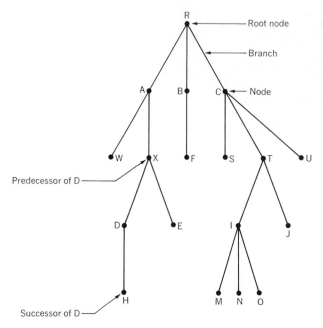

Figure 10·1 A typical rooted tree

Rooted Tree A graph that consists of a collection of nodes and branches, with each branch connecting two nodes. The branch relates the two nodes at its ends such that the node at the upper end of the branch is identified as a *predecessor* of the node at the lower end of the branch. If node **x** is the predecessor of node **y**, then node **y** is said to be a *successor* of node **x**.

A rooted tree also satisfies the following properties:

1. There is a unique node (the *root*) which has no predecessor.

2. Every node other than the root has precisely one predecessor.

3. Every node other than the root is connected to the root by a (unique) path such that the path begins at the root and ends at the node, and such that each node on the path other than the root is the successor of the previous node on the path.

There are no closed loops in rooted trees. For the remainder of this chapter we shall use *tree* to mean rooted tree.

In the tree shown in Figure 10·1 the successors of node T are nodes I and J, and the predecessor of node T is node C. The unique path from the root, node R, to node T is the path R C T.

We have had occasion to make use of trees in earlier chapters. Recall, for example, the data structure for multidimensional arrays using indirection. An example of interest to us is the representation of arithmetic expressions in tree form, as illustrated in Figure 10·2. In forming these graphs we use interior nodes (nodes with successors) to represent the operations $\{+, -, *, /\}$, where each of the successors of an interior node is an operand. Note that some operands are themselves expressions. The leaves of the trees (nodes without successors) are simple variables indicated by A, B, C, ...

Note that each interior node is the root of a tree that consists of the interior node, its successors, the successors of its successors, their successors, etc. We call such a tree a *subtree* of the original tree. There are also subtrees associated with each *leaf* in the tree, namely the subtree that consists of just a leaf by itself.

With each node is associated an integer called the *level* of the node, which is defined to be 1 greater than the length of the unique path in the tree that is directed from the root to the node. By definition, the level of the root is 1, the level of its successors is 2, the level of the successors of the successors is 3, etc. In Figure 10·1 node R is at level 1 and node X is at level 3.

The *degree* of a node is the number of successors of a node. Thus the leaves of a tree have degree 0. In Figure 10·1 node I has degree 3 and node T has degree 2.

An interior node of a tree is called a *branch node*. If a tree has n nodes, then it has $n - 1$ branches. This is because every node except the root has a predecessor, so that there are $n - 1$ nodes with predecessors in the tree. Each predecessor-successor pair is identified with a unique branch.

An *ordered tree* is a tree in which the successors of each node are ordered. For example, in Figure 10·1, if we order the successors of a node from left to right, then node S is the first successor of node C, node T is the second successor, and node U is the third successor.

A special class of trees that is very important for the representation of data is the class known as *binary trees*. Specifically, a binary tree is a rooted tree in which every node has no more than two successors. Moreover, each successor of a node is identified as a *left successor* or a *right successor*, and no node may have two left successors or two right successors. We draw binary trees by slanting branches to the left for left successors and to the right for right successors, so

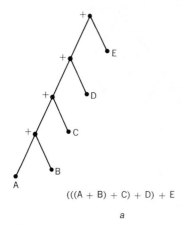

$$(((A + B) + C) + D) + E$$

a

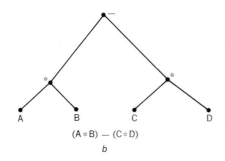

$$(A * B) - (C * D)$$

b

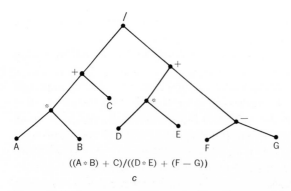

$$((A * B) + C)/((D * E) + (F - G))$$

c

Figure 10·2   Tree representations of arithmetic expressions

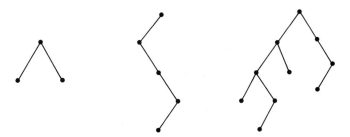

Figure 10·3 Examples of binary trees

that the successor type can be determined by inspection of the drawing. Figure 10·3 shows examples of binary trees.

10·2 Traversing Binary Trees

A *traversal* of a data structure is a scan through the data structure such that each element is examined exactly once. If we consider trees to be a generalization of arrays, then we must find ways to traverse trees in much the same way that the following ALGOL statement allows us to examine each element of the array A:

```
for i := 1 step 1 until N do
    examine(A[i]);
```

An equally natural way to examine arrays is to start at N and index backward through the array.

The corresponding process for trees is best explained for binary trees. Later we shall see how any ordered rooted tree can be represented by a binary tree, so that the traversals presented here are completely general. This presentation follows that of Knuth (1968).

The natural methods for traversing a tree require that we break the tree into three disjoint components: the root, the left subtree of the root, and the right subtree of the root. Tree-traversal algorithms specify the order in which these components are traversed. Since each subtree of the root is again a tree, it too can be broken into a root and a left and right subtree, which are to be traversed in the same specified order. Thus subtrees are broken into smaller and smaller components, until every component has only one node. At this point we have determined the order in which the entire set of nodes is visited.

223

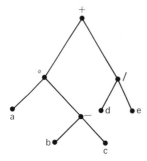

Figure 10·4   Tree representation of a*(b — c) + d/e

The first traversal algorithm, that for postorder traversal, can be informally stated as follows:

Postorder Traversal   Visit the nodes in an order such that, for any node V in the tree, all the nodes in the left subtree of V are visited before V, and all the nodes in the right subtree of V are visited after V.

To traverse the tree in Figure 10·4 in postorder we visit all the nodes in the left subtree of +, then +, and then all the nodes in the right subtree of +. The nodes visited before + have to be visited in the order such that the nodes in the left subtree of * are visited, then *, and then the nodes in the right subtree of *. By following this line of reasoning, the postorder traversal of Figure 10·4 is found to be

$$a*b-c+d/e$$

To simplify the description of the postorder-traversal algorithm, we write it as follows:

Postorder Traversal

1. Traverse the left subtree in postorder.

2. Visit the root.

3. Traverse the right subtree in postorder.

Two other traversal algorithms are of importance to us:

Preorder Traversal

1. Visit the root.

2. Traverse the left subtree in preorder.

3. Traverse the right subtree in preorder.

End-order Traversal

1. Traverse the left subtree in endorder.

2. Traverse the right subtree in endorder.

3. Visit the root.

Traversal of Figure 10·4 in postorder, preorder, and endorder causes the nodes in the tree to be visited in sequence as follows:

Postorder	$a*b-c+d/e$
Preorder	$+*a-bc/de$
Endorder	$abc-*de/+$

In all three cases the relative order in which the leaves are visited is the same. The essential difference in the traversal methods has to do with the sequence in which the branch nodes are visited in relation to each other and in relation to the leaves. Preorder indicates that the root is visited before the left subtree, and postorder indicates that the root is visited after the left subtree. Of the three traversal schemes, the first two are the most important.

The algorithm in Example 10·1 traverses a tree in postorder. By assumption, the tree is represented in the array A, so that all the information about node i in the tree is stored in A[i] as packed data. The notation A[i].leftlink refers to the portion of the data in A[i] that is a link to the left successor of node i and is meant to suggest that the left successor link of node i will be found by unpacking the data in A[i] as described in Chapter 6. Similarly, A[i].rightlink is a link to the right successor of node i. A link in this example is the index of the successor in the array A. Thus if node 10 is a left successor of node 5, then A[5].leftlink has the value 10.

When the tree in Figure 10·4 is represented as shown in Table 10·1, the postorder algorithm produces the results shown in Table 10·2. Table 10·2 lists the state of the stack at the time each node is examined.

The reason Example 10·1 is a correct algorithm is that it reflects the recursive structure of the tree. The order in which nodes are processed is left subtree, root, right subtree. Since a subtree is itself a tree, the instructions for processing the subtrees are precisely the

EXAMPLE 10·1

The procedure PUSHDOWN and POPUP are push-down stack procedures. POPUP has two parameters in this case, rather than one. The first parameter of POPUP receives a copy of the top of the stack before the stack is popped. The second parameter is a label to which POPUP returns if a stack underflow occurs when the stack is popped.

```
Procedure postorder(A);
array A;
comment root of tree is in A[1], left subtree and right subtree are pointed to
by indices contained in A[1].leftlink and A[1].rightlink, respectively;
begin integer i;
    clearstack;
    comment the above procedure clears the push-down stack;
    i := 1;
checkrootempty:
    comment 0 denotes an empty link;
    if i = 0 then go to returntopredecessor;
    PUSHDOWN(i);
    i := A[i].leftlink;
    go to checkrootempty;
returntopredecessor:
    POPUP(i,exitifunderflow);
    examine(A[i]);
    i := A[i].rightlink;
    go to checkrootempty;
exitifunderflow:
comment when stack underflows algorithm terminates here;
end;
```

same as those for processing the tree that contains the two subtrees. Note how the PUSHDOWN and POPUP procedures are used to store and recover the pointer to the root. The pointers must be recovered in last-in-first-out order, so the stack is the appropriate data structure for storing the pointers.

The binary trees as we have represented them are a natural generalization of the one-way linked list. In traversing trees it is the usual case to traverse them both from top to bottom and from bottom to top. Hence a more appropriate representation of a binary tree would be a generalization of the two-way linked list or of the circular

Table 10·1 Representation of the tree in Figure 10·4

INDEX	NODE	LEFT LINK	RIGHT LINK
1	+	2	3
2	*	4	5
3	/	6	7
4	a	0	0
5	−	8	9
6	d	0	0
7	e	0	0
8	b	0	0
9	c	0	0

list. In Example 10·1 we used the push-down stack to remember pointers that are needed when we traverse the tree in the opposite direction from the pointers. We can avoid the push-down stack by using special pointers, similar to those in circular lists, that point back into the tree. These special pointers allow us to traverse counter to the direction of the standard pointers. This pointer structure,

Table 10·2 State of the push-down stack during execution of the postorder algorithm

i	EXAMINE(A[i])	STACK
4	a	2(*)
		1(+)
2	*	1(+)
8	b	5(−)
		1(+)
5	−	1(+)
9	c	1(+)
1	+	empty
6	d	3(/)
3	/	empty
7	e	empty

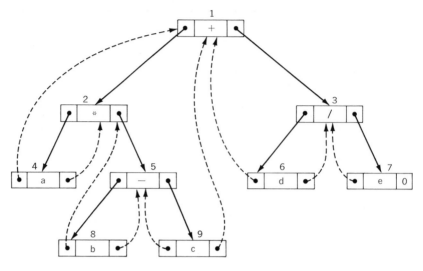

Figure 10·5 Threaded tree representation of Figure 10·4

credited to A. J. Perlis and C. Thornton (1960), is known as a *threaded tree*. Example 10·2 shows how to traverse a threaded tree.

Figure 10·5 illustrates the data structure that is traversed. Links in the tree that would normally be empty are replaced by links into the tree, shown as dashed lines. Dashed lines pointing left are directed from a node n to the node that is the predecessor of n in postorder. Dashed lines pointing right point to the successor of n in postorder. For this procedure to recognize a halting condition, the rightmost dashed link in Figure 10·5 is set to 0 and the leftmost dashed link points to the tree root. Dashed links are distinguished from ordinary links by examining A[i].lefttag and A[i].righttag. The 0 tag denotes a dashed link. If the tree is stored so that successors have higher indices than predecessors, then a magnitude comparison can be used instead.

Table 10·3 shows a data structure for the threaded tree in Figure 10·5, and Table 10·4 illustrates the values of intermediate variables in the threaded postorder procedure as it processes this tree. The values are shown at each point a tag is tested.

The importance of the schemes for traversing binary trees arises from the fact that binary trees can be used to represent arbitrary ordered trees. An example is shown in Figure 10·6. To be more precise, the representation is constructed to satisfy certain properties. If T

EXAMPLE 10·2

```
procedure threadedpostorder(A);
array A;
comment A[1] contains the root. If A[i].lefttag is 1, then A[i].leftlink points to
the left subtree, otherwise the tag is 0 and the link points to the prede-
cessor of the node in postorder. Similarly, A[i].rightlink points to a right
subtree or the successor of A[i] in postorder;
begin integer i, savei;
    i := 1;
traceleft:
    if A[i].lefttag ≠ 0 then
        begin comment move down the chain of left successors;
            i := A[i].leftlink;
            go to traceleft;
        end;
check:
    if i = 0 then go to exit;
    comment 0 link indicates end of tree;
    examine(A[i]);
    savei := i;
    i := A[i].rightlink;
    if A[savei].righttag = 0 then go to check;
    comment 0 indicates a thread. In this case we have the correct successor;
    go to traceleft;
    comment 1 indicates normal link, follow chain of left successors;
exit:
end procedure threadedpostorder;
```

Table 10·3 Representation of the threaded tree in Figure 10·5

INDEX	NODE	LEFT TAG	LEFT LINK	RIGHT TAG	RIGHT LINK
1	+	1	2	1	3
2	*	1	4	1	5
3	/	1	6	1	7
4	a	0	1	0	2
5	—	1	8	1	9
6	d	0	1	0	3
7	e	0	3	0	0
8	b	0	2	0	5
9	c	0	5	0	1

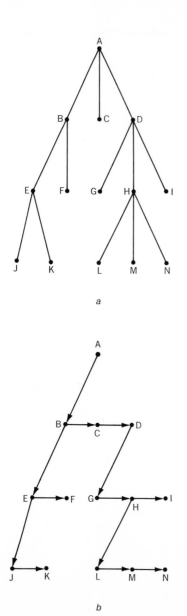

a

b

Figure 10·6 Representation of an ordered rooted tree by a binary tree

Table 10·4 Trace of the execution of the threaded-post-order algorithm

i	LEFT TAG	RIGHT TAG	NEXT i	EXAMINE
1	1		2	
2	1		4	
4	0			a
4		0	2	
2		1	5	*
5	1		8	
8	0			b
8		0	5	
5		1	9	—
9	0			c
9		0	1	
1		1	3	+
3	1		6	
6	0			d
6		0	3	
3	1		7	/
7	0			e
7		0	0	

is an ordered tree, then its representation as a binary tree T′ is as follows:

1. There is a one-to-one correspondence between the nodes in T and the nodes in T′.

2. The first successor of a node in T is the left successor of the corresponding node in T′.

3. The second to nth successors of a node N in T are linked in order in T′ as a chain of right successors. The chain begins at the node in T′ that corresponds to the first successor of N.

Thus to visit the successors of a node in the ordered tree when dealing with the binary representation of the ordered tree, we visit the left successor of the node in the binary tree and then follow the chain of right successors. The binary-tree representation as described here is commonly used for list representations in the programming language LISP. We shall have more to say about binary representation of trees with respect to arithmetic expressions later in the chapter.

10·3 Recursive Programs

Example 10·1 is an iterative program for an algorithm that is easily programmed recursively. In this section we shall explore the concept of recursion and then show methods for implementing recursion in computer programs. Finally we shall relate the flow of control in recursive algorithms to tree structures. To clarify the concept of recursion let us first consider a recursive definition of a function, and then the recursive algorithm for computing this function (Example 10·3).

The term *recursion* indicates that the definition of the function f is defined to invoke properties of itself in an essential way. Recursive definition is valid if the definition includes a basis part which defines the function for some value of its arguments independent of the definition of the function for other arguments, and if the function for all other values of its arguments can be determined from the basis definition.

EXAMPLE 10·3

The recursive definition of $f(x)$ is

$$f(0) = 1$$

$$f(x) = \begin{cases} x \cdot f(x-1) & \text{for integral } x \geq 1 \\ \text{undefined} & \text{otherwise} \end{cases}$$

The ALGOL program to compute $f(x)$ is as follows:

```
integer procedure f(x);
integer x;
begin if x < 0 then f := ∞
      else
          if x = 0 then f := 1
          else
              f := x*f(x − 1);
end procedure f;
```

In the example above $f(0) = 1$ is the basis part of the definition. According to the recursive part, to find the value of the function for any positive-integer argument we must know the value of the function for the next lowest integer. Thus to evaluate $f(x)$ for $x = 10$ we must know $f(9)$; this implies that we must know $f(8)$, etc., until we finally find that $f(1)$ is defined in terms of $f(0)$, which is defined by the basis part of the definition. In spite of the apparent circularity of the definition, we see that the function is truly well defined. What function have we defined?

For every recursive subroutine there must be some set of parameter values for which the subroutine does not call itself recursively. This corresponds to the basis part of a recursive definition. In Example 10·3 no recursive call occurs for $x = 0$. If x is greater than 0, the sequence of recursive calls decreases x until we find the value of $f(0)$, and then all the other values are defined in terms of $f(0)$. If a recursive subroutine calls itself regardless of the values of the parameters, then the subroutine can never reach its exit.

With respect to Example 10·1, we can trivially derive a recursive formulation for algorithms for traversing a binary in preorder, postorder, or endorder.

EXAMPLE 10·4

The following example illustrates tree traversal in postorder:

```
procedure postorder(i);

integer i;

comment A[i] is the root of a tree. Its subtrees are identified by A[i].leftlink
and A[i].rightlink;

begin
    if A[i].leftlink ≠ 0 then postorder(A[i].leftlink);
    examine(A[i]);
    if A[i].rightlink ≠ 0 then postorder(A[i].rightlink);

end procedure postorder;

comment to traverse a tree with root at A[1] use the call "postorder(1)" in
the calling program;
```

The procedure in Example 10·4 can be modified trivially for preorder traversal by exchanging lines 1 and 2 of the procedure body. An exchange of lines 2 and 3 yields a procedure for endorder traversal.

Now we come to the problem of the implementation of recursive procedures in assembly language. If we examine Examples 10·3 and 10·4 carefully we note two potential problems that might arise in a direct translation to assembly language. One is that of saving the return address, and the other is that of saving parameters passed to procedures. Let us consider these problems separately.

Since a recursive procedure can be entered two or more times without an intervening exit, and since the return addresses associated with the entries need not be the same, in general, we cannot use a single memory-storage location for holding return addresses. The natural storage mechanism for saving return addresses is the push-down stack, because the return addresses must be recovered in a last-in-first-out order.

Similarly, sets of parameters cannot be stored in an area that is just large enough to hold one parameter set, where by *parameter set* we mean a set of N values for a procedure that has N arguments. When a parameter set is passed to a recursive procedure it must be stored in a private area, because a recursive call will cause an entirely new set of parameters to be passed, and the new set cannot be allowed to destroy the old set. When a procedure that has been entered recursively reaches an exit, the newest set of parameters is thrown away, and the previous set of parameters becomes current. In fact the sets of parameters must be recovered on a last-in-first-out basis. Consequently the push-down stack is the appropriate storage medium for passing parameters. The methods for using a push-down stack for parameter passing and storing return addresses were discussed in Chapter 7.

One last consideration is important for program implementation. Recursive programs must not be self-modifying in such a way that program self-modification from one entry of the procedure causes the program to misbehave if a recursive entry occurs. This is generally taken to mean that recursive programs must never modify themselves —that is, recursive programs must be reentrant.

The following example shows canonical methods for implementing recursive procedures in assembly language for the HP 2116 and System/360-370 computers.

Figure 10·7 shows the state of the push-down stack during the execution of the instructions in Example 10·5. At RECUR, the subroutine entry point, the top N items in the stack are the N parameters of the subroutine, with the first parameter at the top and the last parameter $N - 1$ words below the top. The first action in RECUR is to push down the return address. After the return address is saved in the stack, the ith parameter can be accessed by decrementing the stack

EXAMPLE 10·5

The following instructions are in HP 2116 assembly language. PUSH and POP are stack procedures, and POINT is the current pointer to the top of the stack.

LABEL	CODE	OPERAND	COMMENTS
RECUR	NOP		Entry to recursive procedure.
	LDA	*—1	Load return address into A register.
	JSB	PUSH	Push down A register (return address).
	. . .		
	LDA	N	Sequence of code to find Nth argument. Argument N is at MEMORY[POINT—N].
	CMA,INA		
	ADA	POINT	POINT—N now in A register.
	LDA	A,I	MEMORY[POINT—N] now in A register.
	. . .		
	LDA	ARGN	Sequence of instructions for passing arguments in stack for a recursive call.
	JSB	PUSH	Last argument stacked.
	. . .		
	LDA	ARG1	
	JSB	PUSH	First argument stacked.
	JSB	RECUR	Recursive call.
	. . .		
	JSB	POP	Preparation for exit. Return address is now in A register.
	STA	RECUR	Store return address while stack is popped.
	LDB	MINUSN	—N, the number of parameters, is placed in B register.
	JSB	POP	Pop the stack N times. A special subroutine might replace this loop.
	ISZ	B	Increment B register, skip if 0.
	JMP	*—2	
	JMP	RECUR,I	Exit.

The program below is the System/360-370 version of a recursive program. PUSH and POP are the stack subroutines, and both use REG[PARAM] for their parameter.

LABEL	CODE	OPERAND	COMMENTS
	. . .		
PARAM	EQU	1	The parameter register for PUSH and POP subroutines.
POINT	EQU	10	The stack pointer.
RET	EQU	14	The return-address register.
TEMP	EQU	6	A temporary register.
RECUR	LR	PARAM,RET	Entry point. Return address is in REG[RET], prepare to stack it.
	BAL	RET,PUSH	Push down contents of REG[PARAM]—that is, stack return address.
	. . .		
	L	TEMP,N	Beginning of a sequence of instructions to access Nth parameter.
	SLA	TEMP,2	Multiply N by 4, the number of bytes per full word.
	LCR	TEMP,TEMP	Negate to create a decrement.
	AR	TEMP,POINT	Add stack pointer, we now point to the Nth parameter.
	L	TEMP,0(TEMP)	Load the parameter into REG[TEMP].
	. . .		
	L	PARAM,ARGN	Beginning of sequence of instructions for a recursive call on RECUR, loads last parameter for the call.
	BAL	RET,PUSH	Push down last parameter.
	. . .		
	L	PARAM,ARG1	Load first parameter.
	BAL	RET,PUSH	Push down first parameter.
	BAL	RET,RECUR	Call RECUR recursively.
	. . .		
	BAL	RET,POP	Sequence of instructions for exit, pop up return address and place in REG[PARAM].
	A	POINT,MINUS4N	Move stack pointer below parameters for this call. MINUS4N = −4·N.
	BR	PARAM	Exit to address in REG[PARAM].

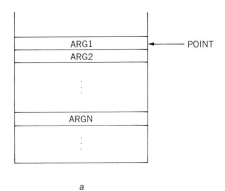

a

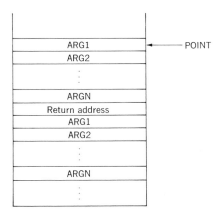

b

c

Figure 10·7 The state of the push-down stack for recursive subroutine RECUR: (a) at entry point and (b) after saving return address. To access the Nth parameter in this state decrement the stack pointer by N. (c) Parameters in stack for a recursive call

pointer by i words, as indicated in the example. When we call the subroutine recursively, we place N new parameters on top of the stack, without destroying the previous parameters. The recursive call is a subroutine call to RECUR, at which point the new return address is placed on the stack. In Example 10·5, at the exit point we first remove the return address from the stack, and then we eliminate the N parameters from the stack by decrementing the stack pointer. The state of the stack after a return from RECUR is identical to the state of the stack just prior to a call on RECUR.

It is interesting to see how several of the concepts introduced in this chapter and in previous chapters are brought together in Example 10·5. These concepts form a basic set of tools for the construction of intricate and rather powerful computer programs.

Before leaving this section we should consider one final relationship of recursive procedures to rooted trees. Compare the rooted trees in Figure 10·2 to the recursive algorithm for postorder traversal in Example 10·4. Each tree provides a graphic representation of the activity of the algorithm when the computation is complete. At any point in the computation the node in process is represented by a node in the tree, and the contents of the push-down stack reflect the unique path in the tree from the root node to the current node. Consequently the maximum stack depth attained during a computation is equal to the maximum level of a leaf in the tree. Every recursive procedure can be represented by a tree like those in Figure 10·2. This is because a predecessor-successor relationship is implied in the recursive definition of a function. In Example 10·3, f(x−1) may be viewed as the successor of f(x). In Example 10·4, f(i.leftlink) and f(i.rightlink) are the successors of f(i).

10·4   Stack Instruction Sets

In this section we shall examine an entirely different concept in machine instructions, the *stack instruction set*. With such an instruction set we can use postorder representations of binary trees, which in turn represent arithmetic expressions. The postorder representation is, in fact, a program for evaluating an arithmetic expression.

The central notion of the stack instruction set is that for each ordered tree there exists a representation of that tree in a linear string of symbols such that the tree can be reconstructed from its linear representation. For each arithmetic expression we shall construct the linearized form of its tree, and that linearized form is a program for evaluating the expression for a stack machine.

To obtain the linearized representation of an arithmetic expression, we perform the following steps:

1. Represent the arithmetic expression as an ordered rooted tree.

2. Represent the ordered root tree as a binary tree, as described in Section 10·2 and Figure 10·6.

3. Traverse the binary tree in postorder. Each time a node is visited, add a symbol for that node to the right end of the linear representation of the tree.

The examples below show the linear representations for typical arithmetic expressions. The ordered rooted tree and binary tree for each expression are shown in Figure 10·8. Our common notation for arith-

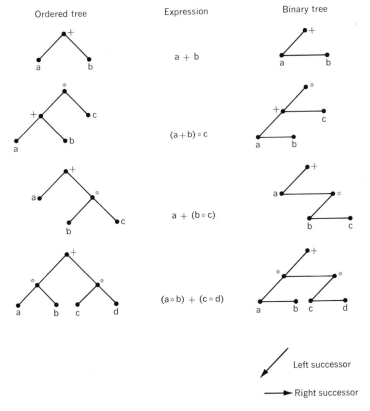

Ordered tree	Expression	Binary tree
	a + b	
	(a+b) ∗ c	
	a + (b ∗ c)	
	(a ∗ b) + (c ∗ d)	

Left successor

Right successor

Figure 10·8 Ordered trees for arithmetic expressions and their corresponding binary trees

metic expressions is called *infix notation,* and the linearized form of the tree representation is called *postfix notation* or *Polish notation* (in tribute to the Polish mathematician Jan Łukasiewicz).

Infix	a+b	(a+b)*c	a+(b*c)	a*b+c*d
Postfix	ab+	ab+c*	abc*+	ab*cd*+

The important aspect of postfix notation is that no parentheses are needed to represent arithmetic expressions. Infix notations must resort to parentheses or some other artifice to reconcile the inherent ambiguity in expressions such as $a + b*c$.

All the arithmetic operators that we use in this chapter are binary operators in the sense that each requires two operands. We can represent nodes of arbitrary degree uniquely in Polish notation, provided that we specify the degree of each operator node. For example, if $\oplus$ represents the operator that forms the sum of three quantities, then the expression

$$\frac{a + b}{\oplus(x,y,z)}$$

has the linearized representation

Entity	a	b	$+$	x	y	z	$\oplus$	$/$
Degree	0	0	2	0	0	0	3	2

The nodes of degree 0 are the leaves of the tree.

Let us now see how the linearized representation can be used to reconstruct the ordered-tree representation. Suppose that we are given a linear string of symbols, and that each symbol has a degree associated with it. The following algorithm translates the linear representation into an ordered rooted tree:

1. Starting with the leftmost symbol in the string, repeat step 2 for each symbol in the string, scanning from left to right, and then terminate the algorithm.

2. If the symbol has degree 0, do steps 3 and 4, otherwise do steps 5 to 7.

3. Create a leaf of the tree labeled by the present symbol.

4. Add the symbol to a push-down stack and then terminate the processing of the present symbol.

5. Create a branch node of the tree labeled by this symbol.

6. Let the node have degree n. The n successors of the branch node are obtained by popping up the stack n times and noting the symbols that appear. The nth successor appears first, the $(n-1)$st appears next, and the first successor appears last.

7. Add the present symbol to a push-down stack and terminate the processing of the present symbol.

The unique characterization is the key to the use of linear representations in stack instruction sets. With this in mind, let us postulate a computer with a push-down stack and the following instructions in its instruction repertoire:

VAL	X	The value of X is placed on the top of the push-down stack.
ADD		The top two entries on the stack are replaced by a single item equal to their sum.
MUL		The same as ADD, except the product replaces the top two entries.
DIV		The same as above, except that STACK[TOP−1]/STACK[TOP] replaces the top two items.
SUB		STACK[TOP−1]−STACK[TOP] replaces the top two items.

With this instruction set, the program to compute

$$\frac{ax^2 + bx + c}{dy + e}$$

can be obtained directly from the postfix representation

$$axx**bx*+c+dy*e+/$$

The program is

```
VAL    a
VAL    x
VAL    x
MUL
MUL
VAL    b
. . .
```

The correct operation of the stack computer depends on the fact that the computer treats VAL as a degree-0 operator and the other operators as degree-2 operators. Degree-0 operators are executed by stacking an item, and degree-n operators for $n > 0$ are executed by replacing the n items at the top of the stack by a single item. Note how this corresponds to the algorithm for constructing an ordered tree from its linear representation.

The instruction set can be extended to include stack equivalents of all the common operators. Among these are

NAME	X	Load name of X to top of stack.
STO		Store top of stack at address given by STACK[TOP—1] and delete both entries.

Now we can form assignment statements. For example,

$$z := a + b + c * d$$

becomes

NAME	z
VAL	a
VAL	b
ADD	
VAL	c
VAL	d
MUL	
ADD	
STO	

To clarify the operation of the machine, simulate the behavior of the stack machine for this example.

Relational operators and conditional branches make use of the following operators:

EQU	Top two items of the stack are compared for equality. If they are equal, the value **true** replaces the top entries, otherwise the value **false** replaces the top two entries.
LSS	Top two items of the stack are compared numerically. If the next-to-top item is less than the top item, the value **true** replaces the top two entries, otherwise the value **false** replaces the top two entries.

$$\left.\begin{array}{l} \text{NEQ} \\ \text{GEQ} \\ \text{LEQ} \\ \text{GTR} \end{array}\right\}$$ The other relational operators.

JMP   label   The program branches unconditionally to label, no stack action occurs.

JT   label   Conditional jump if **true** to label. If the value at the top of the stack is **true,** a jump occurs, otherwise no jump occurs. In either case stack is popped once.

JF   label   Conditional jump if **false** to label. Execution similar to JT.

Before we consider the use of these instructions let us make note of the following instructions for aiding subroutine communication:

CALL   F   Branch to subroutine at location F, store return address at top of stack.

XCH   Exchange top two cells of stack.

RET   n   Return to address at top of stack. Prior to the return pop up stack by n entries (this deletes $n-1$ arguments in stack)

MARK   x   Store name currently at top of stack in location x (used to reference subroutine arguments when top of stack changes).

Now turn to Example 10·6, a program written in the stack instruction repertoire, translated from Example 10·3.

TOP is the current value of the stack pointer; it points to the last item entered in the stack. We use the value of the stack pointer at the entry point of the subroutine as a reference point, q, to access temporary variables and parameters in the stack. Since recursive calls ordinarily destroy this reference point, the example shows how to save the reference-point value by storing it in the stack when a subroutine is entered and restoring it from the stack at the subroutine exit.

At the entry of the subroutine the stack is assumed to have the return address at the top of the stack and the value of the parameter at the next to the top of the stack. The first two instructions store the stack reference pointer at the top of the stack and initialize it to indicate the new top of the stack. Figure 10·9 shows the condition of the stack just before entry into this subroutine, after the execution of the first two instructions, when the instruction labeled exit is reached and when the RET instruction is reached. Note how q, the stack reference pointer, is saved and restored. Note also how the parameter x is accessed in relation to q.

243

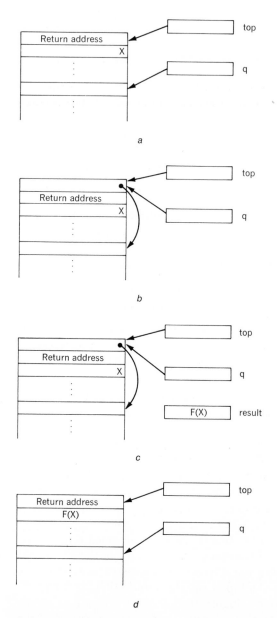

Figure 10·9 The state of the push-down stack during the execution of Example 10·6: (a) at entry to subroutine, (b) after first two instructions, (c) at exit label, and (d) before RET is executed

EXAMPLE 10·6

In the instructions below x[y] means that the effective memory address at execution time is determined by computing the value of MEMORY[x]+y.

	LABEL	CODE	OPERAND	COMMENTS
1.	F	VAL	q	Present value of q is saved in stack.
2.		MARK	q	TOP is stored in q. Now q[0] contains the old value of q, q[−1] contains the return address, and q[−2] contains x.
3.		VAL	q[−2]	Bring x to top of stack.
4.		VAL	zero	Compare x to 0.
5.		LSS		
6.		JF	next	Jump if x $\geq$ 0.
7.		NAME	result	Fetch the name of result.
8.		VAL	infinity	Fetch infinity.
9.		STO		Store infinity into result and exit.
10.		JMP	exit	
11.	next	VAL	q[−2]	Fetch x.
12.		VAL	zero	Fetch 0 and compare to x.
13.		EQU		
14.		JF	recur	Jump if x $\neq$ 0.
15.		NAME	result	Set result to 1.
16.		VAL	one	
17.		STO		
18.		JMP	exit	Jump to exit.
19.	recur	NAME	result	Compute result = x∗F(x−1); place name of result on stack.
20.		VAL	q[−2]	Place x on stack.
21.		VAL	q[−2]	Compute x − 1 and pass it to F.
22.		VAL	one	
23.		SUB		
24.		CALL	F	After this call, the top three cells contain F(x−1), x, and name of result.
25.		MUL		Compute x∗F(x−1).
26.		STO		Store in result.

LABEL	CODE	OPERAND	COMMENTS
27. exit	NAME	q[−2]	Leave the result in the cell now occupied by x, it will be left at top of stack when we exit.
28.	VAL	result	
29.	STO		
30.	NAME	q	Restore value of q.
31.	XCH		Before this instruction is executed stack contains name of q followed by old value of q.
32.	STO		
33.	RET	1	Return address is popped off top of stack; new top of stack contains result.

Several machines have been constructed for stack instruction repertoires, although their number is still insignificant. The most prevalent stack machine in the United States is the Burroughs B-5500 computer.

REFERENCES

The originators of the threaded binary tree and the methods for traversing binary trees are Perlis and Thornton (1960). Knuth (1968) provides a thorough and entertaining discussion of the subject which should not be missed by the serious computer scientist. The importance of trees in data structures cannot be attributed to any one application, or even to just a few applications. McCarthy's programming language LISP, invented circa 1959, uses trees as the principal data structure in the language, although trees had been much used in computation for many years before the invention of LISP. The binary search described in the next chapter is based on a tree structure and is also one of the earliest digital-computer algorithms.

The concept of parenthesis-free notation, originated by Łukasiewicz (cf. Łukasiewicz, 1951), has had an important impact on the development of compilers for high-level languages. The notion of the stack machine is a direct outgrowth of parenthesis-free notation. Barton (1961) described a computer with a stack instruction set that was eventually produced as the Burroughs B-5000 and B-5500. The KDF9 computer was the British version of the stack machine and preceded the B-5500 by a few years (Haley, 1962). Current trends in computer hardware indicate that push-down stacks are becoming common, primarily for storing return addresses and parameters for subroutine calls and for saving the status of a processor when an interrupt occurs. However, the stack instruction repertoire for arithmetic processing is still a rarity.

EXERCISES

10·1 Give a nonrecursive algorithm for traversing a binary tree in preorder.

10·2 Give a nonrecursive algorithm for traversing a binary tree in endorder.

10·3 Threaded links can replace empty links in a binary tree without the need for additional memory space. Give two algorithms for traversing a threaded binary tree in preorder. For the first algorithm assume that the threaded links point to the preorder predecessor or successor, and for the second algorithm assume that the threaded links point to the postorder predecessor and successor.

10·4 Convert the following expression into Polish notation:

$$A+B \cdot C \cdot (D+E+F) \cdot G/(H \cdot I \cdot (J+K))+L/M$$

adding parentheses so that the expression is evaluated from left to right wherever a choice exists. That is, show $X+Y+Z$ as $((X+Y)+Z)$, and not as $(X+(Y+Z))$.
a. Show the ordered-tree representation,
b. Show the binary-tree representation of the ordered tree.
c. Show the linearized form.

10·5 Prove that the leaves of a binary tree are always visited in the same order whether the binary tree is traversed in preorder, postorder, or endorder.

10·6 Write a recursive program for the stack machine that computes the function

$$G(x) = \begin{cases} G(x-1) + G(x-2) & \text{if } x \geq 3 \\ 1 & \text{if } x = 2 \\ 0 & \text{if } x = 1 \end{cases}$$

11

Sorting and Searching

Earlier chapters have been devoted to fundamental aspects of computers rather than to their application to the execution of algorithms. In this chapter we shall discuss several different algorithms for sorting and searching. A rather interesting aspect of algorithms is that the strategies are very different from those that might be employed by a human being doing the same task. The intent of this chapter is to introduce techniques that depend heavily on the capabilities and characteristics of computers.

We shall also consider the analysis of algorithms and the use of some basic combinatorial tools for measuring their relative efficiency.

11·1 Sorting

In this section we consider two different techniques for sorting an array of numbers into numerical order. One, the *bubble sort*, is essentially a "quick-and-dirty" technique. The second, *Floyd's tree sort*, is an elegant method of high efficiency. An interesting result of analysis is that the bubble sort can sort N items in a time proportional to N^2, while the tree sort takes a time proportional to $N \log_2 N$. Thus for sufficiently large N the tree sort is guaranteed to be faster than the bubble sort, regardless of the constants of proportionality.

11·1·1 The Bubble Sort   The name *bubble sort* refers to the characteristic that small numbers "float" to the top of an array if they are placed in the bottom. The bubble sort is very simple to implement, which accounts for its popularity. In applications that require the sorting of very large files, however, its low efficiency makes it unacceptable for use.

The bubble-sort algorithm can be described as follows:

1. Set a flag to 0.

2. Scan the data array from one end to another.

3. Examine pairs of numbers in adjacent words, and if the number with the higher index is numerically smaller, exchange the numbers and set the flag to 1.

4. When the scan is completed, examine the flag. If it is not 0, return to step 1 and repeat the process, otherwise exit.

The claim has been made that this algorithm is inefficient. There remains the problem of justifying this claim. To obtain a machine-independent comparison it is necessary to avoid measures that involve the number of instructions executed or the number of memory accesses. Such measures can vary widely among different computer organizations because they depend strongly on the number of processor registers and on the addressing mechanism. When we analyze an algorithm, we use measures that are not biased by machine organization. Consequently for the bubble sort we choose to count the number of times the comparison and conditional exchange are executed in the central loop of the algorithm.

The analysis is somewhat complicated by the fact that the number of data exchanges is a function of the initial arrangement of the data. Therefore it is necessary to perform an analysis that takes into account the various possible arrangements of data. A natural analysis is a worst-case analysis. For this case we find the maximum number of exchanges that can occur. The analysis of the average case is sta-

---

EXAMPLE 11·1

A version of the bubble-sort algorithm in ALGOL is as follows:

```
procedure sort (A,N);
array A;
integer N; comment lower bound of A is 1 and upper bound is N;
begin integer i; boolean flag; real temp;
    loop:
    flag := false;
    for i := 1 step 1 until N—1 do
        begin
            if A[i] > A[i+1] then
            begin comment interchange;
                temp := A[i];
                A[i] := A[i+1];
                A[i+1] := temp;
                flag := true;
            end;
        end;
    comment another iteration is made if flag is true;
    if flag then go to loop;
comment the array is now sorted in ascending numerical order;
end sort;
```

In the simulation of the bubble-sort algorithm given below the values in the array are shown at the beginning of each loop and at the procedure exit. Note that no exchanges are ever made in the last scan.

ARRAY INDEX	PASS 1	PASS 2	PASS 3	EXIT
1	6	3	1	1
2	3	1	3	3
3	1	6	6	6
4	17	17	17	17
5	18	18	18	18
6	26	23	22	22
7	23	22	23	23
8	22	26	26	26

tistical in nature and involves the calculation of the mean number of exchanges. Since the statistical analysis depends on the initial distribution of data, the usual assumption is that all possible arrangements of data are equally likely. In some instances, however, this assumption is not valid, because it may be the case that the data are "almost" sorted with high probability. Thus our statistical analysis may yield results that are inapplicable to specific situations.

Although we shall analyze only the worst case and the average case here, obviously other analyses may be of interest. For example, we may wish to know the variance of the number of exchanges, as well as higher-order statistical functions. For our purposes the worst-case and average-case analyses are sufficient to illuminate the differences in algorithms.

The worst-case analysis of Example 11·1 is rather simple because of the following observation. If the smallest element in the array happens to be in A[N], then it is moved toward A[1] by one position in each pass. After $N - 1$ passes through the array it is in place, and therefore, counting the last pass, N scans of the entire array might be required, thus bounding the number of comparisons and exchanges by $N \cdot (N - 1)$.

The analysis of the mean number of exchanges is messy by comparison. Nevertheless, it is instructive because it illustrates important techniques. Let us assume that the initial values of A are $a_1, a_2, \ldots, a_N$. Given the initial values, we can compute the set of integers $r_1, r_2, \ldots, r_N$, where r_i is defined to be the number of elements that precede a_i in the sequence and that are greater than a_i. We call r_i the *ranking* of a_i. For the sequence of numbers 2,1,4,3, the corresponding sequence of rankings is 0,1,0,1. It should be clear that the number of exchanges depends only on the sequence of rankings. That is, if two initial conditions of the A array are associated with the same ranking sequence, then both initial conditions require the same number of exchanges when they are sorted.

Simple combinatorial theory tells us that there are $N!$ possible rearrangements of a sequence of N numbers. For each of these rearrangements there is a ranking sequence. It is rather interesting to observe that each of these ranking sequences is distinct. Moreover, for each ranking sequence there is a unique permutation of the N numbers. To see this, consider the different values that each r_i can assume. Since no element precedes a_1, r_1 must be 0. Since one element precedes a_2, r_2 may be either 0 or 1. In general $i - 1$ elements precede a_i, so that $0 \leq r_i \leq i-1$. Then r_i can assume i different values. Thus there are no more than $1 \cdot 2 \cdot 3 \cdots N = N!$ ranking sequences of length N, and for each ranking sequence we can construct one of the $N!$ distinct permutations of N numbers. For example, suppose that the ranking sequence is 0,0,2,1. Which permutation of the integers 1 to 4 is described by this ranking sequence? The last integer in the sequence must be 3, because its rank is 1. The third integer must therefore be 1, because it has a rank of 2 with respect to integers 1, 2, and 4. From this line of reasoning the permutation 2,4,1,3 is the unique permutation of the integers 1 to 4 that has the ranking sequence 0,0,2,1. An algorithm for constructing permutations from ranking sequences is the subject of Exercise 11·1.

The notion of ranking sequence permits us to calculate the average number of times that the label loop is passed, which is the number of executions of the main loop of the program. Note that if a particular element has rank m in a permutation, then the main loop will be repeated at least $m + 1$ times during the sort. In fact we see that the main loop is repeated $k + 1$ times when the maximum rank of an element in the A array is equal to k. The average number of iterations of the main loop is therefore given by

$$\text{Average iterations} = \sum_{i=1}^{N} i \cdot \text{Pr}(\text{max rank} = i-1)$$

where $\text{Pr}(\text{max rank} = i-1)$ is the probability that the maximum ranking of a permutation is exactly $i-1$. Following the same notation, we let

$$\text{Pr}(\text{max rank} \geq i-1) = \sum_{j=i-1}^{N-1} \text{Pr}(\text{max rank} = j)$$

Then the summation for the average number of iterations becomes

$$
\begin{aligned}
\text{Average iterations} &= \sum_{i=1}^{N} i \cdot \text{Pr}(\text{max rank} = i-1) \\
&= \sum_{i=1}^{N} \sum_{j=1}^{i} \text{Pr}(\text{max rank} = i-1) \\
&= \sum_{j=1}^{N} \sum_{i=j}^{N} \text{Pr}(\text{max rank} = i-1) \\
&= \sum_{j=1}^{N} \text{Pr}(\text{max rank} \geq j-1) \\
&= \sum_{i=1}^{N} [1 - \text{Pr}(\text{max rank} < i-1)] \\
&= \sum_{i=0}^{N-1} [1 - \text{Pr}(\text{max rank} < i)]
\end{aligned}
$$

Note the limits on the summations in the second and third lines above. It is easily verified that the double summations treat the same pairs of indices i and j. If we assume that all $N!$ permutations of N integers are equally likely, then the term $\Pr(\text{max rank} < i)$ has a simple form.

To find $\Pr(\text{max rank} < i)$ we shall count the number of ranking sequences that have no ranking with a value i or greater. Since the first i rankings of a ranking sequence cannot exceed $i - 1$, we can select the first i rankings in $i!$ different ways. For j in the interval $i+1 \le j \le N$ each r_j can assume any integer value in the interval $0 \le r_j \le i-1$. Thus for each of the last $N - i$ rankings we have i choices of values for the rankings. Therefore the total number of ranking sequences with rankings that do not exceed i is $i! \cdot i^{N-i}$. From this we find

$$\Pr(\text{max rank} < i) = \frac{i! i^{N-i}}{N!}$$

and

$$\text{Average iterations} = \sum_{i=0}^{N-1} \left[1 - \frac{i! i^{N-i}}{N!} \right]$$

$$= N - \frac{1}{N!} \sum_{i=0}^{N-1} i! i^{N-i}$$

The summation term in this formula is rather messy to evaluate. Although it does not lend itself to simplification, Knuth (1968) has found that it approaches

$$\sqrt{\frac{\pi N}{2}} - \frac{5}{3} + \frac{11}{24} \sqrt{\frac{\pi}{2N}} + \cdots$$

asymptotically as N increases. The terms left out of this expansion contain N^{-1} or higher negative powers of N and are therefore dominated by the leading terms of the expansion for large N. Thus we find that the average number of iterations is given by

$$\text{Average iterations} = N - \sqrt{\frac{\pi N}{2}} + \cdots$$

$$\cong N - 1.25 \sqrt{N}$$

Since each iteration involves $N - 1$ comparisons, the average number of comparisons is approximately

$$(N - 1)(N - 1.25 \sqrt{N}) = N^2 - 1.25N^{3/2} - N + 1.25 \sqrt{N}$$

which grows asymptotically like the maximum number of comparisons, $N^2 - N$, as N becomes large. This suggests that it may be more efficient to eliminate the setting and testing of the flag in Example 11·1 and merely iterate the main loop $N - 1$ times. The flag is supposed to help us eliminate unnecessary comparisons, but our analysis indicates that the work expended in maintaining the flag may exceed the work that is saved.

In order to improve the bubble sort we can use a strategy that moves the small numbers toward A[1] as rapidly as the large numbers are moved toward A[N]. This yields Example 11·2 on page 256.

When the algorithm of Example 11·2 is executed on the array A in Example 11·1, array A attains the following states, shown at the statement

temp := A[j+1];

ARRAY INDEX	j = 1	j = 2	j = 6	j = 7	FINISH
1	6	3	1	1	1
2	3	6	3	3	3
3	1	1	6	6	6
4	17	17	17	17	17
5	18	18	18	18	18
6	26	26	26	23	22
7	23	23	23	26	23
8	22	22	22	22	26

In the inner loop of the algorithm, if a small A[j+1] is encountered, then it is moved toward A[1] as far as possible. The outer loop of the algorithm increases j, so that each inner loop treats an array element that has never been scanned before. The branch to the label endiloop is taken when the proper place has been found for the element A[j+1].

The analysis for this algorithm requires only a minor variation of

EXAMPLE 11·2

```
for j := 1 step 1 until N−1 do
if A[j+1] < A[j] then
    begin
    temp := A[j+1];
    for i := j step −1 until 1 do
        begin if  temp ≥ A[i] then go to endiloop;
            A[i+1] := A[i];
        end;
    i := 0;
    endiloop: A[i+1] := temp;
    end;
```

the analysis of Example 11·1. Clearly in the worst case the interchange will always occur. In this case the element that occupies A[j+1] initially will move j places in the inner loop. Then the maximum number of comparisons is given by

$$\text{Maximum comparisons} = \sum_{j=1}^{N-1} j = \frac{N(N-1)}{2}$$

This is exactly half the comparisons for the worst case of Example 11·1.

To find the average number of comparisons we note that if all permutations are equally likely, then all the possible values of the ranking r_j are all equally likely. Moreover, the values of r_j are independent of the values of every other ranking in a sequence. During the jth iteration of the outer loop of the algorithm A[j+1] will be exchanged r_{j+1} times and will be compared $r_{j+1} + 1$ times. The average total number of comparisons is given by a summation of the average number of comparisons for each A[j], where $2 \leq j \leq N$. That is, if we let the average value of r_j be denoted by $\hat{r}_j$, then

$$\text{Average comparisons} = \sum_{j=2}^{N} \hat{r}_j + 1$$

However, it is equally likely that r_j is any integer in the interval $0 \leq r_j \leq j-1$. Thus

$$\hat{r}_j = \frac{1}{j} \sum_{i=0}^{j-1} i = \frac{j-1}{2}$$

Substituting for $\hat{r}_j$ in the above formula yields

$$\text{Average comparisons} = \sum_{j=2}^{N} \frac{j+1}{2} = \frac{(N+4)(N-1)}{4}$$

In comparing the two versions of the bubble-sort algorithm we see that Example 11·1 requires an average number of comparisons that is dominated by N^2, whereas Example 11·2 requires an average that is dominated by $N^2/4$. Thus for sufficiently large N the second bubble-sort algorithm is likely to be 4 times as fast as the first when all permutations of the data are equally likely.

The analyses in this section are typical. Worst-case analyses are a crude, but often revealing, basis for comparing algorithms. Analysis of the average case is generally more accurate, but it is more difficult. In our examples above the N^2 term was dominant in both the average-case and worst-case analyses, although the multiplicative constant for the N^2 term differed. For some algorithms the dominant term for the worst case can differ from that for the average case by more than just a constant coefficient.

Although the analysis in this section indicates that the algorithm of Example 11·2 is better than that of Example 11·1, the next section shows that Example 11·2 is actually not a very good algorithm at all. We shall see that it is possible to sort N numbers with a number of comparisons proportional to $N \log_2 N$, which grows much more slowly with N than does N^2.

11·1·2 Tree Sort

A very interesting sorting algorithm was reported by Floyd (1964). The strategy in this case is to organize the data in the array into a tree in the first phase and then rearrange the tree into a sorted list in the second phase. Both phases can be executed efficiently, which leads to a very efficient algorithm.

Figure 11·1 shows an example of a tree in the form used in Floyd's algorithm. Each node in the graph represents an element of a data array, and the index of the element associated with each node appears as a node label. Each interior node of the tree has one node above it in the tree—a predecessor node—and one or two nodes below it in the tree—successor nodes. The predecessor of A[i] is A[i÷2] (recall that ÷ denotes integer division), and the successors of A[i] are A[2∗i] and A[2∗i+1].

In the first phase of the algorithm a tree is constructed such that each node is numerically greater than or equal to its successors; that is,

A[i] $\geq$ A[2*i] and A[i] $\geq$ A[2*i+1] for all i. This is done by adding new nodes to the tree one at a time. As each node is added, it is compared to its predecessor and exchanged with it if necessary. If an exchange occurs, then the new item is compared with the predecessor of its current position to see whether another exchange must be made. The process of comparing and exchanging continues until a place is found for the new item at a node within the tree such that it is less than its predecessor. The number of exchanges required to insert one item is bounded by the number of levels in the tree rather than by the number of items in the tree. Thus at most $\lfloor \log_2 N \rfloor$ comparisons and exchanges are needed to find the position of a new item when there are N items in the tree ($\lfloor x \rfloor$ is the largest integer not exceeding x).

Figure 11·1 illustrates a case in which the tenth item is to be placed in the tree. First A[10] is compared with its predecessor, A[5]. If A[10] is greater than A[5], then A[5] will be exchanged with A[10], and the new A[5] will be compared to A[2]. If an exchange occurs after this comparison, the new A[2] will be compared to A[1], and an exchange will take place if necessary.

Once the data are arranged in the form of a tree, they can be sorted by comparing and exchanging from the top down rather than from the bottom up. The largest element in the array is in A[1], so that it can be moved to A[N]. When it is moved to A[N], a new Floyd tree is

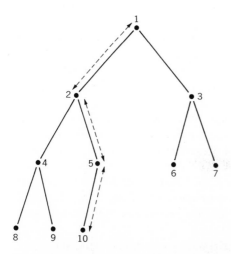

Figure 11·1 Floyd's tree. Dashed lines show comparison which might be made when tenth item is added to tree

formed from the remaining $N - 1$ elements of the tree. The larger of
A[2] and A[3] moves into A[1], and the largest of its successors moves up
one notch in the tree. This process terminates when we find a place
for the element displaced from A[N]. The result of these shifts in the
tree is that the largest number among the $N - 1$ in the new subtree
is found in A[1]. The iteration is repeated by exchanging A[1] and A[N—1]
and forming a new tree with $N - 2$ elements. The entire array is
sorted by finding the largest element among the first i elements of A
and placing this element in position A[i], where the index i runs backward from N to 2.

EXAMPLE 11·3

The following version of Floyd's tree sort is drawn partly from tree sort
and partly from an algorithm called *heap sort*, which stimulated tree sort
and is due to Williams (1964).

```
procedure treesort(A,N);

integer N; array A;

comment the array A is declared [1:N];
    begin
    procedure intree(lim,in);
    integer lim; real in;
    comment procedure for first-phase processing.
    The variable in is the new datum to be placed in the tree;
    begin
        i := llm;
        scan: if i > 1 then
            begin j := i ÷ 2;
                if in > A[j] then
                    begin A[i] := A[j];
                        i := j;
                        go to scan;
                        comment part of an exchange. The variable in is not
                        actually placed into the tree until just prior to exit;
                    end;
            end;
        A[i] := in;
    end procedure intree;
procedure outtree(lim);

integer lim;

comment this procedure finds the largest of the first lim elements in the tree
and places that element in A[1] by exchanging elements along a tree path;
    begin real copy; integer i,j;
```

```
        i := 1;
        copy := A[1];
   loop: j := 2*i;
        if j ≤ lim then
            begin if j ≤ lim then
                begin comment two successors;
                if A[j+1] > A[j] then j := j+1;
                comment select the largest successor;
                end;
            if A[j] > copy then
                begin A[i] := A[j];
                    i := j;
                    comment the larger element is moved up the tree;
                    go to loop;
                end;
            end;
        A[i] := copy;
   end procedure outtree;
   comment the body of procedure treesort begins here;
   integer i; real temp;
        for i := 2 step 1 until N do
            intree(i,A[i]);
        for i := N step −1 until 2 do
            begin
                temp := A[1];
                A[1] := A[i];
                A[i] := temp;
                comment largest element in tree is placed in A[i];
                outtree(i−1);
            end;
   end procedure treesort;
```

Below are some of the intermediate states of the array A as it is sorted by the tree-sort algorithm of Example 11·3. The state of the array is shown at the exit points of the intree and outtree procedures.

ARRAY INDEX	INITIAL VALUE	INTREE i = 4	INTREE i = 8	OUTTREE i = 7	OUTTREE i = 4	FINAL VALUE
1	6	17	26	22	6	1
2	3	6	22	17	3	3
3	1	1	23	18	1	6
4	17	3	17	3	17	17
5	18	18	6	6	18	18
6	26	26	1	1	22	22
7	23	23	18	23	23	23
8	22	22	3	26	26	26

A cursory examination of Example 11·3 reveals that procedures Intree and outtree are very similar. Indeed, Floyd's algorithm is structured so that a single procedure performs both tasks. The Williams algorithm has been presented because the distinction in the procedures adds to the clarity.

The worst-case analysis for the tree sort can be done by assuming that an exchange follows every comparison. We shall count the number of times that the labels scan and loop are encountered in the worst case and use this as a measure of the computational work.

In the worst case an element in a tree of size i will cause loop or scan to be passed $\lfloor \log_2 i \rfloor$ times. Since we deal with a tree of size i for each i in the interval $2 \leq i \leq N$, the maximum number iterations through either scan or loop is given by

$$\text{Maximum iterations} = \sum_{i=2}^{N} \lfloor \log_2 i \rfloor$$

$$= 1 + 1 + 2 + 2 + 2 + 2 + 3 + 3 + \cdots$$

$$\cong \sum_{j=1}^{\lfloor \log_2 N \rfloor} j2^j$$

The last approximation is an equality when N is one less than a power of 2. It is particularly convenient to use this form of the summation, because it can be rewritten in a simple closed form. To derive the closed form we note that the term $j2^j$ is equal to the derivative of the term $2x^j$ when x has the value 2. Consequently we can employ the polynomial

$$g(x) = 1 + x + x^2 + \cdots + x^n = \frac{x^{n+1} - 1}{x - 1}$$

where we let $n = \lfloor \log_2 N \rfloor$. Then the sum we desire is equal to $2g'(x)$ evaluated at $x = 2$. When we take the derivative of $(x^{n+1} - 1)/(x - 1)$, we find

$$\text{Maximum iterations} = 2\, g'(2)$$

$$= \frac{2(n+1)x^n(x-1) - 2x^{n+1} + 2}{(x-1)^2}\bigg|_{x=2}$$

$$= (n-1) \cdot 2^{n+1} + 2$$

When we replace n by $\lfloor \log_2 N \rfloor$ and let N be one less than a power of 2, the formula has the form

$$\text{Maximum iterations} = (\lfloor \log_2 N \rfloor - 1)(N + 1) + 2$$

The general conclusion that we reach here is that the amount of computation in the worst case is asymptotically proportional to $N \log_2 N$. This grows much more slowly with N than does N^2, the function that describes the worst-case computation for the bubble sort. Actually $N \log_2 N$ grows more slowly than $N^{1+\epsilon}$ for any positive ϵ. Thus the worst case for the tree sort will require less computation than the worst case for the bubble sort, provided that N is sufficiently large.

The analysis of the average computation for the tree sort is still an open problem. Nevertheless, there is an information theoretical argument that can be used to provide a lower bound for the average computation. Suppose that on the average $Q(N)$ comparisons are required to sort N numbers. Since each comparison has two possible outcomes, there are essentially $2^{Q(N)}$ different outcomes for the set of $Q(N)$ comparisons. Surely each of the $N!$ permutations of N items must result in a different set of outcomes for the $Q(N)$ comparisons. If not, two different permutations would be treated identically by the sorting algorithm, and the algorithm could not sort both of them. Since each outcome is distinct, we have

$$2^{Q(N)} \geq N!$$

By taking logarithms of both sides and using the Stirling approximation,

$$\log_2(N!) = N \log_2 N - N \log_2 e + \cdots$$

we obtain

$$Q(N) \geq N \log_2 N - N \log_2 e + \cdots$$

Therefore the average number of comparisons grows asymptotically at least as fast as $N \log_2 N$. Since the worst case for the tree-sort algorithm has a computational complexity that grows as $N \log_2 N$, tree sort is at least within a multiplicative constant of being an optimal sorting algorithm.

Our analyses have essentially established that tree sort is a better sorting algorithm than either of the bubble-sort algorithms that we investigated. However, there are several assumptions embedded in the analyses that can be violated in particular cases. It is crucial, for example, that the approximations are asymptotic. When N is small, the asymptotic approximations can lead to erroneous conclusions. It is also crucial that we compute the average of comparisons under the assumption that all permutations are equally likely. If, by chance, data are presented to the sort algorithm only "slightly" disordered, then the bubble sort will be more efficient than our analysis suggests. Moreover, the tree-sort algorithm tends to require higher computation for data that are "almost" sorted than for other data (see Exercise 11·2). Thus there are peculiar cases for which the apparently inefficient bubble sort outperforms the very efficient tree sort. The selection of a sorting algorithm ultimately depends on its behavior in the context in which it is used.

11·2   Search Algorithms

In many different applications it is necessary to search through an array or data structure for a particular datum. For example, in the second pass of a two-pass assembly each reference to a symbol causes the assembler to search a table for an entry containing that symbol. When such an entry is found, other information associated with the symbol in the table is used by the assembler to generate a fragment of an assembled word. This section describes three important and widely used techniques for searching tables.

Novice programmers nearly always write search programs that are similar to the following example:

EXAMPLE 11·4

```
for i := 1 step 1 until N do
    begin if table[i] = searchkey then go to found;
    end;
    go to notfound;
found: whereitsat := i;

    . . .

notfound: . . .
```

Obviously, in the worst case N comparisons are required, and the average number of comparisons is $N/2$. Searches of this type should be avoided in programs where the size of the table searched or the frequency of use of the program places a great deal of importance on running efficiency. Better methods for searching are treated in the sections that follow.

11·2·1 The Binary Search A conceptually simple search technique can be used if the data are sorted numerically in the search table. This technique, called *binary search*, consists of a sequence of iterations such that the area of the table to be searched is halved in each iteration. Eventually either the item is found, or the area to be searched becomes empty. In the latter case the program exits and notifies the calling program that the item is not in the table.

EXAMPLE 11·5

A procedure for the binary search is as follows:

procedure BINARY(A,N, FOUND, PLACE, ITEM);

array A; **integer** N, PLACE, ITEM; **boolean** FOUND;

comment array A is declared [1:N]. If ITEM is in A, then FOUND is set **true** and the index of ITEM in A is stored in PLACE, otherwise FOUND is set **false;**

```
begin integer LOW, HIGH;
    LOW := 0;
    HIGH := N+1;
    FOUND := false;
loop:
    if LOW + 1 ≥ HIGH then go to notfound;
    PLACE:= (LOW + HIGH) ÷ 2;

    if ITEM = A[PLACE] then go to foundit

    else if ITEM < A[PLACE] then HIGH := PLACE

    else LOW := PLACE;

    go to loop;
foundit: FOUND := true;
notfound:
end procedure BINARY;
```

In the program above the variable HIGH is initialized to N+1, because PLACE can attain values only less than or equal to HIGH—1. This is because the function (LOW+HIGH)÷2 can equal HIGH only if LOW equals HIGH, but since LOW is initialized to a number less than HIGH, both PLACE and LOW never attain the value of HIGH.

To illustrate the operation of the binary-search algorithm suppose that the array A contains the integers 1 to 6 in A[1] to A[6]. LOW and HIGH are initialized to 0 and 7, respectively, by the algorithm. If ITEM has the value 0, then PLACE would assume the sequence of values 3 and then 1 before a branch was taken to notfound. If ITEM has the value 4, then PLACE would assume the sequence of values 3, 5, and 4 prior to the branch to foundit. The maximum number of iterations performed by the algorithm is $\lfloor \log_2 N \rfloor + 1$ when A contains N elements. The logarithmic behavior of the algorithm is strikingly better than the behavior of the search in Example 11·4.

Figure 11·2 illustrates how the binary search is related to binary trees. The sequence of probes is shown for an array with 15 elements. When the outcome of a comparison shows that ITEM is less than an array element, the next element to be probed is indicated by an arrow slanting downward to the left. If ITEM is greater than the array element,

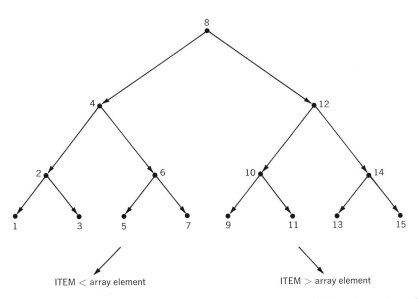

ITEM < array element   ITEM > array element

Figure 11·2 The sequence of probe addresses in a binary search for various values of ITEM

then the next probe of the array is indicated by the arrow slanting downward to the right. The tree in Figure 11·2 is clearly a binary tree, but the links to the successors are not stored in the tree as shown in Chapter 10. In this case we find the successors of a node by manipulating HIGH and LOW.

The analysis of the average number of comparisons is similar to the analysis of Floyd's tree-sort algorithm. If an item is not in the array, then either $\lfloor \log_2 N \rfloor$ or $\lfloor \log_2 N \rfloor + 1$ comparisons are required to discover this fact. When N is one less than a power of 2, the average is exactly $\lfloor \log_2 N \rfloor + 1$, because every item that is not in the array will require this many comparisons, regardless of its value.

If an item is in the array, then there is exactly one position in the array that requires one comparison, there are two that require two comparisons, four that require three comparisons, and, in general, 2^j positions that require j comparisons. Thus the average number of comparisons required to find an item in the array is given by

$$\text{Average comparisons} \cong \frac{1}{N} \sum_{j=0}^{\lfloor \log_2 N \rfloor} j2^j$$

The formula is exact when N is one less than a power of 2. The summation was given in the previous section. Recalling that it is equal to $(\lfloor \log_2 N \rfloor - 1)(N + 1) + 2$, we find

$$\text{Average comparisons} = \frac{(\lfloor \log_2 N \rfloor - 1)(N + 1) + 2}{N}$$

which is approximately $\lfloor \log_2 N \rfloor - 1$ for large N.

Thus the average number of comparisons is approximately one less than the maximum number of comparisons when the item is in the array. Note that it does not make much difference whether or not the item is in the array. The comparisons required for the two cases differ in number by a small constant. For the sequential search of Example 11·4, it makes a great deal of difference whether or not an item is in the array. In fact, on the average, twice as much computation is required when an item is not in the array as when it is in the array.

11·2·2 **Hash Addressing**   The amount of computation required for a binary search is a function only of the number of elements in the array to be searched. For some applications, particularly with large arrays, it is desirable to be able to search faster than is possible with a binary search. There is another search algorithm with the interesting characteristic that the amount of computation required depends both on the size of the array to be searched and on a second parameter which can be selected by the programmer. Thus the programmer can control the amount of computation required for a search by setting the value of the second parameter. The choice of the second parameter reflects a trade off between computation speed and memory requirements.

This search algorithm, commonly called *hash addressing*, is based on the idea that the item that is the search parameter can be used as an index to an array. Suppose, for example, that the variable ITEM can assume only the values 1, 2, . . . , M. Then a convenient way of storing search information in an array A is to store a 1 in A[i] if the number i is present in the array and to store a 0 in A[i] otherwise. Now we can easily search A by direct entry to the array. The test

if A[ITEM] $= 1$ then . . .

constitutes a search for ITEM in the array. This example points out the use of memory to save computation. M could be very large compared to the number of items that are actually stored in A—say, 10^6 times as large. Then a binary search would require only a fraction of the storage required by the direct-entry algorithm, but the binary search would require several comparison iterations instead of the single comparison required by direct entry.

When ITEM can assume a very large number of values, but only a very few different possible values are to be stored in A, a *hash code* can be used somewhat like a direct-entry index. Suppose that ITEM is a string of five or fewer eight-bit characters; for example, it might be the internal representation of a symbol from an assembly language program. Suppose that each character has eight bits, so that there are roughly $(2^8)^5 = 2^{40} \cong 10^{12}$ possible symbols, not all of which are valid assembly language symbols. Clearly we cannot use direct entry with such symbols, because the memory requirements are far in excess of available memory. In the typical case only a few hundred items may actually be stored in a list, so that it is possible to use an algorithm similar to direct entry, but with much smaller memory requirements.

Instead of using the value of ITEM as an index, we shall compute a new value by calling a procedure named HASH, with ITEM as an argument. The value of HASH(ITEM) is some number in a range comparable in size to the number of items in the search list. For example,

HASH(ITEM) might be a number between 1 and 256. We then use HASH(ITEM) as the index to A, as in the direct-entry algorithm. That is, we use the test

if A[HASH(ITEM)] $= 1$ **then** . . .

There is a problem, however. Two or more different values of ITEM may yield the same hash code, but there may be room to store only one of the items in A[HASH(ITEM)]. Thus special steps must be taken to handle the case when two or more entries have the same hash code. We solve this problem as follows. The hash code effectively partitions the possible values of ITEM into disjoint sets such that if there are N different hash codes, then there are N disjoint sets of symbols with the same hash code. Given a list to be searched, we can divide that list into N sublists according to hash code. Then, to see whether a given value of ITEM is in the list, we first compute its hash code and then search the sublist of items that have the same hash code. The search should involve only $1/N$ of the entire list, on the average, if the function HASH is well constructed.

Example 11·6 illustrates how to search a list by hash addressing and how to enter items into a list in preparation for this search. We assume that the hash codes are the integers 1, 2, . . . , N. The array TABLE contains the items. Items with identical hash codes are linked together as one-way linked lists, with the links for these lists stored in NEXT. Thus the item that follows TABLE[i] on a list is TABLE[NEXT[i]]. The beginning of each list of items with the same hash code is identified by the array INDEX. That is, INDEX[h] contains the index in TABLE of the first item on the list of items with hash code h. We use the value 0 in INDEX[i] if there is no item i in TABLE.

To search TABLE we start at INDEX[HASH(ITEM)] and look for a match. Let this index be called the *index of the first probe* of the table. If there is no match, then we trace a linked list of entries that have the same hash code as ITEM. The next entry on the list is determined by using the index of the first probe as an index to NEXT. The entry in NEXT is the *index of the second probe,* the next item to examine. The link tracing is repeated until either a match is found or a 0 is found in the entry of NEXT. The 0 is the signal that the sublist of entries with the same hash code as ITEM has been exhausted.

The procedure ENTER places items in TABLE. We assume that NEXT, INDEX, and the variable AVAIL has been initialized to 0's before the first call of ENTER. When ENTER is called, it computes the hash code of ITEM and places it at the next available place in TABLE, as indicated by AVAIL. ENTER then modifies an entry in INDEX and in NEXT so that the new item is effectively added to the sublist of entries with a hash code equal to HASH(ITEM).

The worst case would be one in which all items have the same hash code. This case reduces to a search of one list, which is essentially equivalent to the sequential search in Example 11·4. Thus in the worst case we may have to inspect all the items in the array.

EXAMPLE 11·6

```
procedure HASHSEARCH(ITEM, PLACE);

integer ITEM;

begin comment if ITEM is in TABLE, then the index of ITEM is put into PLACE,
otherwise PLACE is set to 0;
     integer i;
          PLACE := 0;
          i := INDEX[HASH(ITEM)];
     loop:
          if i = 0 then go to exit;
          if TABLE[i] ≠ ITEM then
               begin i := NEXT[i];
                    go to loop;
               end;
          PLACE := i;
     exit:
end procedure HASHSEARCH;

procedure ENTER(ITEM);

integer ITEM;

begin integer i;
     i := HASH(ITEM);
     comment the value of INDEX[i] is the index of another entry of TABLE
     with hash code i. Place INDEX[i] in NEXT[AVAIL] so that TABLE[INDEX[i]]
     will be scanned immediately after TABLE[AVAIL] is examined during a
     search;
     AVAIL := AVAIL + 1;
     comment there should be a test to guard against table overflow;
     comment this forces the search to look at TABLE[AVAIL] first;
     TABLE[AVAIL] := ITEM;
     NEXT[AVAIL] := INDEX[i];
     INDEX[i] := AVAIL;
end procedure ENTER;
```

Assume that we call ENTER with the sequence of items below. For this case assume that the hash codes are the integers 0 to 6.

ITEM	HASH CODE
ALPHA	4
BETA	2
GAMMA	5
DELTA	5
EPSILON	0
MU	1
NU	5
OMEGA	2

Then the arrays TABLE, INDEX, and NEXT would have the values given below and illustrated in Figure 11·3.

ARRAY ELEMENT	INDEX	TABLE	NEXT
0	5 (EPSILON)	. . .	. . .
1	6 (MU)	ALPHA	0
2	8 (OMEGA)	BETA	0
3	0	GAMMA	0
4	1 (ALPHA)	DELTA	3 (GAMMA)
5	7 (NU)	EPSILON	0
6	0	MU	0
7	. . .	NU	4 (DELTA)
8	. . .	OMEGA	2 (BETA)

A search for GAMMA will scan NU, and then DELTA, before reaching GAMMA.

The analysis of the average case is straightforward and is given as an exercise. Intuition suggests that, on the average, each sublist will contain $1/N$ of the total number of items, where N is the number of distinct hash codes. Statistical analysis supports this reasoning. On the average, we have to search half of a linked list if an item is in the array, and we must search the entire linked list if the item is not there. Com-

INDEX   TABLE   NEXT

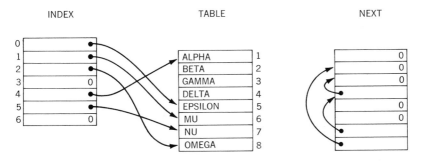

Figure 11·3 An example of a hash table for the hash search algorithm

parison of both of these cases indicates that the hash-addressing algorithm is N times faster than Example $11 \cdot 4$ when the hash codes are well distributed.

The next problem is to determine suitable hash functions. Some experimentation has shown that the function

$$\text{HASH}(x) = (x \text{ MOD } N) + 1$$

yields a number uniformly distributed between 1 and N for many collections of data. The distribution is exactly uniform when x ranges over all integers. Since the items usually encountered in searching applications are composed of characters, it is well to consider this in the selection of N. For example, if characters are eight bits, then the choice of $N = 256$ effectively causes the hash code to depend only on the last character in an item. It is safest to select N to be a prime or a number that is not highly composite to avoid the possibility of nonuniform distributions.

Other functions that work well are the logical EXCLUSIVE OR function and ordinary addition. These are usually implemented by breaking an item into several fields of equal size—say, r bits each—and then combining the fields into a single r-bit field with the EXCLUSIVE OR operation or addition. If addition is used, then carries outside the field are disregarded. The result is a hash code between 0 and $2^r - 1$. The reason addition or EXCLUSIVE OR is used is that the final hash code depends on every r-bit field. We should not choose r to be equal to the number of bits per character if items are derived from character strings, because the nonuniform distribution of characters in text will tend to yield a nonuniform distribution of hash codes.

N must be selected to balance search time against memory utilization, since the size of the array INDEX increases in proportion to the size of N. In System/360-370 computers a large memory is available, so that N as large as 1000 might be used to decrease search time in large arrays. However, this is far too large for the HP 2116 computer, which has a very small memory.

The most serious disadvantage of the hash search algorithm is the use of memory for storing linked-list pointers. In Example 11·6 the pointers are stored in the array NEXT. In most implementations of the hash search algorithm the pointers will be part of a packed data structure in order to conserve memory. There is an alternative hash search algorithm that needs no pointer storage at all. Since pointers are necessary only when two or more items have the same code, we can dispense with them by developing a different method for dealing with hash-code duplications. One method that has been widely used is the following:

1. Use a hash code to determine the address of the first probe of a table.

2. If the table entry is empty, halt, indicating that the item is not in the table.

3. If the table entry matches the item, halt, indicating the index of the match.

4. If the table entry is neither empty nor equal to the item, then generate a new address for another probe of the table. (The algorithm for generating addresses is discussed later.)

5. Go to step 2.

The interesting aspect of this hash search algorithm is that during a search of the table items with many different hash codes may be encountered. The hash code merely determines where to start the search, and may possibly influence the sequence in which addresses are examined (see Exercise 11·7). Because there is no pointer information, the search cannot be directed to a specific set of items that share a single hash code.

When the table to be searched is sparsely populated, the algorithm behaves like the hash search algorithm of Example 11·6. We expect to match the item or find an empty cell in a few probes of the table. When the table becomes full or nearly full, the algorithm behaves more like the sequential search of Example 11·4. Since few cells are empty, each new probe will be directed to a nonempty cell with high probability, and the search will rarely reach a termination point. Thus when we use the algorithm without pointers, the table should be partially empty—say, no more than 90 to 95 percent full. The unused memory in the table represents parts of the memory requirements of the algorithm. As such, it partially negates the memory savings achieved by eliminating pointers.

The algorithms for searching a table and for entering a new item into a table are given below.

EXAMPLE 11·7

By convention, if TABLE[i] contains a 0, then that element of the table is empty. The principal difference between this algorithm and Example 11·6 is the technique for generating the next address to search. In Example 11·6 we used the pointers in the data structure. Here we call the function NEXTADDRESS, which when given the address of the present search address, produces the next address to be examined.

```
procedure hashwithoutpointers(ITEM,PLACE);

integer ITEM, PLACE;

begin comment if TABLE[i] contains a 0, then no item has been placed there;
     integer i;
          PLACE := 0;
          i := HASH(ITEM);
     loop:
          if TABLE[i] = 0 then go to exit;
          if TABLE[i] ≠ ITEM then
               begin i := NEXTADDRESS(i);
                    go to loop;
               end;
          PLACE := i;
          exit:

end procedure hashwithoutpointers;

procedure ENTER(ITEM);

integer ITEM;

begin integer i;
     i := HASH(ITEM);
     comment search for an empty place in the table and place ITEM in the
     first space available;

loop:
     if TABLE[i] ≠ 0 then
          begin comment look for a new place to insert ITEM;
               i := NEXTADDRESS(i);
               go to loop;
          end;
     TABLE[i] := ITEM;

end procedure ENTER
```

The only part of the algorithm left unspecified is the procedure NEXTADDRESS. One candidate for this function that has often been used is

```
i := (i+1) MOD TABLESIZE;
```

Thus the array is searched sequentially, beginning at HASH(ITEM). The MOD operation causes the indexing to continue at 0 when i reaches the last element in the table. Other functions with better statistical properties are mentioned below.

To analyze this method of hash searching we shall make some assumptions that simplify the analysis, but which are not generally valid. Thus our analysis will not be rigorously correct, but it will be an accurate lower bound on the average computation.

Let α, the *load factor*, be the ratio of the number of entries in the table to the total size of the table. Then with probability α the first probe of the table will find a nonzero entry, and with probability $1 - \alpha$ the first probe will find an empty entry. Suppose that we wish to search for a given item. How many probes are necessary to determine that the item is not in the table? This is the number of probes required to find an empty cell. The algorithm terminates after i probes of the table when the first $i - 1$ probes reach nonempty cells and the ith probe reaches an empty cell.

If we assume that the probability of finding an empty cell is the same for any probe in a sequence of probes, then the probability of finding an empty cell on the ith probe is $\alpha^{i-1}(1 - \alpha)$. (This assumption is normally violated because the probability of finding an empty cell during any probe is not statistically independent of the outcomes of the previous probes.) Our assumption leads to the following asymptotic formula for E, the average number of probes to search for an item not in the table:

$$
E = \sum_{i=1}^{\infty} i\alpha^{i-1}(1 - \alpha)
$$

$$
= (1 - \alpha) \sum_{i=1}^{\infty} i\alpha^{i-1}
$$

$$
= \frac{1 - \alpha}{(1 - \alpha)^2} = \frac{1}{1 - \alpha}
$$

The average number of probes required to search for an item in the table is approximately half the average required to determine that an item is not in the table. The reason is that the list of items to be examined has length E, and it is equally likely that we will find our item anywhere on that list. Hence on the average we would expect to search half the list.

There are various ways that we can compare the behavior of Example 11·7 with Example 11·6. The most important point of comparison is related to the behavior when the table becomes full. As α approaches 1, the average number of probes required by Example 11·7 increases rapidly, approaching the size of the table. However, for Example 11·6, the average number of probes is $1/N$ the number of entries in the table. For smaller values of α, particularly for α less than 3/4, the number of probes required by Example 11·7 is sufficiently small to make the algorithm competitive with Example 11·6.

The analysis of Example 11·7 relies heavily on the assumption that the outcomes of successive probes are statistically independent. The NEXTADDRESS function given above, which effectively causes the table to be searched linearly, will lead to a violation of our assumption, so that the algorithm will be less efficient than our analyses indicate. Clusters of items tend to accumulate in the table, so that if a probe hits somewhere in the cluster, a large number of probes is required to move the search beyond it.

Other functions for NEXTADDRESS have been reported in the literature. The functions that lead to the most efficient behavior are those which tend to randomize the address sequences produced by NEXTADDRESS. Maurer (1968) and Bell (1970) report methods based on quadratic equations that have good randomization properties. One good method, due to Bell and Kaman (1970), is called the *linear-quotient method*. In this method the initial probe is made at the index given by the hash code, but successive probes are made at addresses that depend on the value of ITEM. Thus two items with the same hash code will generally produce different probe sequences, which tends to eliminate the clustering problem.

In the linear-quotient method we assume that the hash code is ITEM MOD TABLESIZE, and the probe sequence depends on ITEM ÷ TABLESIZE. That is, we use both the remainder and the quotient of the integer division of ITEM by TABLESIZE. In many computers, such as System/360-370, the quotient and remainder are both computed during the execution of a divide instruction.

We obtain the next address in a probe sequence from the present address by adding the quotient (that is, ITEM÷TABLESIZE) to the present address and taking the result modulo the size of the table. Thus the sequence of probe addresses is

```
HASH(ITEM)
[HASH(ITEM)+quotient] MOD TABLESIZE
[HASH(ITEM)+2·quotient] MOD TABLESIZE
[HASH(ITEM)+3·quotient] MOD TABLESIZE
    . . .
```

The sequence of addresses will cover the entire table if, and only if, TABLESIZE is a prime number (see Exercise 11·8).

EXAMPLE 11·8

The linear-quotient method is given below:

integer quotient, remainder;

integer procedure HASH(ITEM);

value ITEM;

integer ITEM;
    begin comment this procedure produces the address of the first.probe and initializes variables for successive probes;
        HASH := remainder := ITEM MOD TABLESIZE;
        quotient := ITEM ÷ TABLESIZE;
        if quotient = 0 **then** quotient := 1;
    end procedure HASH;

integer procedure NEXTADDRESS(address);

value address;

integer address;

begin integer temp;
    temp := (address + quotient) MOD TABLESIZE;
    if temp = remainder **then**
        begin comment we have searched the entire table. Notify search routine by setting address to −1;
            NEXTADDRESS := −1;
        end
    else NEXTADDRESS := temp;
end procedure NEXTADDRESS;

The interested reader is referred to Bell (1970) and Bell and Kaman (1970) for the combinatorial properties of Example 11·8. The statistical behavior of the example when it is used in a search algorithm is closely approximated by our analysis.

Before closing this section we must consider one final point concerning hash searching with and without pointers. When pointers are used, as in Example 11·6, it is possible to delete items from the table by the standard techniques for deleting items from lists. The memory that holds the deleted item can then be linked to a list of available memory for reuse. Search time diminishes when items are deleted. In Example 11·7 an item cannot be eliminated, leaving an empty cell in the table, because this empty cell can cause searches to stop prematurely. Thus items should be deleted by marking them with a special tag. New items can be entered in tagged cells, but searches cannot stop on these cells. Deleting items by tagging them does not improve search time and does not lead to efficient reuse of memory. Thus the hash search with pointers is more desirable than the search without pointers when items are to be deleted with high frequency from the table.

11·2·3 AVL Trees   For many applications neither hash search nor binary search are suitable algorithms. In particular, there are many situations in which we wish to accomplish the following three processes efficiently:

1. Search for a specified item.
2. Enter a new item.
3. Delete a specified item.

The binary search is efficient for searching, but insertion and deletion of new items are extremely costly, since the table must be maintained in numerically ascending order. Hash searching with pointers is efficient for the last two items, but the efficiency of the search depends on the amount of memory that we wish to allocate. When tables become very large, the memory required for efficient searching can become excessive. Hash searching without pointers has a similar problem related to the inefficient use of memory. More important, the deletion process is a serious disadvantage, because the memory for deleted items cannot easily be returned to use, and deletions do not decrease search time.

A method for accomplishing all three of these processes efficiently has been developed by Adel'son-Vel'skii and Landis (1962). Foster

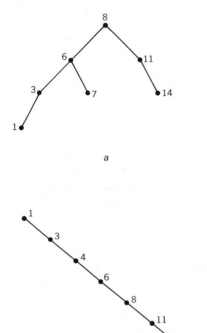

a

b

Figure 11·4 Two search trees: (*a*) a nearly balanced tree and (*b*) a badly balanced tree

(1965) provides a detailed analysis of their work and supplies the name *AVL tree* after the authors.

To understand the AVL tree algorithm consider the binary tree shown in Figure 11·4*a*. In this tree we use the convention that the number stored at each node of the tree is smaller than those at the nodes in its right subtree and larger than those at the nodes in its left subtree. Thus we search for the number *i* as follows:

1. If the node contains the number *i*, halt.

2. If *i* is less than the number at the node, examine the left successor link, otherwise examine the right successor link.

3. If the link is empty, halt, indicating that the number *i* is not in the tree, otherwise follow this link to the successor node and return to step 1.

Figure 11·4*a* suggests that, on the average, we would expect to do no more than $\lfloor \log_2 N \rfloor$ comparisons if there are N items in the tree. Unfortunately Figure $11 \cdot 4b$ shows a case for which the worst case requires N comparisons when there are N items in the tree. Since there is a large difference between $\log_2 N$ and N, we wish to prevent trees from becoming badly unbalanced, as in Figure $11 \cdot 4b$, as we insert items into the tree. The AVL tree insertion algorithm does indeed accomplish this. The longest path in an AVL tree is guaranteed never to exceed $K \log_2 N$, where K is a small constant.

Specifically, we define an AVL tree as one that has the following property:

> **AVL Tree** For every node of an AVL tree, the length of the longest path in the left subtree differs from the length of the longest path in the right subtree by no more than one branch.

The tree in Figure $11 \cdot 4a$ is an AVL tree; the tree in Figure $11 \cdot 4b$ is not.

First we shall see how to maintain trees that satisfy the AVL property with successive insertions, and then we shall see how both the insertions and the searching can be done in a time proportional to $\log_2 N$. The deletion algorithm is the subject of Exercise $11 \cdot 4$.

Let us assume that a new item inserted into the tree is always inserted as a leaf. To do this we trace a path through the tree until we find the predecessor node of the item to be inserted. Typical cases are shown in Figure $11 \cdot 5$. The insertion may cause the tree to fail to satisfy the AVL property. To help us detect such a failure, at each node in the tree we include information about the longest paths in the two subtrees of the node. A node is said to be *balanced* if the longest paths in each of its two subtrees are equal. If the longest path in the left subtree is one longer than the longest path in the right subtree, then we say that the node is *left heavy;* we define *right heavy* similarly. Every node is in one of these three states.

When an item is added to an AVL tree, one or more nodes in the tree will change state. Examination of Figure $11 \cdot 5$ shows that the nodes that do change state are all on the path between the root of the tree and the new node of the tree. One of three changes of state may occur to a node on that path:

1. The node was formerly balanced and has become left heavy or right heavy.

2. The node was formerly heavy in one direction and has become balanced.

3. The node was formerly left heavy or right heavy, and the new node was inserted in the heavy subtree.

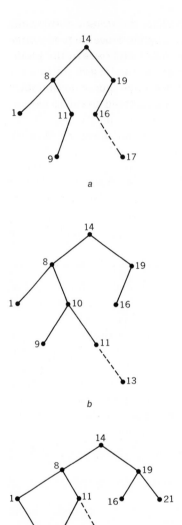

Figure 11·5 Insertion of new nodes into AVL trees. (*a*) Insertion of node 17 makes node 19 a critical node. (*b*) Insertion of node 13 makes node 8 a critical node. (*c*) Insertion of node 13 leaves no node critical

If condition 1 applies to a node, then the predecessor of this node undergoes a change of state. If condition 2 applies, then the predecessor node does not change state, nor does any other node above the predecessor node change state, because the length of the longest path in the subtree is unchanged. If condition 3 applies, then the node no longer satisfies the AVL property. Such a node is said to be a *critical node*.

These observations suggest that a suitable insertion algorithm should check predecessors on the path to the root to see which of the three conditions applies. When condition 2 applies, the algorithm changes the state of the node and exits. When condition 1 applies, the algorithm changes the state of the node and then checks the predecessor node. When condition 3 applies, the algorithm must rearrange the tree. If the rearrangement of the tree returns the critical node to its original state, then no node in the tree above the critical node need be examined.

The next problem concerns tree rearrangement when a critical node is encountered. How might this be done efficiently to leave the tree in AVL form? Figure 11·6 illustrates the three different cases that might occur and the rearrangements that bring these trees into AVL form. In the first case the tree rooted at the critical node has only three nodes after the new item is inserted. The new item becomes the root of the tree after rearrangement. In the second case the node marked N is the new node, and the boxes labeled S_1, S_2, and S_3 are each trees. The number in parentheses indicates the length of the longest path in these trees after node N is inserted. Since A is the critical node in this example, node B originally must be in the balanced state. The second case covers the situation when B becomes heavy in the same direction in which A is heavy. The third case is similar to the second, except that B becomes heavy in the direction opposite from that in which A is heavy. For this case it must be that node C is originally in the balanced state. The new node can be added to either subtree of C. Figure 11·6 shows the new node added to the left subtree, but the algorithm in Example 11·9 also treats the instance in which the new node is added to the right subtree. Notice that the tree-rearranging computation involves the modification of no more than four pointers in the worst case. The complete details of the algorithm are given in Example. 11·9.

To prove that the AVL tree algorithm is as efficient as claimed we need only show that the longest path in the tree does not exceed $K \log_2 N$ for a tree with N nodes, where K is a small constant. If this is the case, then neither the search process nor the insertion process can exceed a number of steps proportional to $\log_2 N$. Although we do

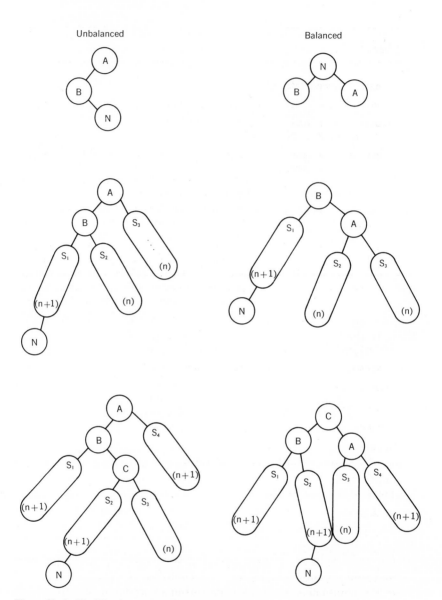

Unbalanced

Balanced

Figure 11·6 Modifications at a critical node that restore the AVL property

EXAMPLE 11·9

integer balanced, left, right;

comment these integers have values 0, 1, and 2, respectively;

integer array nodevalue[1 : n], nodeweight[1 : n],
link[1 : n,1 : 2], path[1 : m], direction[1 : m];

comment	nodevalue	contains the value associated with a node.
	nodeweight	contains the state of the node. The value 0 indicates balanced, 1 indicates left heavy, and 2 indicates right heavy.
	link	contains pointers to the left and right subtrees of a node. The left subtree of node i is in link[i,1].
	path	contains pointers to nodes that form a path from the root to the point of insertion of a node.
	direction	shows the direction of the path. The node at path[i] is always a left or right successor of path[i−1]. The value of direction[i−1] is 1 or 2 to indicate path[i] is a left or right successor, respectively;

integer root;

comment root is a pointer to the root node of the tree;

integer level;

integer procedure opposite(dir);

value dir;

integer dir;
  if dir = left **then** opposite := right **else**
  opposite := left;

procedure changehead(j);

value j;

integer j;

begin comment this procedure does a portion of the link rearranging required to maintain the AVL property. It links the subtree rooted at the critical node to the rest of the tree. Special consideration is given to the case in which the critical node is the root of the entire tree;
  if level = 1 **then**
      begin comment the critical node is the root of the tree, and the new root is the node at position j on the path;
          root := path[j];
      end
  else
      begin comment in the normal case the node at path[level−1] is made to

have the node at path[j] as its successor. The direction of the pointer to the successor is given in direction[level—1];

```
    link[path[level—1],direction[level—1]] := path[j];
end;
```

end procedure changehead;

procedure exchange(a,b);

value a,b;

integer a,b;

begin comment this procedure changes the links of a pair of nodes in the tree as part of the process of making the tree into an AVL tree;

```
    link[path[a],direction[a]] := link[path[b],opposite(direction[a])];
    link[path[b],opposite(direction[a])] := path[a];
```

end procedure exchange;

procedure savepath(place,dir);

value place, dir;

integer place, dir;

begin comment this procedure places entries in the arrays path and direction as a path is traced from the root to a point of insertion;

```
    level := level+1;
    path[level] := place;
    direction[level] := dir;
```

end procedure savepath;

integer procedure search(item);

value item;

integer item;

begin comment this procedure searches for an item in the tree. If the item is not in the tree, the procedure returns the value 0. If the item is in the tree, the procedure returns the index of the node that holds the item;

```
        integer where;
        where := root;
        level := 0;
    testequal:
        if where = 0 then go to exit;
        comment the tree is empty or we have reached a leaf if the previous
        test is satisfied;
        savepath(where, if nodevalue[where] ≥ item then left else right);
        if nodevalue[where] = item then go to exit;
        comment the preceding test is satisfied if the item is found in the
        tree;
        where := link[where,direction[level]];
        go to testequal;
    exit:
        search := where;
```

end procedure search;

procedure insertnode(item);

value item;

integer item;

begin comment this procedure inserts a node into the tree. If the new tree fails to satisfy the AVL property, then the procedure rearranges the linkages at the critical node to make the tree into an AVL tree;

    integer where, weight;

    where := search(item);

    if where $\neq$ 0 **then go to** exit;

    comment the branch to exit is taken when the item is already in tree;

    where := avail;

    comment avail is a procedure that returns the index of an available cell for a new tree node. The following statements enter the item into the new tree node;

    nodevalue[where] := item;

    link[where,left] := link[where,right] := 0;

    nodeweight[where] := balanced;

    savepath(where,balanced);

    comment the following statement links the new node into the tree;

    changehead(level);

    comment in the following loop we check and modify the state of each node on the path to the root. If a critical node is found, the branch is taken to the statement labeled move;

    for level := level−1 **step** −1 **until** 1 **do**

        begin weight := nodeweight[path[level]];

            if weight = direction[level] **then**

                begin comment node is critical;

                    go to move;

                end;

            nodeweight[path[level]] := direction[level];

            if weight $\neq$ balanced **then**

                begin comment a node has been found that has changed into a balanced state. Record this fact and exit the loop and the procedure;

                    nodeweight[path[level]] := balanced;

                    go to exit;

                end;

        end for-loop;

    go to exit;

move:

    if direction[level] = direction[level+1] **then**

        begin comment this is the second case;

            changehead(level+1);

            exchange(level,level+1);

            nodeweight[path[level]] := nodeweight[path[level+1]] := balanced;

        end

```
      else
          begin comment the next four statements apply to both cases 1 and 3;
              changehead(level+2);
              exchange(level,level+2);
              exchange(level+1,level+2);
              nodeweight[path[level+2]] := balanced;
              if direction[level+1] = direction[level+2] then
                  begin comment one possibility for the third case;
                      nodeweight[path[level]] := balanced;
                      nodeweight[path[level+1]] := opposite(direction
                          [level+1]);
                  end
              else
              if direction[level+2] ≠ balanced then
                  begin comment the other possibility for the third case;
                      nodeweight[path[level]] := opposite(direction[level]);
                      nodeweight[path[level+1]] := balanced;
                  end
              else
                  begin comment the first case;
                      nodeweight[path[level]] := nodeweight[path[level+1]]
                          := balanced;
                  end;
          end;
    exit:

    end procedure insertnode;
```

not include the deletion algorithm in Example 11·9, the hint given in Exercise 11·4 suggests that deletion also requires a number of steps proportional to $\log_2 N$.

For the proof we construct a sequence of trees T_1, T_2, T_3, . . . such that the longest path in tree T_i is length i and no AVL tree with a path of length i has fewer nodes than T_i. Figure 11·5 shows T_1, T_2, T_3, and T_4. To construct T_i we construct a tree with T_{i-2} and T_{i-1} as the left and right subtrees, respectively, of a single node. This is shown in Figure 11·7. For each i, T_i has the AVL property. Moreover, if we delete a node from T_i, either the derived tree will no longer have the AVL property, or the longest path in the derived tree will not be of length i. This can be shown by an inductive argument which is left as an exercise.

Each of the trees we construct is an AVL tree that is more nearly unbalanced than any AVL tree with an equal number of nodes. Thus each tree in the sequence has the longest path of any AVL tree with an equal number of nodes. We shall count the number of nodes in each of these trees and establish the relation between the length of the longest path and the number of nodes in the tree.

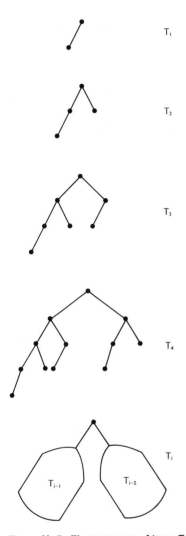

Figure 11·7 The sequence of trees T_1, T_2, T_3, . . .

Let $t(i)$ be the number of nodes in T_i. Then Figure 11·7 indicates that the following relations hold:

$$t(1) = 2$$
$$t(2) = 4$$
$$t(i) = t(i-1) + t(i-2) + 1 \qquad \text{for } i > 2$$

These relations are very similar to the relations that define the Fibonacci numbers (cf. Knuth 1968):

$$F(0) = 0$$
$$F(1) = 1$$
$$F(i) = F(i-1) + F(i-2) \qquad \text{for } i > 1$$

Close inspection of the first few terms in the series reveals that

$$t(i) = F(i+3) - 1$$

This last equation can be shown to be an identity by substituting for $t(i)$ in its defining equation. It is well known that the Fibonacci numbers satisfy the asymptotic formula (cf. Knuth 1968)

$$F(i) \cong \frac{\phi^i}{\sqrt{5}}$$

where

$$\phi = \frac{1 + \sqrt{5}}{2}$$

From this we obtain

$$t(i) \cong \frac{\phi^{i+3}}{\sqrt{5}} - 1$$

Now we solve for i in terms of $t(i)$. For this we find

$$\phi^{i+3} \cong \sqrt{5}\,[t(i) + 1]$$
$$i + 3 = \log_\phi \sqrt{5} + \log_\phi [t(i) + 1]$$

From the identities

$$\log_2 x = \log_\phi x / \log_2 \phi$$

and

$$\log_2 \phi = .694$$

we obtain the bound

$$i < \tfrac{3}{2} \log_2 [t(i) + 1] - 1$$

Since $t(i)$ is the number of nodes in the tree, we see that for a tree with N nodes, the longest path cannot exceed $\tfrac{3}{2} \log_2 (N + 1)$, which is the result we set out to prove.

REFERENCES

Other sorting algorithms exist that have the same computational behavior as Floyd's tree sort. In particular, Hoare's quicksort (1961) and its later modifications (Singleton 1969) are algorithms for sorting in a time proportional to $N \log_2 N$ that can be more efficient than Floyd's tree sort in many contexts.

Hash addressing, like so many other algorithms in computer lore, appears to have been invented early in the history of computers and is not traceable to a particular individual. Dumey (1956) describes the use of hash addressing for maintaining data files. The first detailed analysis of hash addressing appears in an article by Peterson (1957). Morris (1968) has provided an excellent survey of many different hash-addressing techniques.

EXERCISES

11·1 Give an algorithm for constructing a permutation of the integers 1 to N when given a ranking sequence for that permutation.

11·2 Simulate the tree-sort algorithm on an array containing 15 integers 1, 2, . . . , 15. Assume that the data are initially sorted in ascending sequence so that A[i] contains i.

11·3 Assume that the hash codes for data are integers uniformly distributed in the interval $0 \leq$ hash code $\leq N-1$. If an array to be searched contains M items, show that the average length of a list of items with the same hash code contains M/N items. (Hint: Assume that the probability that an item has hash code h_0 is $1/N$, and the probability is $1 - 1/N$ that the item has some other hash code. Show that the length of the list of items with hash code h_0 is binomially distributed.)

289

11·4   Write an algorithm that deletes a specified item from an AVL tree. (Hint: If the item is not located in a leaf, find its postorder predecessor and see if it can be deleted.)

11·5   Prove the following assertion:

If a leaf node is removed from T_i, then either the new tree fails to satisfy the AVL property, or the longest path in the new tree has a length less than i.

11·6   Binary searching is not efficient when new items have to be added to the table. A programmer suggests that the table be stored as a linked list rather than as a contiguous array in order to facilitate insertion of new items. In this case how many steps are required in the worst case to search for an item? How many steps are required to enter a new item, given the position at which it is inserted?

11·7   Let TABLESIZE = 13 in Example 11·8. Show the sequence of addresses probed for quotients with the values 1, 3, and 4. For each sequence assume a remainder of 0.

11·8   In Example 11·8 prove that the entire table is searched if, and only if, the value of TABLESIZE is prime. [Hint: If probes i and j reach the same address, $j > i$, then $(j - i) \cdot$ quotient is a multiple of TABLESIZE.]

Appendix

Explanation of the Algol-Like Notation

The notation in this book is an extension of ALGOL 60 that includes coroutines. This appendix contains a short summary of the notation. A full report on the revised ALGOL 60 language appears in *Comm. ACM*, vol. 6, no. 1, January 1963, pp. 1–23.

A·1   Basic Symbols

The basic entities from which statements are constructed are

> Constants
> Identifiers
> Reserved words

Constants have real, integer, or boolean values, and these values cannot change during program execution. Examples are:

Real constants	1.2	3.14159268	-7.99983
Integer constants	1, 2, 3, . . . ,	$-1, -2, . . .$	
Boolean constants	**true, false**		

Identifiers are user-defined names. The meaning of an identifier depends on the context in which it is used. The various meanings that can be assigned to identifiers are described in later sections. Identifiers are strings of alphanumeric symbols that begin with a letter. Examples of identifiers are:

A   I   J   MAX   quotient   notfound

Reserved words are words that have a fixed meaning in programs. They are printed in boldface. The meaning of each reserved word is discussed in later sections. Examples of reserved words are:

begin   end   procedure   if   then   else

A·2 Simple Variables

Simple variables are named entities that occupy one unit of memory storage. They can be assigned values during the course of computation, and any particular simple variable may have its value changed by assigning it a new value. Declaration statements for simple variables are used in programs to reserve space for the variables and to indicate their type. Variables declared to be boolean can assume only the values **true** and **false**. Similarly, integer variables can attain only integer values, and real variables can attain only real values. Examples of declarations are:

real   X, Y, Z;
integer   I, J, MAX;
boolean   found, erroroccurred;

A·3 Arrays

Arrays are data structures in which individual elements are specified by subscripts. A one-dimensional array X with lower bound LB and an upper bound UB is a data structure that consists of the variables X[LB], X[LB+1], . . . , X[UB]. That is, X is a vector in which the least index is LB and the greatest index is UB. Higher-dimensional arrays are data structures which have two or more indices. The two-dimensional matrix M, with rows indexed from LB1 to UB1, and columns indexed from LB2 to UB2, consists of a set of variables M[I,J] for all pairs I,J such that LB1 ≤ I ≤ UB1 and LB2 ≤ J ≤ UB2.

The size, dimension, and data type of an array are specified in array declarations. Examples of array declarations are:

real array   A[LB1 : UB1, LB2 : UB2];

integer array   X[LB : UB], Y[1 : 10];

boolean array   V[0 : 7, 0 : 7, 0 : 7];

A·4 Expressions

Values of variables, array elements, and constants can be combined by arithmetic and boolean operators to produce new values. Expressions fall into two categories:

1. Arithmetic expressions (combinations of entities of type real and integer)

2. Boolean expressions (combinations of boolean variables, boolean constants, and arithmetic relations)

Arithmetic expressions are constructed from the following operators:

ARITHMETIC OPERATOR	MEANING
+	Addition
−	Subtraction
*	Multiplication
/	Division
÷	Integer division
MOD	Modulus, the remainder after an integer division
↑	Exponentiation

Examples of arithmetic expressions are:

A+B*(C/D)↑2   (N MOD TABLESIZE)+1

The arithmetic expressions can be compared to each other in magnitude by using a construction known as an arithmetic relation. The relation involves an operator which can be any of the following:

$$= \quad \neq \quad > \quad < \quad \geq \quad \leq$$

When an arithmetic relation is evaluated during program execution it has a value of either **true** or **false,** depending on whether or not the relation holds. Examples of arithmetic relations are:

B = A+6   A∗4 < B−1

When A and B have the values 1 and 7, respectively, both relations hold, and are said to have the value **true.** When A and B have the value 5 and 6, respectively, both relations have the value **false.**

Boolean expressions are combinations of relations, boolean variables, and boolean constants with the following boolean operators:

NOT   AND   OR   EXCLUSIVE OR

The operators are defined by the table below:

X	Y	NOT X	X AND Y	X OR Y	X EXCLUSIVE OR Y
false	false	true	false	false	false
false	true	true	false	true	true
true	false	false	false	true	true
true	true	false	true	true	false

Examples of boolean expressions are:

((NOT X) AND (I < J)) OR (I = 3∗K)   Z AND ((I ≠ J) OR (I > K + 2))

In these examples we assume that I, J, and K are arithmetic variables and X and Z are boolean variables.

A·5 Assignment Statements

The values of variables can be changed by means of assignment statements. We use the symbol ← (and := , its ALGOL version) to indicate the transfer of data. The variable to the left of the arrow represents the name, or the memory location, of the variable. The expression to the right of the arrow is evaluated, and its value is placed in the indicated memory location. Examples of assignment statements are:

```
A[I] ← 3+X/Y[2,6];
B := (5*N) MOD J;
FOUND := false;
FOUND := NOT FOUND AND ITEMSEEN;
```

A·6 Control Statements

The three types of control statements are the unconditional branch, the conditional statement, and the iteration.

An unconditional branch is a statement of the form

```
go to targetlabel;
```

where targetlabel is the label of some statement in the program. Examples of unconditional statements are:

```
go to compute;
. . .
compute: x := y;
go to skiponestatement;
next: a := b;
skiponestatement: c := d;
```

A conditional statement can either execute or skip a statement, depending on the value of a boolean expression. Conditional statements have one of the following two forms:

```
if booleanexpression then S else T;
if booleanexpression then S;
```

Here S and T are statements. In both forms, if the boolean expression has the value **true**, then statement S is executed, otherwise statement S is skipped. In the first form of the conditional statement statement T is executed if, and only if, the boolean expression has the value **false.**

Examples of conditional statements are:

if I $\neq$ J **then** X[I] := X[I]+1;
if I $>$ 3 **then** I := I $-$ 1 **else go to** finish;
if pagenum $=$ 0 **then** M := 0 **else** M := P;

Iteration statements are statements of the general form

for LOOPVARIABLE := FIRSTVALUE **step** INCREMENT
    until LOOPLIMIT **do** S;

Here S is a statement. The iteration statement causes S to be executed zero or more times, depending on the values of FIRSTVALUE, LOOPLIMIT, and INCREMENT. If INCREMENT is positive, then S is executed iteratively, with LOOPVARIABLE assuming the sequence of values FIRSTVALUE, FIRSTVALUE + INCREMENT, FIRSTVALUE + 2·INCREMENT . . . , FIRSTVALUE + K·INCREMENT, where K is the largest integer for which FIRSTVALUE + K·INCREMENT does not exceed LOOPLIMIT. In this case if FIRSTVALUE is greater than LOOPLIMIT, then S is not executed at all. The value of INCREMENT can also be negative, in which case the values assumed by LOOPVARIABLE decrease instead of increase. The iteration terminates when the value of LOOPVARIABLE falls below LOOPLIMIT. FIRSTVALUE, INCREMENT, and LOOPLIMIT need not be simple variables or constants, but can be arbitrary arithmetic expressions. The expressions are reevaluated before each execution of S, so that the execution of S can change these values and affect the iteration statement.

Examples of iteration statements are:

for i := 1 **step** 1 **until** MAX **do** A[i] := 0;
for j := i+1 **step** m **until** MAX—m **do** X[j] := X[j+m];

A·7 Compound Statements

Iteration and conditional statements are used to control the execution of individual statements. To control the execution of a group of two or more statements the statements can be collected together into a compound statement which can be treated as an individual statement. The general form of a compound statement is

begin $S_1;S_2;S_3;$ . . . ;S_n **end**

where $S_1,$ . . . , S_n are each assignment, control, or compound statements.

Examples of compound statements are:

```
if I = J then
    begin if I ≠ K then
        begin I := 2;
                J := 1;
        end
    else
        K := 3;
    end
for I := 1 step 1 until 10 do
    begin A[I] := 0;
            B[I] := B[I+1] + B[I];
    end;
```

In the first example the compound statement

```
begin I := 2;
        J := 1;
end
```

is executed when I = J and I ≠ K. In the second example the compound statement is

```
begin A[I] := 0;
        B[I] := B[I+1] + B[I];
end
```

This statement is executed 10 times as I assumes the values 1, 2, . . . , 10.

A·8 Procedures

Procedures are the ALGOL version of subroutines. These are subprograms that are invoked from arbitrary points in a program and return control to the calling point. The entry point is always the first statement of the procedure.

The least complex form of procedure is the procedure without parameters. It has the general form

```
procedure proc; S;
```

where S is a statement. Wherever the procedure call statement proc;

appears in a program the effect of the call is the same as replacing the call by the statement S.

An example of a parameterless procedure is

```
procedure BUMPI;
    begin I := I+1;
        if I > MAX then go to error;
    end procedure BUMPI;
```

A typical program that uses this procedure might have the following appearance:

```
    . . .
    if x = y then BUMPI;
    . . .
    BUMPI;
    . . .
error:
    . . .
```

The use of parameters for procedures greatly increases their utility. Procedure parameters are specified as part of the procedure declaration. Dummy parameters called *formal parameters* are used for the declaration, and these parameters are replaced by *actual parameters* when the procedure is invoked.

An example of a procedure with parameters is:

```
procedure BUMP (index, maxval, errorlabel);

integer index, maxval;

label errorlabel;

begin index := index+1;
    if index > maxval then go to errorlabel;

end procedure BUMP;
```

The formal parameters of this procedure are index, maxval, and errorlabel. The statements

```
integer index,maxval;

label errorlabel;
```

are specification statements that describe the type of the formal parameter. Specification statements differ from declarations in that declarations cause space to be reserved for the entity declared and specifications describe entities for which space has already been reserved.

Typical calls on BUMP are:

```
integer I,J,M,N;
    . . .
BUMP(I,N,error);
    . . .
error:
    . . .
BUMP(J,M,stop);
    . . .
stop:
    . . .
```

Array specifications do not include the lower and upper bounds of the array. An example of array specification is

```
procedure SEARCH(ITEM,A);
integer ITEM;
integer array A;

    . . .
```

Parameters can be transmitted either by name or by value. When the value is transmitted, the actual parameter is evaluated at the time of the call, and the resulting value is the parameter manipulated by the procedure. When the name of the parameter is transmitted, the resulting computation is what would be obtained if all occurrences of the corresponding formal parameter name were replaced by the actual parameter (see Chapter 7 for a complete discussion of this point). Value parameters are indicated in the specification part. Parameters that are not specified as value parameters are name parameters by default.

An example of value and name parameters is

```
procedure change (N,I);
value N;
integer N,I;
    . . .
```

In this procedure N is called by value and I is called by name.

Procedures can transmit values back to the calling program through parameters called by name. Another convenient method of returning values is to treat the procedure as a function. Examples of this method are the procedures SINE(X) and SQRT(X) for computing the sine and square root of a number. Function procedures are specified by indicating a type for the procedure in its declaration. The functional value is transmitted back to the calling program by assigning a value to the procedure name in the body of the procedure.

An example of a function procedure is:

```
integer procedure BUMP(I);
integer I;
begin
BUMP := I+1;
end procedure BUMP;
```

A typical call on this procedure is

```
J := BUMP(I);
```

Function procedures need not have parameters. The rules for transmitting parameters to function procedures are identical to the rules for transmitting parameters to ordinary procedures.

A·9 Coroutines

Coroutines are subprograms that are entered at the point of their last exit rather than at a beginning point. The initial entry to a coroutine is made to the first statement in the coroutine. An example of coroutine declarations is

```
coroutine X;
    begin
        . . .
        RESUME Y;
        . . .
        RESUME Y;
        . . .
        RESUME Y;
end coroutine X;
coroutine Y;
begin
    . . .
    RESUME X;
    . . .
    RESUME X;
    . . .
end coroutine Y;
```

We use RESUME to indicate a coroutine call. In coroutine X the statement

    RESUME Y;

causes control to pass from X to Y, entering Y at its last call to X. (If Y is entered for the first time, control passes to the beginning of Y.) When the statement

    RESUME X;

is reached, control passes to the statement immediately following the last coroutine call to Y.

Bibliography

Adel'son-Vel'skii, G. M., and E. M. Landis, 1962: An algorithm for the organization of information, *Dokl. Akad. Nauk SSSR, Mathemat.*, vol. 146, no. 2, 1962, pp. 263–266.

Barton, R. S., 1961: A new approach to the functional design of a digital computer, *Proc. WJCC*, 1961, pp. 393–396.

Bell, C. G., and A. Newell, 1971: "Computer Structures: Readings and Examples," McGraw-Hill Book Company, New York, 1971.

Bell, J. R., 1970: The quadratic quotient method: A hash code eliminating secondary clustering, *Comm. ACM*, vol. 13, no. 2, February 1970, pp. 107–109.

Bell, J. R., and C. H. Kaman, 1970: The linear quotient hash code, *Comm. ACM*, vol. 13, no. 11, November 1970, pp. 675–677.

Burks, A. W., H. H. Goldstine, and J. Von Neumann, 1946: Planning and coding of problems for an electronic computing instrument, parts 1 and 2. Institute for Advanced Study, Princeton, N.J. Reprinted in *Datamation*, vol. 8, no. 9, September 1962, pp. 24–31, and vol. 8, no. 10, October 1962, pp. 36–41.

Conway, M., 1963: Design of a separable transition compiler, *Comm. ACM*, vol. 6, no. 7, July 1963, pp. 396–408.

Davis, Martin, 1958: "Computability and Unsolvability," McGraw-Hill Book Company, New York, 1958.

Dijkstra, E., 1958: "Communication with an Automatic Computer," dissertation, Technische Hochschule Eindhoven, 1958.

Dumey, A. I., 1956: Indexing for rapid random access memory systems, *Computers and Automation*, vol. 5, no. 12, December 1956, pp. 6–9.

Floyd, R. W., 1964: Algorithm 245, treesort 3, *Comm. ACM*, vol. 7, no. 12, December 1964, p. 701.

Foster, C. C., 1965: Information storage and retrieval using AVL trees, *Proc. ACM Natl. Conf.*, 1965, pp. 192–205.

Haley, A. C. D., 1962; The KDF9 computer system, *Proc. AFIPS Conf. FJCC*, vol. 22, 1962, Spartan Books, Washington, D.C., pp. 108–120.

Hoare, C. A. R., 1961: Algorithm 63, partition, and algorithm 64, quicksort, *Comm. ACM*, vol. 4, no. 7, July 1961, p. 321.

Ingerman, P. Z., 1961: Thunks, *Comm. ACM*, vol. 4, no. 1, January 1961, pp. 55–58.

Kent, W., 1969: Assembler language macro-programming, *Computing Surveys*, vol. 1, no. 4, December 1969, pp. 183–196.

Knuth, D. E., 1968: "The Art of Computer Programming," vol. I, "Fundamental Algorithms," Addison Wesley, Reading, Mass., 1968.

Lampson, B., 1968: A scheduling philosophy for multiprocessing systems, *Comm. ACM*, vol. 11, no. 5, May 1968, pp. 347–360.

Leiner, A. L., 1952: Buffering between input/output and the computer, *Proc. EJCC*, 1952, pp. 22–30.

Lin, S., and T. Rado, 1965: Computer studies of Turing machine problems, *J. ACM*, vol. 12, no. 2, April 1965, pp. 196–212.

Lukasiewicz, J., 1951: "Aristotle's Syllogistic from the Standpoint of Modern Formal Logic," Oxford University Press, Oxford, 1951.

Maurer, W. D., 1968: An improved hash code for scatter storage, *Comm. ACM*, vol. 11, no. 1, January 1968, pp. 35–38.

Minsky, M., 1967: "Computation: Finite and Infinite Machines," Prentice-Hall, Inc., Englewood Cliffs, N.J., 1967.

Mock, O., and C. J. Swift, 1959: The SHARE 709 System, programmed input/output buffering, *J. ACM*, vol. 6, no. 2, April 1959, pp. 145–151.

Morris, Robert, 1968: Scatter storage techniques, *Comm. ACM*, vol. 11, no. 1, January 1968, pp. 38–44.

Newell, A. (ed.), 1961: "Information Processing Language V: Manual," Prentice-Hall, Englewood Cliffs, N.J., 1961.

——— and J. C. Shaw, 1957: Programming the logic theory machine, *Proc. WJCC*, 1957, pp. 230–240.

Perlis, A. J., and C. Thornton, 1960: Symbol manipulation by threaded lists, *Comm. ACM*, vol. 3, no. 4, April 1960, pp. 195–204.

Peterson, W. W., 1957: Addressing for random access storage, *IBM J. Res. Dev.*, vol. 1, no. 2, April 1957, pp. 130–146.

Rogers, H., Jr., 1967: "Theory of Recursive Functions and Effective Computability," McGraw-Hill, New York, 1967.

Rosen, S., 1969: Electronic computers: A historical survey, *Computing Surveys*, vol. 1, no. 1, March 1969, pp. 7–36.

Ross, D. T., 1961: A generalized technique for symbol manipulation and numerical calculation, *Comm. ACM*, vol. 4, no. 3, March 1961, pp. 147–150.

Shaw, J. C., A. Newell, H. A. Simon, and T. O. Ellis, 1958: A command structure for complex information processing, *Proc. WJCC*, 1958, pp. 119–128.

Singleton, R. C., 1969: Algorithm 347, sort, *Comm. ACM*, vol. 12, no. 3, March 1969, pp. 185–186.

Tarski, A., 1956: "Logic, Semantics, Metamathematics," Clarendon, Oxford, 1956.

Turing, A. M., 1936: On computable numbers with an application to the Entsheidungsproblem, *Proc. London Math. Soc.*, ser. 2, vol. 42, pp. 230–265.

Van Wijngaarden, A. (ed.), B. J. Mailloux , J. E. L. Peck, and C. H. A. Koster, 1968: "Draft Report on the Algorithmic Language ALGOL 68," Mathematish Centrum, Amsterdam, 1968.

Wirth, N., and C. A. R. Hoare, 1966: A contribution to the development of ALGOL, *Comm. ACM*, vol. 10, no. 6, June 1966, pp. 413–432.

Williams, J. W. J., 1964: Algorithm 232, Heapsort, *Comm. ACM*, vol. 7, no. 6, June 1964, pp. 347–348.

Index

To IBM System/360-370 Instructions

CODE	DESCRIPTION	PAGE
C	Compare	55
CR	Compare (register)	55
D	Divide full word	51
DC	Define constant (pseudo-instruction)	94
DD	Divide floating-point double word	54
DDR	Divide floating-point double word (register)	54
DE	Divide floating-point full word	54
DER	Divide floating-point full word (register)	54
DR	Divide (register)	53
DROP	Drop base register (pseudo-instruction)	94
DS	Define storage (pseudo-instruction)	94
END	End of program (pseudo-instruction)	94
ENTRY	Entry symbol (pseudo-instruction)	106
EQU	Equate (pseudo-instruction)	94
EXTRN	External symbol (pseudo-instruction)	106
L	Load full word	50
LCR	Load (two's) complement (register)	53
LD	Load floating-point double word	54
LDR	Load floating-point double word (register)	54
LE	Load floating-point full word	54
LER	Load floating-point full word (register)	54
LH	Load halfword	53
LR	Load (register)	53
LTR	Load and test (register)	55
M	Multiply full word	51
MACRO	Begin macro (pseudo-instruction)	110
MD	Multiply floating-point double word	54
MDR	Multiply floating-point double word (register)	54
ME	Multiply floating-point full word	54
MEND	End macro (pseudo-instruction)	110
MER	Multiply floating-point full word (register)	54
MR	Multiply (register)	53
N	Logical AND	79
NR	Logical AND (register)	79
O	Logical OR	79
OR	Logical OR (register)	79
ORG	Origin (pseudo-instruction)	94
READ	Read (channel command)	186
S	Subtract full word	51
SD	Subtract floating-point double word	54

Index

To Hewlett-Packard Instructions

CODE	DESCRIPTION	PAGE
EXT	External symbol (pseudo-instruction)	106
HLT	Halt	87
I	Suffix for indirect addressing	65
INA	Increment A	32
INB	Increment B	32
IOR	Logical INCLUSIVE OR with A register	78
ISZ	Increment, skip if zero	25
JMP	Unconditional jump	25
JSB	Jump to subroutine	25
LDA	Load A register	23
LDB	Load B register	23
LIA	Load input to A	169
LIB	Load input to B	169
MIA	Merge input to A	169
MIB	Merge input to B	169
NOP	No operation	137
OCT	Octal convert (pseudo-instruction)	90
ORG	Origin (pseudo-instruction)	89
OTA	Output from A	169
OTB	Output from B	169
RAL	Rotate A left (cyclical shift)	81
RAR	Rotate A right (cyclical shift)	81
RBL	Rotate B left (cyclical shift)	81
RBR	Rotate B right (cyclical shift)	81
REP	Repeat (pseudo-instruction)	109
RSS	Reverse sense of skip	25
SEZ	Skip if E is zero	34
SFC	Skip if flag clear	168
SFS	Skip if flag set	168
SOC	Skip on overflow clear	31
SOS	Skip on overflow set	31
SSA	Skip on sign of A positive	25
SSB	Skip on sign of B positive	25
STA	Store A register	23
STB	Store B register	23
STC	Set control	168
STF	Set flag	168
XOR	Logical EXCLUSIVE OR with A register	78

Index